CREATING YOUR LIBRARY'S BUSINESS PLAN:

A How-To-Do-It Manual with Samples on CD-ROM

JOY HP. HARRIMAN

facet publishing

Copyright © 2008 by the Medical Library Association.

"A How-To-Do-It Manual®" and "A How-To-Do-It Manual for Librarians®" are registered trademarks of Neal-Schuman Publishers, Inc.

Published by
Facet Publishing
7 Ridgmount Street
London WC1E 7AE

Facet Publishing is wholly owned by CILIP: the Chartered Institute of Library and Information Professionals.

First published in the USA by Neal-Schuman Publishers, Inc., 2008.
This simultaneous UK edition 2008.

British Library Cataloguing in Publication Data
A catalogue record for this book is available from the British Library

ISBN 978-1-85604-656-5

Printed and bound in the United States of America.

CONTENTS

LIST OF FIGURES, TABLES, AND WORKSHEETS

FIGURES

TABLES

WORKSHEETS

CD-ROM CONTENTS

Section I: Worksheets and Templates

Section II: Library Business Plan Models

Digital Library Federation (DLF) Aquifer Business Plan (2005)
Jacaranda Public Library Business Plan (2006)
Kenosha Public Library Business Plan (2006)
Kenosha Public Library Business Plan (2007)
London Health Libraries Strategy and Development Group electronic
    Knowledge Access Team (eKAT) Performance Measures (2005–2008)
London Health Libraries Strategy and Development Group & London
    Workforce Development Group Business Plan Agreement (2006–2007)
Maroochy Shire Council Library Strategy (2006)
NHS London Health Libraries electronic Knowledge Access Team (eKAT) &
    Strategy and Development Group Business Plan Agreement (2005–2006)
NHS South East London Strategic Health Authority Workforce Development
    Confederation Business Plan (2006–2007)
Oakville Public Library Business Plan (2007–2009)
Red Deer Public Library Business Plan (2006–2008)
Stockport Metropolitan Borough Council Library and Information Service
    Business Plan (2006–2007)
Strategic Alliance of Federal Science & Technology Libraries (AFSTL)
    Federal Science eLibrary Business Case (2005)
Torbay Council Library Services Business Plan (2006–2007)
University of Otago Library Business Plan (2004)
University of Wollongong Library Professional Unit Business Plan (2006)
U.S. Environmental Protection Agency Business Case for Information
    Services: EPA's Regional Libraries and Centers (2004)
Wombatta Public Library Service Marketing Plan

Section III: Searchable Single File of All Business Plans

PREFACE

Creating Your Library's Business Plan: A How-To-Do-It Manual with Samples on CD-ROM will help librarians demystify the business planning process. A good business plan can guide your library's operations and ensure its viability and growth by helping you to:

- clarify goals,
- set reasonable time frames for service introductions and changes,
- articulate standards,
- measure performance according to predetermined criteria,
- attract supporters, and
- announce your successes.

I give frequent workshops on business planning, and I designed this guide to help my colleagues better connect organizational vision with everyday practice. The key to this connection is a well-thought-out and well-implemented business plan. The creation of a business plan will focus your thinking on specific goals, step by step, allowing you to develop services that are well conceived and appealing to stakeholders.

Many libraries conduct business planning but don't necessarily recognize it as such. Many misconceptions surround the term "business plan," and many view the planning process as being unnecessarily complicated. At its core, a business plan is simply a tool to describe a project, and it includes information on the organization's mission, markets, marketing strategies, and needs of clients. A good plan describes a service, outlines objectives, allocates resources, and measures the results of actions taken along the path toward your organization's goal.

Understanding how to utilize a business plan will help you become more flexible, more proactive, and more accountable. A good business plan will help you attract support, talented individuals, partners, and capital. *Creating Your Library's Business Plan* can be used by any library planning group to assess community needs; evaluate current library services; determine the library's role in the organization; establish goals, objectives, and priorities; design and implement strategies; and develop an ongoing monitoring system for organizational control.

ORGANIZATION OF BOOK CONTENTS

Creating Your Library's Business Plan is divided into ten chapters; together, these chapters comprise a step-by-step approach to the process. The book begins with an overview of the whys and wherefores of writing a plan, including descriptions of the function of each component - from the cover page to the appendix and everything in between. Individual chapters then discuss each step in detail and offer an array of real-world examples used by successful libraries. Each chapter begins with a review of that essential component's purpose and addresses why that information is necessary, how it will impact the project, the manner in which it should be presented, and how it will help develop a competitive advantage supportive to the parent organization.

- Chapter 1, "Why Write a Business Plan?," introduces readers to the full range of benefits to be garnered from business planning.

- Chapter 2, "The Components of a Business Plan," describes each element of a successful business plan in straightforward, easy-to-understand terms.

- Chapter 3, "Describing Your Service Concept, Vision, and Mission Statements," explains how to craft client-focused statements that will highlight your service's competitive advantage in the marketplace.

- Chapter 4, "Conducting Assessments and Creating a SWOT Chart," examines the use of internal (strengths and weaknesses) and external (opportunities and threats) environmental assessments in choosing, designing, monitoring, and revising services suitable to your market.

- Chapter 5, "Clarifying Objectives," discusses how to quantify the end results desired and create the strategies to achieve them.

- Chapter 6, "Determining Strategies and Action Plans," describes the steps involved in turning strategies into actions that will grow your service.

- Chapter 7, "Creating a Marketing Plan," focuses on developing strategies that will build awareness of your service, communicate how it meets clients' needs, and generate new or continued use.

- Chapter 8, "Evaluating Your Business Plan's Success," describes strategies for continual reassessment of plan implementation to keep services fresh and relevant and to maintain competitive advantage in your target market.

- Chapter 9, "Forming a Financial Plan," introduces the reader to recordkeeping basics, profit and loss statements, balance sheets, break-even analysis, cash flow projections, and more.
- Chapter 10, "Writing an Executive Summary and Communicating the Plan," discusses how to summarize the information gathered from the preceding steps to clearly, effectively, and successfully communicate your plan to your organization and its stakeholders.

Every component may not be necessary for a given plan. Depending on your institution's needs, these components may be combined, reordered, or eliminated. A larger plan with great impact may require all of the components, whereas a simple plan with less impact may require only a few of them. Your individual circumstances, intended impact, organizational imperatives, and staff capabilities will determine the complexity of the plan. What is important is that you understand each component's raison d'être; cover key matters in a focused, logical, and comprehensive way; and present the relevant information in a consistent manner.

I have included more than 50 templates and worksheets, and more than 25 real-world examples from a wide variety of successful libraries. The worksheets and templates provided are designed to assist in clarifying and focusing your thoughts and intentions.

The real-world examples included in each chapter need not be followed verbatim; they provide models and patterns that you can customize and build upon when developing your own business plan. All worksheets and templates in this book are included, in Word format, on the accompanying CD, along with complete versions of over 20 business plans developed by libraries around the world.

CD-ROM: STRUCTURE AND USAGE

The CD-ROM comprises three sections. The first includes Word files representing every worksheet and template found in the printed book. These files may be freely distributed throughout your library and may be edited, augmented, and otherwise adjusted as needed in response to your particular library's needs. Each worksheet and template is clearly labeled and arranged in accordance with its description in the book.

The CD's second section is devoted to the full text of over 20 actual business plans successfully drafted and implemented by a wide variety of libraries. Business plans are listed alphabetically on the CD.

A third section contains a single file representing the entire collection of business plans from section two. This allows for easy searching across documents, and may be helpful to readers interested in comparing similar elements of various business plans.

I designed *Creating Your Library's Business Plan* to provide a comprehensive framework for library operations, with an emphasis on understanding the effects the internal and external environments have on new and expanded services. I hope that you will see how a solid business plan will help you develop a successful service. I trust that it will prove invaluable as it guides, prompts, measures, communicates, and focuses staff members by building the necessary components of fact, shared vision, and mutual understanding. Without a shared vision, staff members and participants in the development of the new service will be left to their own means to interpret your library's purpose and goals. A shared vision creates trust, understanding, communication, and commitment. You no longer need to wonder if a service will work; writing a business plan will map your road to service success.

ACKNOWLEDGMENTS

In grateful acknowledgment to Grace King and Sonya Haynie—two talented intra- and entrepreneurs—for their support, inspiration, and encouragement; to the MLA Book Panel for shepherding this book to Neal-Schuman; and to the many librarians who have contributed hours of hard work and risk taking in creating business plans and budgets to fund their dreams and visions:

I can no other answer make but thanks, and thanks.
—*Twelfth Night* (Act III, Scene iii)

1

WHY WRITE A BUSINESS PLAN?

> Even if you don't need one, write it anyway. It will force you
> to think in a disciplined way about what you are doing.
> —"What It Takes to Launch Your Own Business" (2007)

Every library needs a written business plan to guide its operations and ensure its viability and growth. Most well-run corporations operate in accordance with a business plan that defines their goals, strategy, and tactics for achieving objectives. Day-to-day operations are subject to short-term ups and downs. Side issues may temporarily appear more important than they are. The "squeaky wheel" will consume resources and distract you from the main focus of activity. A good business plan guards against these distractions and keeps you focused on your major objectives.

Libraries are about people and their aspirations. A library creates services to meet the needs of those who comprise its constituency. In order to create any viable service, the customer's needs, the library's particular market, and the broader information industry have to be understood. Once these things are understood, it is possible to create a service whose success, while not guaranteed, is at least well conceived and able to be communicated with stakeholders. Writing a business plan ensures that your library's management is clearly focused on reaching success and recognizes possible situational advantages and disadvantages. Writing a business plan ensures that you will pay attention to your operation and financial objectives as well as to the details of budgeting and marketing. It means you have covered your bases and are generally well equipped to deal with change.

The intent of a business plan is to develop a successful service. A business plan guides, prompts, measures, communicates, and focuses staff by coordinating the necessary components of fact, shared vision, and mutual understanding. Without a shared vision, the staff and participants in the development of a new venture are left to their own devices when interpreting the purpose and goals of the service. A shared vision creates trust, understanding, and communication, and paves the way for greatly increased productivity.

A business plan also includes a clear recognition of the effects of the internal and external environment on a service. There is no sense in wondering if a service will work after writing a business plan; you will know it will work because you will have gathered and sifted through all of the components necessary for its success, or you will know why it should not be implemented. As this process improves weaker areas of your organization, the chance of success for any given service you offer increases. If you have identified potential risks or threats that cannot be altered, a service may be cancelled based on the results of information gathered when writing the plan.

"Measure twice, cut once" is the mantra of carpenters creating a new piece, and is a valuable lesson in planning. Evolving technology, diminishing budgets, and seriously competitive environments compel libraries to apply this mantra to planning efforts. If you cannot show effectiveness or quantify the library's value to justify funding, the funding may cease. A library may initiate, continue, or cease services despite experiencing a loss of use or without having established a clearly defined need met by that service. There may be no defined measures of progress or success. Without clear measurements, no reason exists to establish priorities to maintain any service. If cutbacks become necessary, then any service can be eliminated without a prioritized need to substantiate saving the best.

Libraries can learn from business competitors and counterparts. Determining the viability of a plan is essential given the competition libraries face. Choosing a reasonable direction in tune with the library's strategic advantage of altruism can only assist in creating a successful venture. It does not make good sense to keep services available that are not relevant to the library's mission.

Many libraries already conduct business planning, but may not call it by this term. Some of the other terms used *are strategic business plan, direction planning, strategic planning, business imperatives and objectives*, or *plans and priorities* (Jones, 2000). Some of these terms, such as strategic planning, technically refer to different processes, but are often used interchangeably with business planning. Regardless of the term used in a particular organization, business planning is planning conducted by using the core components that will help a given service reach its goal.

Publications and instruction on business planning in libraries are widely available, but the technique has not been widely recognized in U.S. libraries. U.K., Canadian, and Australian libraries have written business plans since April 1991, when the NHS trusts introduced business planning into the management process (NHS Management Executive, 1990). Publications on strategic planning or planning in general for U.S. libraries are readily available, but a strategic plan is not a business plan.

A strategic plan provides the foundation and framework for a business plan. Generally, the strategic plan is produced at the corporate level, while business planning occurs at the service level. A business plan generally applies to activities whose scope ranges from one to three years. It develops from strategic planning and SWOT (strengths, weaknesses, opportunities, and threats) analysis, and includes a mission statement and vision statement (Adams Six Sigma. n.d.). A new library will most likely find that its business and strategic plans share the same intent. As the library or service matures, the business plan will become the bridge between its current position and its vision for the future.

A business plan is just as important for an established library, regardless of its size, as it is for a new service. Every library is dynamic—change and growth occur and new goals or plans are set. This is a good thing. The plan enables monitoring of a library's historic performance, or what new direction a library should take. The evaluation, monitoring, or measurement component of a plan provides the overview and guidance necessary to correct problems, identify opportunities, and keep the plan current. Frequently, evaluation or output measures will let you know when the industry or client's need is changing. Because the environment in which your library operates is always changing, periodic reviews will allow time to react or to alter your plans (Clark, 2001).

Intrapreneurs—those who innovate from within an organization—rely every bit as much on sound analysis as those entrepreneurs who create their own start-ups. Inside a larger library or organized system, the intrapreneur should take advantage of any opportunity to identify weaknesses and strengths in the beginning to ensure internal support and success. He or she should present managers with information about the relation of the proposed service to the vision, mission, goals, and strategies of the parent company.

Creating a business plan helps planners make good decisions based on the recognition of how a particular service fits into the scheme of the parent organization. A business plan communicates direction, establishes a framework for delegation of authority and responsibility, and tracks expectations and performance. The creation of the plan brings discipline to your thinking and helps to bring your idea or concept into focus (Ernst & Young LLP, 1997). A good business plan describes a service, allocates resources, and measures the results of planned actions, which, when taken, then drive the next set of choices. The "map" of the plan exists to guide you to reach specific goals, saving time, money, and grief.

Using the steps outlined in the business planning process encourages proactive decision making. You might create, alter, or remove services as a result of the increased awareness gained from an internal and external assessment. The assessment responses, derived from your clients, your knowledge of the opportunities and challenges of the library's capabilities in your particular community, and the current state of the information industry describe your choice of services.

The overriding purpose here is to find out what your clients want, to satisfy those wants, and to generate a successful service according to the measures your organization uses to define success. The plan is used to implement and manage the service. It is important to recognize that all businesses are fluid. A business plan identifies and measures only one aspect of many unfolding possibilities. People, opportunity, technology, outside environment, and internal dynamics all create movement. Any and all of these factors are subject to change over time. A business plan by nature incorporates the process of change.

Throughout this book, reference to the "service" is used only for ease. Your business plan may relate to a new collection, a single service, or to many services. You may want to establish new divisions, reinvigorate established systems, or plan for a whole library or an existing department in a library. A business plan can be used for any of these purposes and more, but, for consistency, all choices referred to here are the "service." This book also refers to library patrons, guests, customers, visitors, or users as clients.

FUNCTIONS OF A BUSINESS PLAN

CLARIFIES EFFORTS AND PROVIDES A CONSISTENT FOCUS

A business plan identifies the idea you are trying to develop, helps clarify your thinking, forces a stronger understanding of what you want to achieve, and names how and when all of this can be done. It plays a vital role in helping avoid costly mistakes. It generates enthusiasm and builds consensus by focusing efforts. While its success lies in offering a consistent message, the business plan is not static. It evolves with the library and the environment, becoming a circular process.

A business plan clarifies efforts by analyzing aspects and possibilities of success and failure. It reviews the need, possible deliverables, cost and benefits, and the industry, among other elements. After analyzing the results of questions asked during the planning process, a clear picture develops of what will work and what will not. The plan becomes a reality check and performance tool as you define goals and establish milestones. It forces you to think in a focused, methodical manner about the next best step and about the bigger picture.

Creating the plan results in market knowledge and determination of the service's competitive advantage. The mission, objectives, and action plans will be interlinked and consistent with one another. This is not always an easy process. Some libraries do not have clear goals or concise missions. However, at the end of the planning process, if you choose to offer the service in question, you will know that the service is connected to the overall strategy of the library and so is something that both the library and its culture can embrace and commit to.

An ideal service leverages core competencies and builds on staff assets (Ramachandran, n.d.). This will not guarantee success, but your ideas will go much further than without the planning foundation. Creating an atmosphere of change, trust, commitment, and involvement is essential for successful planning and managing (Spears, 1995; Dow and Cook, 1996).

Effective planning results in consistency and evenhanded management. A challenge for the information industry noted by Outsell, Inc. "will be continuing to grow revenue while maintaining profitability and continuing to invest for growth. Firms will need to keep a steady hand on the wheel while driving for growth and not flinch when making critical investments to sustain growth..." (Outsell, Inc., 2006). Anticipating change and incorporating flexibility ensures a stronger entity.

Gathering the information for a business plan requires time spent learning about the market. Market demand must be established. The more understood about the various market factors, the more likely your plan is to succeed. In doing the research required to write a business plan, you will learn about the market's history and about making projections of future market trends.

PROVIDES THE FRAMEWORK

A business plan provides the framework for action. A plan guides a business through the growth process, identifying risks to avoid and reasonable alternatives to pursue. Planning is the start, but the real work is in the implementation. The components of a business plan must be reality-based, customer-focused, simple to understand and communicate, and flexible enough to change with the times. The implementation itself must be a part of the organization's strategic plan.

For example, e-business has altered the view of work and what staff and clients expect from libraries. New expectations related to e-business have included doing business with other libraries electronically, real-time interaction, immediate information resources, single-step processing, and personalized marketing and service. For a library trying to meet these expectations, a business plan can help answer essential questions:

- How can you incorporate changing expectations into library services?
- Can you build a calendar-dated picture of when you will roll out the activities that will ensure these ventures occur?
- Can you write a method to evaluate the performance of these ventures against the plan's calendar projections?
- Can you identify the duties of each staff involved with the hands-on efforts and delivery?
- What training will your staff require?
- What specific goals and strategies do you want the staff to clearly understand?
- How would you know the staff heard what you said?
- How would you know the staff bought into your plan?
- When would you know to move on to initiating, evaluating, or expanding other services?

TRACKS AND MEASURES PERFORMANCE

The business plan helps track, monitor, evaluate, and shape progress by establishing realistic expectations, identifying timelines and milestones, and then measuring the progress. Any planning process is continuous and dynamic by nature. A business plan provides a foundation for making decisions; the plan evaluates progress at preset times and determines what alterations, if any, will push you toward success. Throughout the planning process, you will add in time to review, refine, and redesign the plan's elements.

Measuring or evaluating a service attracts, motivates, and retains quality staff, the true assets of any organization. All staff members need to understand where their service is going, what is expected of them individually, and how their efforts fit into the big picture (Granger, 1970). Managing with a steady hand and being able to identify success provides staff with a valuable sense of stability. Staff morale has a significant impact on productivity, quality, and customer service. Satisfied staff will want their plan to succeed, and their attitudes will dramatically alter the bottom line. If staff have a clear picture of the quality of a service, are proud with their association with the library, and believe you offer reasonable job security, you will have a stronger chance of retaining them.

In summary, measurable impacts of business plans include:

- Increased speed of change
- More commitment to the service
- A stronger focus on relationships within and outside of the organization
- A focus on internal strengths and weaknesses relative to external opportunities and threats

A business plan builds communication channels, refocuses staff, and brings the library together. This process works at all levels of the organization. For example, in 2005, eight national libraries negotiated collaborating on a joint approach to access to their digital libraries. The results of using a business plan fully supported the methodology of business planning to "achieve mutual agreement among partners with widely different aims and characteristics" (Collier, 2005: 608).

THE IMPORTANCE OF STAFF SUPPORT

A plan can take you only so far. It isn't useful unless staff support and buy-in, increased awareness, increased focus on results, and attraction of possible clients are considered equal priorities. Lines of communication must be kept open during the entire life span of the business plan, as much information as possible must be shared. Input gathered from all levels contributes to success; all stakeholders should contribute to the new planning effort and should be accountable for meeting objectives. When everyone is focused in the same direction, objectives can be accomplished (Clark, 2001).

If you really believe that your staff and personnel are your strongest assets, then put your money where your plan is. When it comes to business planning, nobody likes surprises. Include staff in the entire planning process and obtain buy-in as early as possible. They are a part of the team—and if you're writing a business plan, you need a team. In addition to your staff team, you will need to gain management buy-in early and often. Involve stakeholder groups in the planning.

The business plan is shared widely in an effort to communicate a broader understanding of where the library is going and what its goals are. The business plan serves as a core communications tool in obtaining advice and constructive criticism, reaching agreement, and developing effective partnerships. It informs everyone about your intentions. It is also an essential tool in developing stronger understanding among staff. Staff participation in creating a business plan results in staff confidence in their value as organizational members who understand operations and whose individual objectives and goals match the library's overall strategies. When everybody understands what is important and what is expected of them, tremendous growth can take place (Studer, 2003).

When starting to build a new plan, the staff will identify past successes and failures. It is important to unemotionally assess what currently works and what doesn't work in the library. Staff concerns must be addressed. For example, if communication is poor between any groups, progress on a plan will be very difficult. Unrecognized disputes will be brought up and dragged into the results of the planning (Dougherty, 2002).

Consistency and communication form the bottom line. Any improvement is influenced and sustained by building strong, trusting relationships between people and groups who are interested in the library's success. Any organization that expects to perform well in the long run must pay attention to the needs of all of its relationships, especially those with staff. Managers can easily create an environment with positive relationships, trust, and mutual respect by using the techniques of open communication and stability. Delegation allows others to have a sense of ownership and involvement in the outcomes, increasing the chance of success (Clark, 2001). When developing an action plan, all staff must be involved in order to understand what they are to do and when.

Commitment is also important. A lack of commitment results from lack of involvement by key personnel. Without widespread commitment to a plan, the chances of achieving something worthwhile will greatly diminish. Commitment springs from two factors: understanding and involvement. If either is missing, achieving an effective plan is doubtful.

If the business plan doesn't generate staff support, then the potential exists for a reduced staff buy-in. An immediate result of staff not sharing the same base of information is that they will not see the whole picture. The worst-case scenario is for staff to focus on activities and not on results. An overly rigid or inflexible implementation plan can also affect staff buy-in. It is difficult to remain motivated during a tedious process, and the focus may fall away from results. Keeping a plan short and concise and modifying it as necessary will keep it from becoming written in stone. Overly ambitious plans result in exhaustion and being overwhelmed (Sakzwedel, 2000).

As a principal communication tool, the impact of a business plan is unparalleled. It will document activities supporting your intentions, help you gain advice and constructive criticism, and secure participation or support (Budapest Open Access Initiative, 2003). Each library organization evolves. As changes occur and the size of the staff grows or individuals become replaced, it is difficult for all employees to stay on the "same page." Even with an understanding of the core mission and vision, it can be difficult to reconcile individual personal beliefs with the library's focus. Increased levels of open communication will help all recognize and understand the common view of the library. The clear communication will help determine the true improvements or changes that ensure the library's success. Not everyone will agree, but the majority of staff will come closer to consensus.

Change can be influenced by many external and internal forces. Understanding these forces can help you formulate plans that are realistic and appropriate to each unique situation (Sakzwedel, 2000). It is essential to develop flexibility in recognizing change and allowing it to happen. Actively keeping aware of market changes and embracing flexibility allows discovery and exploitation of better ways to operate and increase effectiveness. Libraries should develop the skills to investigate, evaluate, and either accept or reject change based on reason. If there is a level of trust within the library, the organization can develop and expand as well as accept its mistakes and missteps as a part of change.

WRITING A BUSINESS PLAN

Drawn up correctly, a plan will help you articulate your five or six critical success factors. Not providing enough time or giving enough priority to the process will have negative results. The objective is to learn about your market, meet its needs, and get focused. Try to find the middle road: don't create a counterproductive elaborate planning process heavy with form-filling and unnecessary information-gathering, but don't underestimate the amount of time the planning will take.

Write for the audience by reflecting your audience's shared interests and do not get too technical. Use illustrations and exhibits to make your points, and avoid clutter and complexity in the main body of the text. Build your design on the plan that defines your future, not operational processes that reflect the needs of the past. This planning technique will result in basic systems that can be rapidly implemented and shifted more easily than older, more restrictive structured systems.

Short attention spans need high-end graphic tools to make it easier to feed the data to readers. Sprinkle color graphs and charts, and pull quotes, text boxes, and other visual aids liberally throughout your plan, "punching up" or breaking up the text as much as possible.

Fine-tune and polish key individuals' resumes and include information about any professional advisors. This enhances credibility. The management section of the plan should illustrate experience, balance, ability, and commitment. If a new service is involved, then management may be its only real asset. Consider the formation of a management team or strengthening management as part of the plan.

Build your business plan on a carefully considered outline, with the goal of providing information about your library. Workable business plan template software can be found and is fine to use as long as you change it to suit your goals. Otherwise, it may begin to sound more like a term paper rather than a tangible, real-life business plan.

BUSINESS PLAN DOs AND DON'Ts

DO:

- Use a business plan to set concrete goals, responsibilities, and deadlines to guide your service.
- Flesh out each section with as many specific details as possible.
- Keep the plan as simple as possible; keep it short and eminently practical.
- Keep it flexible and usable; allow it to evolve as needed through modifications.
- As a part of the implementation, provide a forum for regular review and course corrections.
- Make sure you work out all the financial details with tangible results.
- Assign tasks to people or departments and set milestones and deadlines for tracking and evaluating implementation.
- Include five to ten parts implementation for every one part strategy.
- Submit a complete plan: include client descriptions, products and services, operations, marketing and promotion, the management team, competitors, and a discussion of the industry (particularly industry trends).
- Include a detailed financial projection (monthly cash flow and income statements as well as annual balance sheets for two years).
- Identify the various stages of your new service and describe how you'll get from one to the next. Establish measurable milestones or targets.
- Get plenty of feedback on the written draft of the plan, especially from those not invested in the plan.
- Solicit recommendations, endorsement, or approval.

- Present your plan as cleanly and crisply as it's written. Do not allow for sloppiness.
- Make sure that your finished plan has consistent margins and no missing pages, that charts have labels and correct units and tables have headings, and that technical terminology is defined, acronyms are introduced at first use, and an accurate table of contents is included.
- Secure the services of a qualified proofreader.
- Keep in mind your library's overall strengths and needs—no single business model successful elsewhere is the right one for your library.
- Focus on people rather than technology. The user's needs must be at the center of the planning process.
- Take into consideration past planning efforts and ongoing projects. When it comes to planning, blank slates don't exist.
- Remember that ultimately the planning process doesn't matter at all. What matters is that the plan is implemented. The crazy truth: people often draw up a business plan and then promptly forget it or never read it. That doesn't do any good!
- Create the future; do not try to forecast it (Jones, 2006).

DON'T:

- Use a business plan to show how much you know about your business.
- Go on too long—nobody reads a long-winded business plan, not bosses or bankers.
- Be vague or too detailed.
- Dumb it down, but do write in language simple enough for a non-librarian to understand.
- Rely on unfounded or unrealistic assumptions—support your assumptions with facts that are facts, and double check the accuracy of your research and be ready to recognize your own bias.
- Neglect to identify the competition—competition exists for every new service so if you can't identify it, do you really need to start a new service?
- Expect the first draft to be perfect—really.

REFERENCES

Adams Six Sigma. n.d. "Business Plans Develop from Strategic Planning, SWOT Analysis and Includes Mission Statements and Vision Statement." Available: http://www.adamssixsigma.com/Newsletters/ strategy_vision_values.htm.

Budapest Open Access Initiative. 2003. *Guide to Business Planning for Launching a New Open Access Journal*, 2nd ed. July. Available: http://www.soros.org/openaccess/oajguides/business_planning.pdf.

Clark, Jacquel K. 2001. "Keys to Successfully Implementing a Business Plan." *Business Credit* (September): 58.

Collier, Mel. 2005. "The Business Aims of Eight National Libraries in Digital Library Cooperation." *Journal of Documentation* 61, no 5: 602–622.

Dougherty, Richard. M. 2002. "Planning for New Library Futures." *Library Journal* 127, no. 9: 38–41.

Dow, Roger and Susan Cook. 1996. *Turned On: Eight Vital Insights to Energize Your People, Customers, and Profits*. New York: HarperCollins.

Granger, Charles H. 1970. "How to Set Company Objectives." *Management Review* (July): 3.

Ernst & Young LLP. 1997. "Outline for a Business Plan: A Proven Approach for Entrepreneurs Only." Available: http://www.techventures.org/resources/docs/ Outline_for_a_Business_Plan.pdf.

Jones, Rebecca. "Business Plans: Roadmaps for Growth and Success." *Information Outlook*. Alexandria, VA: Special Libraries Association (December 11, 2000). Available: http://www.sla.org/content/Shop/Information/infoonline/2000/dec00/ jonesr_dec00.cfm.

Jones, Rebecca. 2006. "Accelerated Planning: Not an Oxymoron." Paper presented at the Ontario Library Association, February 2–4, 2006, Toronto, Ontario, Canada.

NHS Management Executive. 1990. *NHS Trusts: A Working Guide*. London: HMSO.

Outsell, Inc. 2006. "Information Industry Outlook: FutureFacts 2007." Available: www.outsellinc.com/store/products/281.

Ramachandran, Subramanian. n.d. "Strategy in a Competitive Landscape." The CEO Refresher. Available: http://www.refresher.com/Archives/!sbrstrategy.html.

Sakzwedel, Beth A. 2000. *The MLA Guide to Managing Health Care Libraries*. New York: Neal-Schuman Publishers.

Spears, Larry C. 1995. *Reflections on Leadership: How Robert K. Greenleaf's Theory of Servant Leadership Influenced Today's Top Management Thinkers*. New York: Wiley.

Studer, Quint. 2003. *Hardwiring Excellence*. Gulf Breeze, FL: Fire Starter Publishing.

"What It Takes to Launch Your Own Business." 2007. *Money*, 36, no. 1: 71–72.

2 THE COMPONENTS OF A BUSINESS PLAN

THE ESSENTIAL COMPONENTS

Just as no two libraries are exactly alike, no two library business plans are perfectly identical. But every business plan includes a series of core components. Some issues may be more relevant to some libraries than to others. Some libraries may follow every detail of the following sections while others will not. It is important to tailor the plan's contents to suit your individual circumstances. Whatever format you use, all key matters should be covered in a logical and comprehensive way, and information should be presented consistently throughout (Scholarly Publishing and Academic Resources Coalition, 2002).

Strategy forms the basis of a business plan. The first half of a business plan is geared to reviewing the market, industry, clients, and competitors; looking at client needs and the benefits of current products and services; evaluating the strengths and weaknesses of each competing service; and looking for opportunities in the marketplace. All of these components help create a strategy. The second half of a plan details the strategy's execution. All products and services, marketing, and operations will closely tie in with the strategy (Gumpert, 2000).

The essential components of a business plan include:

1. Cover page, introduction, table of contents
2. Executive summary
3. Description of the service concept, vision and mission statements
4. Internal and external assessments and a SWOT chart (market analysis)
5. Objectives
6. Organizational strategy and plans
7. Marketing and promotional strategy
8. Evaluation
9. Financial plan

Rigorous thinking through the whole process about how a service will start up and what processes are necessary to maintain it remains the most essential part of a business plan.

COVER PAGE, INTRODUCTION, AND TABLE OF CONTENTS

Introduce the service and use a few sentences to explain what you do or plan to do. Explain who wrote the plan and when. Provide contact details.

EXECUTIVE SUMMARY

The executive summary is the first part of the business plan, but must be written last, so it is covered in Chapter 10 of this book. It presents the highlights and key facts of the plan; it is the business plan in miniature (Inc.com, 2000). This section sells a service to those who may offer support or funding. It is brief and to the point; since readers may pay more attention to this section than to other sections, the facts must be presented concisely, persuasively, and in an upbeat manner. The focus here is on matters of strategic importance, such as your objectives, strategies, and overall plans. Avoid the details, which will be presented later. The summary allows someone to speed-read your vision, secure in the knowledge that it is backed up elsewhere with facts.

DESCRIBING THE SERVICE CONCEPT AND CREATING OR HONING THE VISION AND MISSION STATEMENTS

The description of the service concept presents a high-level picture of how the different elements of a service fit together: who you are, what you plan to offer, why, and to whom. It identifies client needs, current services designed to meet those needs, and the primary success factors that give the service a competitive advantage over other information providers competing for client interests (U.S. Small Business Administration, 2007). This component of the business plan will be covered in Chapter 3.

The vision statement is expansive and idealistic, detailing specific objectives and goals. If you do not already have a vision statement, the intent and words will emerge from the environmental assessment and SWOT chart you will develop. More detail on creating vision statements and examples of vision statements will be included in Chapter 3. The mission statement describes the central purposes of the service from the client's perspective. It defines the fundamental, unique purpose that the service attempts to serve and identifies its products or services and clients. This powerful statement focuses on intent and aspiration, values and creed. More detail on mission statements and examples of mission statements are given in Chapter 3.

ASSESSING THE INSTITUTION AND DESIGNING A STRENGTH-WEAKNESS-OPPORTUNITY-THREAT (SWOT) CHART

A strength-weakness-opportunity-threat (SWOT) chart results from an environment assessment, also known as situational or community analysis or profiling.

The chart focuses on identifying why or how the service has an advantage over other competitive, available information services. Conducting a SWOT analysis prompts strategic thinking to determine your strengths and weaknesses (from the internal environment assessment) or opportunities and threats (from the external environment assessment) of the service. This in turn assists in developing a viable marketing strategy. Assessments and SWOT charts are covered in Chapter 4.

CLARIFYING OBJECTIVES

Objectives focus on achieving specific results within established time frames. They have well-defined targets with easily measured quantifiable elements. The accomplishment of each objective moves the service toward its goals, as they are the end result or focal points for directing strategies. More detail on objectives is provided in Chapter 5.

DETERMINING ORGANIZATIONAL STRATEGY AND ACTION PLANS

When you know where you are (from the assessments) and what you want (from your vision, mission, and objectives), then you can figure out what you need to do to achieve your objectives. Strategies describe this process, and they identify how the service will grow or what will make your library successful over time. This section, the focus of Chapter 6, tells what specific initiatives you will use to achieve your vision.

Strategy involves the entire library and concerns itself with the basic direction for the future: the library's purpose, ambitions, resources, how it interacts with the community in which it operates, and, very important, how it interacts with other businesses in the marketplace within which it competes. The plan creates an advantage over your competitors by identifying and exploiting the added value of the service. It covers the range and depth of the library's activities and guides the changing and evolving relationship of the library with its environment (International Federation of Accountants, 2006).

Action-oriented plans identify broadly the work to be done, and they also define specific tasks and their associated deadlines. Each action plan directly relates to an objective and a strategy.

MAKING MARKETING PLANS

Developing a marketing strategy requires assessing your service's competitiveness in terms of price, quality, and features, then clarifying how you will enter the market and how you will advertise or promote your services to clients, identifying packaging or how you will present deliverables, physical or electronic access, service support, and specific forecasts of the related costs. This section tells why you think clients will use your service and how you plan to let them know about it. More details on marketing can be found in Chapter 7.

ESTABLISHING AN EVALUATION PROCESS (PERFORMANCE MEASURES)

Measurements of success, both tangible and intangible, are integral to successful implementation of any plan. Measuring success requires a realistic assessment and creating a feedback loop to repair or restructure tasks as the situation evolves to make sure that your service stays on track toward a goal. Evaluation is covered in Chapter 8.

FORMING A FINANCIAL PLAN

The financial plan, detailed in Chapter 9, translates everything you have said throughout the business plan into numbers. It presents a fiscal picture of the market strategy and implementation plans.

Included are the following:

- An income statement providing an overview of revenue, costs, and profits for two years
- A current and projected balance sheet listing what the service owns, liabilities, and the value of the service at the time the business plan is drafted—complete these for the start-up and annually for two years
- At a minimum, monthly projections for the first year plus quarterly (or annual) projections for the next 12 months— include in the business plan only high-level financial projections in summary tables, and all detailed schedules and analyses should be placed in appendices after the plan
- A cash flow statement describing how the income is received, distributed, and net amounts accessible by month for the first two years (Small Business Development Centers/SCORE, 1998)

FIVE BUSINESS PLAN PRESENTATION FORMATS

The complete business plan can take several different formats. These examples show possibilities for presenting the information in your business plan.

PRESENTATION POSSIBILITY 1

I. Executive summary—business description, marketing strategies, management/key personnel, financial needs/application of funds, earnings/projections

II. Library information
   A. History/significant achievements
   B. Vision/mission statement/goals/objectives/plans/desired image
   C. Legal form of organization
   D. Organization hierarchy
   E. Services (and characteristics)

III. SWOT analysis
   A. Organizational—strengths and weaknesses (competitive advantages, key success factors, value to clients)
   B. Environmental—opportunities and threats (industry overview, trends, growth rate, outlook for future)

IV. Manufacturing and operations
   A. Location
   B. Physical facility/layout
   C. Capital equipment
   D. Sources of supply
   E. Availability of labor

V. Marketing
   A. Total market analysis
   B. Target market
   C. Competition
   D. Distribution
   E. Pricing
   F. Promotion

VI. Management
   A. Human resource management
   B. Duties/responsibilities of principals
   C. Board of directors (if applicable)
   D. Resumes of principals and key managers

VII. Financial
   A. Budget

      B. Balance sheet

      C. Income statement

      D. Cash flow statement

      E. Key business ratios

      F. Loan proposal—amount, purpose, repayment schedule

PRESENTATION POSSIBILITY 2

1. Executive summary
2. Situational analysis
3. Project history, status, and schedule
4. The journal or service description
5. The business and/or funding model
6. Editorial, content and copyright considerations
7. Technology considerations and production platform
8. Online user considerations
9. Markets, marketing, sales, and pricing
10. Organization and staffing
11. Financial plan: budget and forecast
12. Operating plan
13. Business risks, contingencies, and midcourse corrections
14. Conclusion (or end notes)
15. Exhibits (Open Society Institute, 2003)

PRESENTATION POSSIBILITY 3

- Mission, vision, values, and goals
- Executive summary
- Product or service description
- Needs assessment or market research
- Environment and competition
- Markets and services
- Pricing
- Distribution
- Communication
- Organizational structure
- Operations, including facilities and equipment, management and staffing, and legal issues

- Financial plans
- Product evaluation and usability assessment (excerpted from Bishoff and Allen, 2004)

PRESENTATION POSSIBILITY 4

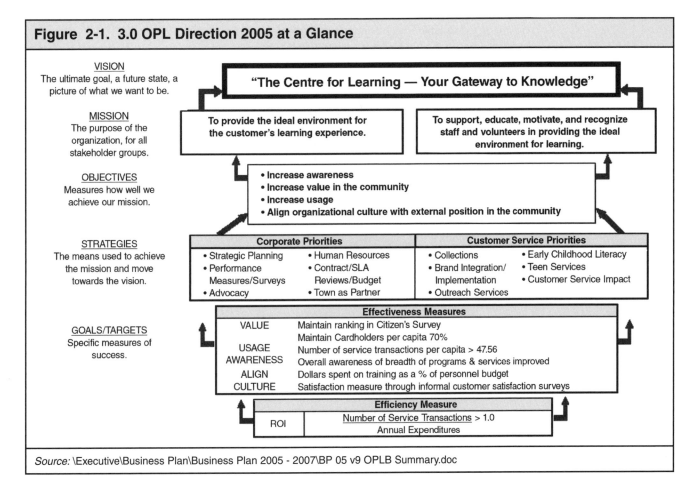

Figure 2-1. 3.0 OPL Direction 2005 at a Glance

Source: \Executive\Business Plan\Business Plan 2005 - 2007\BP 05 v9 OPLB Summary.doc

PRESENTATION POSSIBILITY 5

- Outline of product/services—cost/fees
- Vision/goals
- Personnel (decision-making authority)
- Target audience
- Competition
- Measurement of success (tangible and intangible, marketing)
- Evaluation/assessment (Norlin, 2004)

REFERENCES

Bishoff, Liz and Nancy Allen. 2004. "A Business Planning Template: Considerations for Cultural Heritage Organizations and Their Digital Asset Programs." In *Business Planning for Cultural Heritage Institutions*, by Liz Bishoff and Nancy Allen. Washington, DC: Council on Library and Information Resources, pp. 29–48. Available: www.clir.org/pubs/reports/pub124/pub124.pdf.

Gumpert, David E. 2000. "Executive Summary As a Guiding Light." Inc.com (October 2000). Available: www.inc.com/articles/2000/10/14875.html.

International Federation of Accountants. 2006. "Business Planning Guide: Practical Applications for SMES." New York: IFAC. Available: www.cpaireland.ie/UserFiles/File/Technical%20Resources/SME%20Resource/Business%20Planning%20Guide%20%20Practical%20Application%20for%20SMEspdf.pdf.

Inc.com. 2000. "Pointers on Putting Together Your Business Plan." BusinessTown.com (April 2000). Available: www.inc.com/articles/2000/04/18474.html.

Norlin, Elaina. 2004. "Non-Profit Business Plan—Simplified. Business Plans for Dummies." PowerPoint presentation presented at Internet Librarian conference, November 17, 2004, Monterey, California.

Oakville Public Library Executive Directors Team. 2005. "3.0 OPL Direction 2005 At A Glance." In "Oakville Public Library Business Plan 2005 Summary." Oakville, ON: Oakville Public Library, pp. 5–6. Available: www.opl.on.ca/BP_05_v9_OPLB_Summary.pdf.

Open Society Institute. "Open Access Journal: Model Business Plan: A Supplemental Guide for Open Access Journal Developers and Publishers." (July 2003). Available: www.soros.org/openaccess/oajguides/oaj_supplement_0703.pdf.

Scholarly Publishing and Academic Resources Coalition. 2002. "Gaining Independence: A Manual for Planning the Launch of a Nonprofit Electronic Publishing Venture." Washington, DC: SPARC. Available: www.arl.org/sparc/GI/SPARC_GI_MANUAL_VERSION1.0.PDF.

Small Business Development Centers/SCORE. 1998. "Entrepreneurs' Guide to Business Success: Writing Your Business Plan." November 30. Available: www.sba.gov/smallbusinessplanner/plan/writeabusinessplan/SERV_WRRITINGBUSPLAN.html; www.sba.gov/ smallbusinessplanner/plan/writeabusinessplan/SERV_USINGBUSPLAN.html.

U.S. Small Business Administration. "Small Business Planner: Write a Business Plan." U.S. Small Business Administration. (2007). Available: www.sba.gov/smallbusinessplanner/plan/writeabusiness plan/serv_bp_compd esc.html.

3 DESCRIBING YOUR SERVICE CONCEPT, VISION, AND MISSION STATEMENTS

DETERMINING INTENTIONS

Business plans are written to communicate your library's intentions. As you begin to formulate your business plan, it is best to start by taking a step back to be sure that everyone is on the same page. Begin by describing who you are and how your library is managed (does a participatory, matrix, or classic style of management predominate?); include your mission and vision statements, as they further inform readers about your intentions and beliefs; and identify your clients and their needs. Present the benefits of current services; what you plan to offer in the future, why, and to whom; evaluate the strengths and weaknesses of each service competing for your client's attention and time, and look for opportunities to reach more deeply into your market. Your description is a high-level picture of how the different elements of your service fit together. Here, you identify the primary success factors that give the service a competitive advantage over other information providers competing for client interests (U.S. Small Business Administration, 2007).

The mission statement describes the central purposes of the service from the client's perspective. It defines the fundamental and unique purpose that the library attempts to serve and identifies your products or services and clients. The vision statement is expansive and idealistic, detailing your specific objectives. Together these statements and the description provide the foundation for building a strategy designed to reach your objectives.

DESCRIBING THE SERVICE CONCEPT

BASIC DEFINITIONS

The description of the service presents a high-level picture of the relationship among market needs, current services designed to meet those needs, and the primary success factors that give the library an advantage over other information providers (U.S. Small Business Administration, 2007). The description includes the library mission statement, current status, and major successes or achievements. In short, it identifies the library's reason for being.

The description also identifies who will do what for the proposed service. The working team is introduced here, and their roles are noted. A simple organizational chart can illustrate the team's structure and explain its communication patterns, reporting lines, and positions of responsibility (examples of organizational charts can be found below). Including individual profiles and resumes will identify experience and strength, demonstrating that the team has both the knowledge and necessary skills to run the service. If there are any gaps in the team's expertise, this section may explain how the gaps will be filled or how problems generated by the gap will be handled. It may also be appropriate here to introduce and profile the library committee or board and outline their role in the service's management.

Include what information technology or technical expertise must be acquired by the library or will be needed in the future. Describe the backgrounds and qualifications of currently employed technical staff (an example of a staff description can be found below). This will allow you to more easily anticipate future needs and how best to meet them.

If the business plan focuses on a service, describe what you offer, writing in short and clear sentences. Emphasize your service's distinguishing features (its competitive advantage in the market). Include a description of the service, what it does, the specific needs it meets, the market potential for growth, which clients will use it, and pricing information. Indicate how you will perform the service.

If the business plan focuses on a library, describe the essence of the library, defining its unique or distinguishing (competitive advantage) features, the market needs it meets, the potential for growth, which clients will use it, and pricing information. Pricing is an important element of the description that many libraries may not be familiar with or comfortable with. Pricing information covers all direct and indirect costs (Association of Specialized and Cooperative Library Agencies, 2007; Weingand, 1999). Ideally, business planning should include information on the full cost of providing products and services, even if the parent organization decides not to recover that cost. The types of cost data collected should include both direct and indirect costs, as illustrated in Table 3-1.

- Define the price level. This is based on development, production, packaging, storage, delivery, and promotion costs as well as determining how much clients value the service.
- Define the pricing plan to identify decisions about pricing. Will you provide single, multiple, or differential pricing? Specify whether clients will commit funds up front, through a subscription plan or deposit account. Describe the structure of your various price levels for different client groups and geographical locations.

- Specify retail costs and pricing, including competitive position, pricing below competition, pricing above competition, price lining, and service costs.
- Identify and define the circumstances appropriate to offering a discount.
- Identify the nonprice costs of using or purchasing the service, such as travel time, wait time, etc. How important are the nonprice costs to the user?
- Identify any legal restrictions established by funding sources.

For example, if funded by state grants, then in-state clients may need a payment rate lower than that for out-of-state clients.

Table 3-1. Types of Cost Data	
Direct Costs	**Indirect Costs**
Rent/space	Building operations, including heating, air-conditioning, and lighting; depreciation costs
Salaries for continuing and temporary personnel	Salaries of permanent staff only indirectly involved, such as: • accounting • legal • human resources
Other areas involved in producing the product or service, such as technology, marketing, or educational services	
Supplies specifically for the product or service	Supplies from general stock
Promotional expenses	Supplemental services (e.g., printing, billing)
Source: Weingand (1999: 106).	

Due to their missions, some libraries have no experience in this area. A key point to remember when venturing for the first time into new waters is to recognize the value that different clients or their groups place on different libraries or services. Use this understanding as a starting point for developing your pricing strategy.

Bishoff and Allen (2004) note that some projects develop cost models by dividing total costs by the number of objects generated for the product or service (for instance, the number of digital images created). While this may be a relatively easy method of cost assessment, it is not fully accurate. Instead, take an approach that includes not only the expenses just noted but also capital expenses. Hardware and software must be depreciated over a period of time that generally extends beyond the time frame for a single project. When amortized, project costs will vary. Other questions to ask include:

- Is the initial investment intended to be used for other projects?

- Was product research included in the overall cost?

- Have staff costs been appropriately allocated to the project?

- Are staffing costs higher than anticipated because of the learning curve or delays in the product development? (This will drive up project and product costs and could have an impact on the cost per item if the simple calculation method noted above is used.) (Bishoff and Allen, 2004)

KEY POINTS TO INCLUDE

When writing a description of the service, cover these points (see also Worksheet 3-1 ⓒⓓ :

- Describe the service in terms of what the client gets, not the product. For example, "We provide access to clinical medical information for answering diagnostic and treatment questions," not "My service connects you to the Internet."

- Build the description around clients' needs and how the service will solve their problems and fulfill their needs, keeping within the scope of the library's mission and objectives.

- Describe the extent of the demand for the service.

- Identify everything being provided in terms of what the client will use. For example, describe what jobs or problems the service eliminates for the client. Identify all unique characteristics of the service. What does it offer? Identify its special advantages or name the benefits offered. What will the service do for the client? Does it do what the client needs?

- Clearly state the service's special qualities and why it gives clients a better value than any other service available to your clients.

- Define any technical terms and introduce all acronyms.

- Describe the status of all discussions of legal aspects such as patents, copyrights, and trademarks, and address the necessary government clearances. (*List continues on page 26.*)

Worksheet 3-1. Describe Your Service
Describe the structure of your library including management style, locations, annual budget, staff profiles, your mission statement, and any other pertinent information.
Describe the community you serve, including its needs, how you have identified its needs, and what services you have designed to meet them.
State the current capabilities of the library and any successes or achievements.
Discuss the objectives of the current plan at hand, identifying why it will be successful; identify your success factors that will give this service an advantage over other similar services; identify the current status in reaching any of the objectives noted in this plan, including any beta test strategies or other attempts to assess your market's response to the plan.
Introduce the team members working on this particular service, noting their roles, capabilities, experiences, or strengths.
If it will aid in identifying overall staff support or communication channels, then include a simple organizational chart.
If you have any gaps in staffing, IT, or any other core support group, then identify these in high-level terms and state how they will be overcome.
If you will charge for this service, then briefly establish the pricing structure for the service; if you will not charge, then briefly identify how the service will be funded.
Refine your description here:

- If appropriate, include photographs.
- Describe the unique marketability of the service.
- Describe how the service will be produced in a timely and consistent manner, and by whom.
- Describe how the service will be produced in a cost-effective manner; explain how you know this will happen.

EXAMPLES OF DESCRIPTIONS OF LIBRARIES AND SERVICES

Digital Library Federation Aquifer Business Plan (CD)
Pricing Statement
Source: Kott, 2006; © Digital Library Federation.

In the first phase of the initiative, DLF Aquifer collections and services will be made available to DLF Aquifer participants, DLF members, the library community, and beyond without cost to the user. Future project phases may include a modeling fee for service scenarios.

George Eliot Hospital NHS Trust
Staff Description
Source: Brook, 2007: 12; reprinted courtesy of Nigel Brook, Library Services Manager, William Harvey Library, George Eliot Hospital NHS Trust.

Staff

The Library Service Manager is a Chartered Librarian who is employed full time. The Clinical Librarian acts as the service deputy manager and is currently working toward full Chartership and is also a full-time post. Administrative support is provided by one full-time Senior Library Assistant and one part-time Library Assistant. The Librarian and Clinical Librarian are funded through MADEL; the Library Assistants are funded through Trust funds with a L9631 contribution form the SHA to support half of the Senior Library Assistant post.

All Library staff participates in training programs organized both by the George Eliot Hospital and by the West Midlands Regional Library Unit. Library staff also attends regular appraisal interviews and have individual training plans, in line with KSF guidelines, to help them to develop their skills and knowledge.

During 2005, the Senior Library Assistant post was upgraded from a part-time to a full-time post: the vacant Clinical Librarian (KBPF) post was also successfully filled. The Review of Library and Knowledge Services from Coventry and Warwickshire 2005 has highlighted that the North Warwickshire patch is under-resourced in terms of staffing.

Increase in staffing levels has meant that a full-service relaunch was achieved in 2005, with all Library Services reinstated with immediate effect. In addition, the extra staff time has enabled us to address the serious flaws and inconsistencies inherited by the new Library Team. We have also reinitiated the formal link with PALS service and are joint-working on a database of patient-information leaflets to help the Trust meeting its CNST standards.

Library staffing needs were reviewed earlier this year, taking account of the greater demand for outreach services to support evidence-based practice and increased use of both literature search and training services.

We have already received requests for extended staffed opening hours and access to professional services during the evening. We project that extra posts will be required if demand continues to rise exponentially. For more information see the 2007 "Staffing Review."

London Health Libraries electronic Knowledge Access Team (eKAT)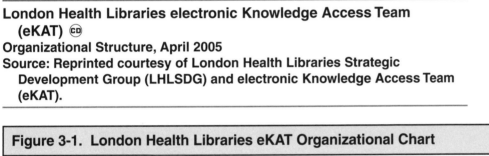
Organizational Structure, April 2005
Source: Reprinted courtesy of London Health Libraries Strategic Development Group (LHLSDG) and electronic Knowledge Access Team (eKAT).

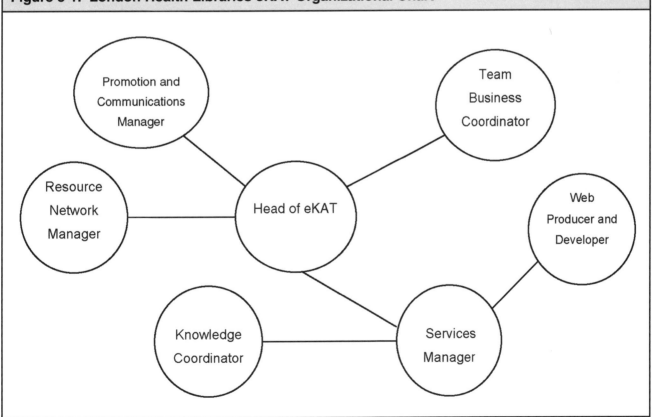

Figure 3-1. London Health Libraries eKAT Organizational Chart

Kenosha Public Library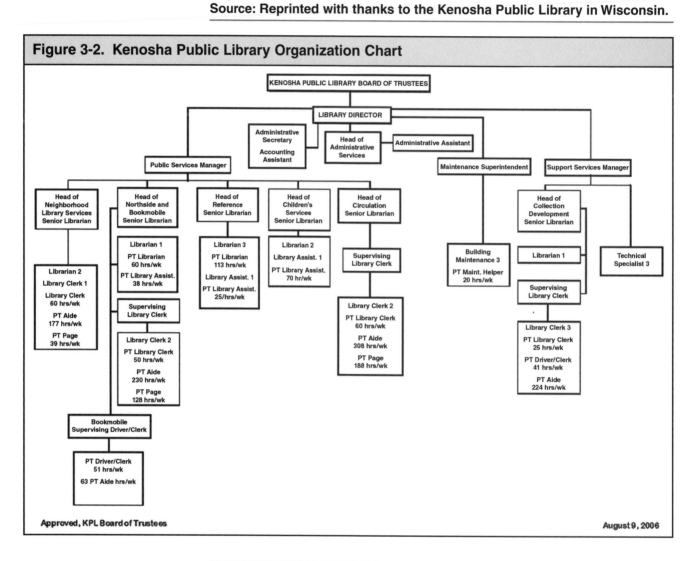
Organizational Structure
Source: Reprinted with thanks to the Kenosha Public Library in Wisconsin.

Figure 3-2. Kenosha Public Library Organization Chart

Association for Library Collections & Technical Services (ALCTS) Business Plan 2005 ⓒ
Management Summary
Source: Association for Library Collections & Technical Services, 2005; reprinted courtesy of Association for Library Collections & Technical Services (ALCTS).

1.0 Management Summary

1.1 Organizational Structure

ALCTS has positively positioned itself organizationally to move forward on this plan. The Membership Committee is actively seeking new outlets for its promotional and marketing projects. The ALCTS board has supported funding for the library support staff plan for its initial year, and funding is in the proposed FY 2002 budget for the second year. Through its sections and their committees, ALCTS has a solid support structure for its products and services.

1.2 Management Team

After an initial period of adjustment from the dissolution of its partnership with LAMA [Library Administration and Management Association], ALCTS should have in place appropriate staff resources to pursue this plan.

1.3 Management Team Gaps

Again, with the split of LAMA and ALCTS, some previously held expertise would have to be replaced, and staff responsibilities reconfigured. This is a temporary situation, which will be resolved in time.

Marketing General could be used to help structure a marketing program. Several ALA units could be called on to provide necessary support services such as Web design, publication production help, and publicity support. ALCTS anticipates that the knowledge-management function within ALA will help define some of the information gaps that might exist and provide assistance in resolving those gaps.

U.S. Environmental Protection Agency's Regional Libraries and Centers (2004) ⒸⒹ
Source: U.S. Environmental Protection Agency, 2004.

II. Background

Established in 1971, the Environmental Protection Agency's Library Network is composed of 28 libraries serving 10 regional offices, 2 research centers, 12 research laboratories, and 4 separate libraries in headquarters. The libraries differ in function, scope of collections, extent of services, and organizational reporting structure. Each library also differs with respect to the amount of support they offer for pubic access, their use of new technologies, and their level of budgetary support. Each library supports a collection of materials that have been chosen over time. These collections contain a wide range of information resources on environmental protection and management, basic sciences such as biology and chemistry, applied sciences such as engineering and toxicology, environmental law and regulation, and issues unique to specific regions or ecologies.

The combined EPA collections include 504,000 books and reports, 3,500 journal titles, 25,000 maps, and 3,600,000 information objects on microfilm. The Online Library System (OLS) provides the shared catalog for all of these resources and is available to both EPA staff and the public via the Internet. The EPA Web site, with over 60,000 PDF files indexed, provides searchable access to full text, online EPA documents. In addition, for EPA staff, the "Desktop Library" provides an electronic collection of over 430 mostly commercial information resources. It can be accessed by all agency staff directly from their desktop computers via the Intranet. The Desktop Library (http://intranet.epa.gov/desktop) includes the full text of scientific and policy journals, reports, newspapers, reference works, and databases.

Separately, each library is charged with providing services to EPA staff and external users with access to their location. However, each library within the network has always leveraged the capabilities of the other libraries to assist patrons with information not available at their own locations. This cooperation allows the agency to extend the value of its materials and services to create an "institutional value" greater than the sum of its parts.

Finally, some libraries contain materials that the agency must make publicly available under law. Two examples are the Regional National Priorities List Public Dockets and the risk management plans for chemical facilities.

Sandwell Metropolitan Borough Library Council
Source: Sandwell Metropolitan Borough Council, 2005: 1–2; reprinted courtesy of Sandwell Metropolitan Borough Library.

Section 1: Service Description

1. The Objectives and Core Services of the Library and Information Service in 2004/05

1.1 Our objective and core services are:

Our mission: "Open to everyone: to explore, discover and enjoy"

Our objectives:

- To increase the numbers of people reading and learning in Sandwell by providing access to books, IT [information technology], and activities in a welcoming and safe environment
- To encourage Sandwell people to develop digital kills and use electronic resources, including e-government resources, by providing free public access to the Internet and other electronic resources with support from knowledgeable staff
- To support local communities by working with partners to reach excluded groups, removing barriers to library use and promoting resources that encourage a sense of community and personal pride
- To preserve the documented record of the communities and neighborhoods that have been part of the Sandwell area in the past, now, and in the future
- To provide public value by deploying resources effectively to achieve the greatest benefits to all people living, working, and studying in Sandwell

Core services:

Libraries and CHAS [Community History Archives Service]

- Support from trained and knowledgeable staff
- Printed and electronic access to reference materials, information sources, and council information
- Provision of learner support, including taster sessions, Information Advice and Guidance accreditation, and promotional activities (e.g., Adult Learners' Week)
- Public access PCs that are free to use and have standard office applications, e-mail, and Internet access at minimum
- Disability access through use of special formats, supportive software, equipment, or building adaptations

Libraries

- Lending of books, CDs, spoken word, video, DVDs, and CD-ROMs with electronic access to the catalog and online renewals and reservations

- Program of reader development activity for children and adults
- Newspapers and magazines
- Provision of resources in community languages—staff, books, newspapers, electronic, audiovisual
- Local history resources in all libraries supported by local history resources at CHAS
- Homework clubs and study space
- Toy library and Bookstart
- Specialist collections of items for loan (e.g., Basic Skills Tutor materials, GCSE resources, parents information)
- Loans of resources to community groups and Tutors, Volunteer Readers
- Space for others to use, (e.g., Joblink, Pension Surgeries, learning providers)
- Photocopying and fax facilities

CHAS

- Public access to records through the Search Room and electronically
- Collecting, documenting, preserving, and conserving records relating to the geographical area covered by Sandwell MBC
- Holding records relating to public bodies operating in Sandwell
- Supporting local studies provision in libraries
- Providing information about local and family history for fact to face and remote enquiries
- Holding national information that relates to Sandwell
- Creating surrogates via microfilm, digitization to increase access

These are delivered through:
- Sandwell Central Library
- A network of 18 community libraries
- Special Library Services—2 mobile libraries and Housebound Library Service
- Community History and Archive Service
- Library support services providing essential services that can be delivered more cost effectively on a Borough-wide basis

What are our core strengths?
- Putting the customer at the heart of what we do
- Being open to everyone and used by all communities
- Supporting information, independent, voluntary learning
- Reaching into local communities and providing a space that can be used by others
- Supporting and working with partners and local networks (e.g., Local Learning Panels)
- Delivering what we say we will
- Promoting the pleasures of reading as well as supporting literacy development

Calgary Public Library
Source: Calgary Public Library, 2006: 4; (c) Calgary Public Library, All
    Rights Reserved.

About the Calgary Public Library

The Calgary Public Library is a network of 17 locations offering library services, collections, and access to technology and programs to Calgarians of every age, ability, ethnocultural group, and socioeconomic status.

Calgarians hold their Library in high regard as a welcoming neighbor and focal point in their communities. Comfortable and convenient, the library is full of options to read, watch, or listen to. Every library location prides itself on personal service, and has exciting new dimensions through technology. In 2004, 98 percent of Calgarians rated the library as an important resource in their community, and 96 percent said the library was a good investment of tax dollars.

The Calgary Public Library attracted more than 65,000 new members in 2004, and over 73 percent of all Calgary households now have a library user. High-quality collections, diverse programs, and inviting facilities all added to this significant increase.

Among library users, satisfaction levels are high. In 2004, 90 percent of the respondents to the library's independently conducted Annual Satisfaction Survey said they were satisfied or completely satisfied with the library overall. Respondents reported similar high levels of satisfaction with the knowledge and helpfulness of library staff, information services provided, as well as the convenience, cleanliness, and location of library facilities. Satisfaction levels with electronic resources, collections of library materials, and hours of opening were only marginally lower.

Use of library services, programs, and collections is also high. In 2004, a total of 27.4 million library transactions were made, including in-library use of materials, in-person visits to library facilities, Web site visits, and requests for information. Circulation of library materials represented nearly half of total uses in 2004. Calgarians borrowed more than 13.3 million items in a wide variety of formats, making the Calgary Public Library the second busiest system in Canada.

The library contributes to community vitality in several ways. Encouraging children's imaginations. Promoting literacy. Supporting the development of well-educated and competitive workforce. Providing the information resources that help make local businesses profitable. Helping Calgarians relax with the latest bestsellers. These are just some of the many ways the library enriches its customers' lives, helping to build both community and capacity.

The Calgary Public Library is an efficient operation, managed with prudence and resourcefulness. Costs are among the lowest and productivity at or near the highest in comparison with libraries of similar size in Canada. Recent capital projects, including the construction of the Crowfoot Library, the construction of the Country Hills Library, and the expansion of the Forest Lawn library, have been completed on time and under budget.

Fifth Judicial Circuit-Library System, United States Court of Appeals
Source: Fifth Circuit Court of Appeals Library, 2005–2006: 1.

The Circuit Library System

The Fifth Circuit Library System supports the information needs of the federal judges in Louisiana, Mississippi, Texas, and their staffs. To a lesser extent, the library also supports the information needs of the practicing federal bar in those states. The library system is composed of one headquarters library in New Orleans and ten satellite libraries located in Baton Rouge, Lafayette, and Shreveport, Louisiana; Gulfport and Jackson, Mississippi; and Austin, Beaumont, Brownsville, Houston, and San Antonio, Texas. Thirteen staff members are in New Orleans and twelve staff members are located in satellite libraries.

London Health Libraries Strategy and Development Group and the London Workforce Development Group, Business Plan Agreement, 2006–2007 ⓒ
Source: London Health Libraries Strategic Development Group and London Workforce Development Group, 2006: 2; NHS London, formerly South East London Workforce Development Confederation (SELWDC).

Background

London Health Libraries is a network of health libraries serving the health (and increasingly the social care) workforce in London. There are over 70 NHS-funded library sites managed either by the NHS or higher education, with a workforce of 450, and a total investment of £6 million from the five London Strategic Health Authorities. In addition to the NHS and higher education-managed services, there is active participation by a number of libraries in the voluntary sector.

London Health Libraries Strategy and Development Group (LHLSDG) was set up by the five London Workforce Development Confederation Chief Executives (from April 2004, the London Workforce Development Group). Its members are the five SHA library leads plus the head of the pan-London electronic Knowledge Access Team (eKAT).

Working groups with formal representation from the five London sector library networks are informing and embedding networks at the local level.

In addition to NHS Trusts, LHLSDG works with a range of other partners to deliver its mission. These include colleagues in higher education, social care, the London Deanery, and the public library sector. Coordination with national library initiatives is ensured through active participation in the national Library and Knowledge Development Network (LKDN).

Kenosha Public Library Business Plan (2007) ⓒ
Service Highlights by Location
Source: With thanks to the Kenosha Public Library in Wisconsin.

The KPL board and staff provide top quality service to our customers at our buildings and the bookmobile.

SOUTHWEST LIBRARY [see also Table 3-2]
7979 38th Avenue
Traditional one-story brick and stone structure. Originally constructed in 1981 and expanded and renovated in 2004. Used as the headquarters for the delivery of major KPL services to the public. Gross area—42,300 square feet.

Table 3-2. Highlights of Southwest Collections: Primary KPL collections for reference, children, and young adults; largest circulating collections and foreign language collections; and last copy respository for KPL

Southwest Library	2003 actual	2004 actual	2005 actual	2006 est.	2007 goal
Checkout of library materials	402,554	515,011	666,388	694,000	695,000
Reference and information questions	33,595	68,188	103,958	106,000	107,000
Computer workstation sessions	36,107	118,903	186,114	196,000	209,000
Library visits	205,082	337,836	467,207	460,000	461,000
Hours open per week	69	69	69	69	69

NORTHSIDE LIBRARY [see also Table 3-3]
1500 27th Avenue
Traditional one-story brick and stone structure. Built in 1993. Used for general library services and Bookmobile and Outreach Service. Gross area—24,600 square feet.

Table 3-3. Highlights of Northside Collections: KPL general circulation collections for all ages and main KPL adult special needs collection

Northside Library	2003 actual	2004 actual	2005 actual	2006 est.	2007 goal
Checkout of library materials	441,632	409,641	357,905	350,000	350,000
Reference and information questions	41,859	40,313	36,488	40,000	41,000
Computer workstation sessions	35,933	42,126	46,384	78,000	87,000
Library visits	256,053	255,590	219,639	226,000	227,000
Library collections (by volume)	136,246	120,490	121,712	118,000	120,000
Hours open per week	69	69	69	69	69

UPTOWN LIBRARY [see also Table 3-4]
2419 63rd Street
One-story Flemish style structure compatible with the residential area in which it is located. Built in 1925. Used for general library services to adults and children and as the

headquarters for the Kenosha Literacy Council, Inc. Occupancy is approximately 50 percent Library, 50 percent Kenosha Literary Council, Inc. Gross area—4,073 (2,274 upstairs, 1,799 downstairs) square feet.

Table 3-4. Highlights of Uptown Collections: General circulating collections for all ages

Uptown Library	2003 actual	2004 actual	2005 actual	2006 est.	2007 goal
Checkout of library materials	47,443	42,490	32,809	34,000	35,000
Reference and information questions	25,368	22,928	10,488	9,000	9,000
Computer workstation sessions	6,146	7,815	6,701	7,000	8,000
Library visits	32,155	35,928	29,526	30,000	31,000
Library collections (by volume)	27,375	19,556	19,514	18,500	20,200
Hours open per week	40	40	40	40	40

BOOKMOBILE [see also Table 3-5]
Headquartered at Northside Library
Forty-foot rear engine bus type vehicle acquired in 2004. Provides general library services throughout the City and County of Kenosha.

Table 3-5. Highlights of Bookmobile Collection: General circulating collections for all ages

Bookmobile	2003 actual	2004 actual	2005 actual	2006 est.	2007 goal
Checkout of library materials	56,727	51,090	51,615	57,000	58,000
Reference and information questions	3,940	3,195	3,151	4,000	4,000
Library visits	20,947	20,193	19,186	23,000	24,000
Library collection (by volume)	13,584	11,344	11,706	10,300	7,000
Hours open per week	30	30	30	30	30

CIVIC CENTER BUILDING [see also Table 3-6]
812 56th Street
Former police station owned by the City of Kenosha. KPL rents approximately 14,000

square feet here for library administration, support, maintenance, and storage. Ten-year lease for this space extends from 2001 through 2011.

Table 3-6. Highlights of Storage Collection: Archival reference materials and overflow collections

Civic Center Building	2003 actual	2004 actual	2005 actual	2006 est.	2007 goal
Library collection (by volume)	13,197	10,662	1,422	1,700	1,800
Hours open per week	42.5	42.5	42.5	42.5	42.5

Franklin Templeton Global Research Library
Library Competencies and Services Leveraged by or Transferred to Research Groups Worldwide
Source: Brigevich, 2004; Franklin Templeton Global Research Library.

The competencies and services listed below are unique, and the library, managed by a professional librarian, is the only entity in the organization that offers them.

Content Management
- Identify, evaluate, and purchase high quality, cost-efficient print and electronic information sources and services accessible from the research analysts' office, home, on the road, or in the library.
- Leverage global contract agreements, corporate discounts, and vendor support teams to obtain maximum benefit and ROI [return on investment] from partnerships with third-party information providers.
- Customize vendor products through effective use of technology to reduce information overload and increase relevancy of information in the context of investment research process. Examples: Research Portal, Virtual Library, LexisNexis Express Search, automated news alerts.
- Provide training on the use of external databases and online services including searching techniques and strategies, best searching practices, matching requests to the right sources, etc.

Information Research
- Research, analyze, format, synthesize and personalize information from a large number of disparate sources, including commercial research systems, broker research repositories, subject experts, academic press, business and trade publications, and Internet.
- Supply research analysts with different types of information including company filings, broker recommendations, financials, independent research, macroeconomics and statistics, government and academic studies, trends and forecasts, biographical profiles, news analysis, etc.
- Balance street research with independent, academic, and government information to ensure a holistic view.
- Support industry teams with industry related information research.

Research Portal

- Integration of the third-party sources for a seamless access to qualitative research and information in the context of company, industry, and country research. This can be modified for each research group based on their unique specifications.
- Conceptual design of the portal "gears," views, and functionality based on research process and the analysts' information-seeking behavior patterns.
- Search strategies and queries designed to produce the most relevant results and filter out irrelevant material.
- Quality control through testing and communication with the portal team.

Virtual Library

- Phase I: VL provides a Web-based catalog of all information assets available within the library and the Global Equity Group, including databases, online services, publications, books and Web sites. This application is flexible for rolling out on a global scale.
- Phase II: VL will provide industry and country views where internal information is displayed along with external research and material from disparate sources.

Country and Industry Information Packages (CIIPs)

- Customized for each analyst, the packages consist of documents manually selected from disparate sources, some not available on desktops through the standard group subscription. CIIP saves the analysts' time by assembling important pieces of screened and evaluated information, including independent industry and country analysis, broker research, trends, forecasts, news articles, statistical data, and select Web resources. CIIPs assist research analysts in preparation of their semiannual research reports.

Automated News Alerts

- Personalized news alerts are available via e-mail to monitor analysts' companies, industries, countries, or any topic of interest to the receiver. The most precise search strings are developed to produce highly relevant and targeted news, saving time, reducing information overload on analysis, and increasing relevance of information received.

THE VISION STATEMENT

BASIC DEFINITIONS

The expansive and idealistic vision statement details the service's specific objectives. The vision identifies where you want the service to go, becoming the compass for your future aspirations without specifying the means used to achieve those ends (International Federation of Accountants, 2006: 9). With short and succinct verbiage, this inspiring statement describes what your organization intends to become. A frequently reported pitfall in expressing vision statements is the failure to boil things down to a manageable list of initiatives. Culling this list involves thinking through and then making difficult choices. These choices communicate volumes about how staff should be spending their time (Kaplan, 2007).

In the following section, you will find questions whose answers will help create your vision statement. If not already created, the vision statement can emerge from the environmental assessment and SWOT analysis conducted in the next stage of the planning process. If you are part of a larger organization, the vision statement supports the parent organization's vision. In essence, the service exists to help the larger organization reach its goals. Your focus, intentions, and efforts take their cue from the parent organization's vision.

KEY POINTS TO INCLUDE

Answering some of the following questions may assist in constructing a vision statement (see also Worksheet 3-2 ⓒ). To answer these questions, research may be needed on markets, competition, and potential for growth—elements addressed in Chapter 4.

WHO?

- Identify the clients. Describe them by identifying their needs and how the service will meet them.
- With whom can you partner?
- Who can provide professional and strategic advice to help grow this service properly?
- What background experience does the team have that will lead the service to success?

WHAT?

- What exactly is the service? What are you building: a library, products, services, or all of these?
- What will the service be known for among its clients?
- What is the manager's role? How will time be spent?
- What will you see two years from now?
- What are the central purposes and activities of the service?
- What are its strengths, weaknesses, opportunities, or threats?
- What are its major objectives and key strategies?

- What is the business environment like?
- What benefits will you offer your clients?
- What is unique about the service? What will set it apart from its competitors?

WHY?

- Why are you creating the service?
- Why will your clients use the service?
- Why will the administration allocate money to this service?
- Why is anyone interested in this particular service?
- Why is the library uniquely qualified to provide this service?

WHEN?

- When will the service be operational?
- When will space be required?
- When will equipment be required?

WHERE?

- Where does the service provide coverage (department, school, city, region, local, regional, national, or international)?
- Where are the administrative offices and location of service offered?
- Where do you want to be; where are you taking your service?
- Where is the service located? Describe the physical space in terms of size, layout, parking, image, appearance, ambiance, etc.

HOW?

- How will this service be financed?
- How does management plan to interact with staff, suppliers, and clients?
- How will the service be run, and by whom? How will it be structured?
- How will clients obtain the access to the services?
- How did the idea for the service originate? What has been done to develop the idea? How and from whom will component goods and services be obtained?
- How do you want the service to look in 18 to 24 months?

Worksheet 3-2. Write Your Vision Statement

Within the next _____ years, grow _____
                                                          (Service)

into a $ _____ local, regional, national, or international

_____
(Type or description of service)

providing _____

to _____
                              (Describe clients)

Source: Excerpted with Permission from *The One Page Business Plan for Non-Profit Organizations* by Jim Horan, Copyright 2007, The One Page Business Plan Company, Berkeley, CA. www.onepagebusinessplan.com.

EXAMPLES OF VISION STATEMENTS

Calgary Public Library
Source: Calgary Public Library, 2006: 5; © Calgary Public Library, All Rights Reserved.

A world of information and ideas within reach of every Calgarian.

State Library of Ohio
Source: Budler, 2006; reprinted courtesy of the State Library of Ohio.

The State Library of Ohio will lead in ensuring the delivery of all information and library services to all Ohio residents, anywhere, anytime.

University of Wollongong Library Library Business Plan (2006) ⓒⒹ
Source: University of Wollongong Library, 2006; reprinted courtesy of University of Wollongong Library 2006.

Vision—Where we want to be in the future

Our Vision is to be recognized as a knowledge resources center of distinction, integral to the realization of the University's Mission, Vision, and goals. We will:

- Develop education and training programs to equip staff and students with the skills for lifelong learning

- Structure systems and develop gateways to provide integrated, convenient, and client-friendly access to resources
- Foster staff to become innovative information specialists, skilled in providing exceptional service, customized to meet individual needs and preferences
- Contribute to the development and enhancement of a knowledge-based society

SLA Vision, Mission, and Core Value Statements
Source: Special Libraries Association, 2004; reprinted with permission of Special Libraries Association, 2004. www.sla.org. © Copyright Special Libraries Association. All rights reserved.

Vision

The Special Libraries Association is the global organization for innovative information professionals and their strategic partners.

Mission

The Special Libraries Association promotes and strengthens its members through learning, advocacy, and networking initiatives.

Core Values Leadership

Strengthening our roles as information leaders in our organizations and in our communities, including shaping information policy.

Services

Responding to our clients' needs, adding qualitative and quantitative value to information services and products.

Innovation and Continuous Learning

Embracing innovative solutions for the enhancement of services and intellectual advancement within the profession.

Results and Accountability

Delivering measurable results in the information economy and our organizations. The association and its members are expected to operate with the highest level of ethics and honesty.

Collaboration and Partnering

Providing opportunities to meet, communicate, collaborate, and partner within the information industry and the business community.

Montana State Library
Source: Montana State Library Business Plan 2006–2011; reprinted courtesy of Montana State Library.

The Montana State Library's information resources are supported by professional librarians, content specialists, and information technology professionals. We efficiently and effectively provide high-quality, user-centric library services and content. We are funded commensurate with our users' needs. We work collaboratively, partnering with other regional, national, and international organizations.

Port Stephens Library
Source: Port Stephens Library, 2004: 6; reprinted with thanks and acknowledgment to Port Stephens Library, NSW, Australia.

Port Stephens Library will be a vibrant center, enriching community life, providing a focal point for community activity. It will be a welcoming and convivial space, offering opportunities for social interaction and connection. A diverse range of programs to educate and entertain will be available, inviting community participation and creativity. Equitable, unbiased access to information, leisure, and technology resources will be provided, facilitating independent decision-making, lifelong learning, and information literacy. Friendly staff with expertise in information management will be available to assist anyone with an information need.

The library will have a strong, positive image, forming relationships with other council sections to develop and deliver innovative services. Partnerships with community groups will also contribute to vital services targeted toward specific audiences.

Ontario Digital Library
Source: Ontario Digital Library, 2003: 8; reprinted courtesy of Ontario Library Association, the Ontario Digital Library Businesses Plan, Toronto.

The ODL will coordinate the purchase and delivery of electronic information and virtual services on behalf of all Ontarians and Ontario libraries. The ODL is a partnership among the 6,500 public, school, college, and university libraries in the Province of Ontario working in cooperation with the education, university, training, business, and medical communities. The ODL seeks to serve Ontario citizens with the assistance of all levels of government. The goal of the ODL is to assist information users in seeking, navigating, and using electronic information through the effective management and delivery of electronic resources to Ontarians. The services provided are geared toward assisting Ontarians at all ages to learn about, find, and locate the information they need.

The ODL will provide to Ontarians seamless access to information anywhere they need it and at any time. The ODL will be part of each step of their lives, as they move from early reading to study and research, to professional and business initiatives, to gathering health and consumer information, to caring for children and the elderly, to learning more about the world they live in and the opportunities available to them.

The ODL will be based on the following guiding principles or values:

Equitable Access for All Ontarians

- The ODL will bring high-quality electronic resources and services to over 12 million Ontario citizens, eliminating some of the barriers that now exist in accessing information and creating more consistent services for library users.

Shared Decision Making and Accountability

- The ODL will balance the interests and realities of small and large, rich and poor communities and institutions through shared decision making.

Shared Funding

- Leverage provincial, institutional, and local dollars to realize economies of scale and to put Ontario dollars to work for everyone.

Local Points of Entry

- The ODL will work to provide the licenses, infrastructure, services, and support that will enable local libraries to provide exceptional services to their clientele.

THE MISSION STATEMENT

WHAT IT IS

The mission statement identifies what is really offered in clear and compelling language. Present your mission statement by explaining, from the client's perspective, why the service exists. Define the service's core activities, aims, and objectives clearly and concisely. Unlike the vision statement, which speaks to your long-term wishes, the mission statement is one that can be lived daily. If you do not already have a mission statement, begin to create one by writing down phrases describing, from the client's point of view, why your service exists (see Worksheet 3-3 ⊕). Then use those phrases to create your statement.

KEY POINTS TO INCLUDE

Core activities to include in your mission statement:

- Target market and services offered
- Competitive advantage—or what sets it apart from competitors
- Major milestones in the next one to three years (International Federation of Accountants, 2006)

Answering these questions may clarify your thoughts about why the service exists:

- What activity is being performed, where, how, etc.?
- Why does this service exist?
- Why will clients use this service? What's in it for the client?
- What does the service offer, and how is it unique?
- What value does it provide the client? What unique benefits does it provide?
- What existing demand is the service trying to satisfy?
- What can the service promise? What are you committed to providing?

Worksheet 3-3. Write Your Mission Statement
Who are you and what do you do?
What is your service or library?
Who are your clients?
What are you committed to providing?
Write your statement. After writing, ask yourself, does this statement support our vision?
Refine your mission statement on this page.
Source: Adapted from *The One Page Business Plan* by Jim Horan, Copyright 2004, The One Page Business Plan Company, Berkeley, CA. www.onepagebusinessplan.com.

EXAMPLES OF MISSION STATEMENTS

Oconomowoc Public Library
Source: McKenna, 2004: 5; reprinted courtesy of Oconomowoc Public Library.

The Oconomowoc Public Library provides materials, services, facilities, technology, and up-to-date resources and programs to meet the educational, informational, cultural, and recreational needs of the community. The library is a free and vital resource, providing the community with the opportunity to explore, discover, learn, and grow, ultimately enriching individual lives and the community as a whole. The library actively promotes an interest in and appreciation for reading and encourages lifelong learning.

Aurora Public Library
Source: Abbott, 2006: 2; reprinted with the permission of Aurora Public Library, Ontario, Canada.

Our **Mission** describes our purpose, or raison d'être . . .

Discovery and inspiration . . .

Connecting Aurora to information, lifelong learning, literacy, and the love of reading.

Oakville Public Library ⓒⒹ
Source: Oakville Public Library, 2007: 4; reprinted courtesy of Oakville Public Library.

Mission

To provide the ideal environment for our customer's learning experience and to support, educate, motivate, and recognize staff and volunteers in providing the ideal environment for learning.

Association for Library Collections & Technical Services (ALCTS) ⓒⒹ
Source: Association for Library Collections & Technical Services, 2001; reprinted courtesy of the Association for Library Collections & Technical Services (ALCTS).

ALCTS provides leadership to the service and information communities in developing principles, standards, and best practices for creating, collecting, organizing, delivering, and preserving information resources in all forms. It provides this leadership through its members by fostering educational, research, and professional service opportunities. ALCTS is committed to quality information, universal access, collaboration, and lifelong learning.

Montana State Library
Source: Montana State Library Business Plan 2006–2011; reprinted courtesy of Montana State Library.

The Montana State Library meets the information needs of Montana government agency management and staff, ensures all Montana citizens' have access to information created by their government, supports the role of all Montana libraries in delivering quality library content and services to their patrons, works to strengthen local community public libraries, and ensures that Montanans who are blind and physically handicapped are provided access to library resources.

University of Otago Library ⓒⷰ
Source: University of Otago Library, 2004: 1; reprinted courtesy of University of Otago Library.

The Library is committed to the University's goal for the advancement of knowledge, scholarship, and lifelong learning in partnership with scholarly and professional communities, both local and international, by providing:

- Access to excellent information resources
- Information literacy skills programs
- A stimulating learning environment

The Library is a prime contributor to the University's distinctive "repository of knowledge" characteristic as defined in the Education Act 1989.

Sandwell Metropolitan Borough Library Council
Source: Sandwell Metropolitan Borough Council, 2005: 1; reprinted courtesy of Sandwell Metropolitan Borough Library.

"Our mission: Open to everyone: to explore, discover and enjoy."

EXAMPLES OF MISSION AND VISION STATEMENTS TOGETHER

The vision and mission statements together identify where a library wants to be in the future and how it plans to get there.

OCLC
Source: Online Computer Library Center, n.d.; OCLC Online Computer Library Center, Inc. Mission and Vision Statement. Used with Permission.

Mission
OCLC exists to further access to the world's information and reduce library costs by offering services for libraries and their users.

Vision

OCLC will be the leading global library cooperative, helping libraries serve people by providing economical access to knowledge through innovation and collaboration.

Society of Competitive Intelligence Professionals
Source: Society of Competitive Information Professionals, 2004; reprinted with permission from the Society of Competitive Information Professionals, available at www.scip.org.

Vision

Better Decisions Through Competitive Intelligence

Mission

The mission of the Society of Competitive Intelligence Professionals is to enhance the success of our members through leadership, education, advocacy, and networking.

Second Life Library
Source: Pope, 2006: 2; reprinted courtesy of Second Life Library, Alliance Library Service.

Vision

To serve the citizens of an online world and build community using traditional and nontraditional library services and serving as a model for the twenty-first century library to determine how virtual library services will affect traditional libraries.

Mission

The mission of the Second Life Library is to:

- Explore the issues of providing library services in a virtual world
- Evaluate services currently offered by real-world libraries in the light of features offered in virtual-reality [VR] environments and the information needs of VR residents
- Examine how libraries will remain relevant when more business and education activities take place virtually
- Promote the real library and online library services to residents of Second Life
- Learn what kinds of library services are desired in virtual space.

REFERENCES

Association for Library Collections & Technical Services. "Membership Business Plan Outline FY 2002–2005." Chicago: American Library Association (February 26, 2001). Available: www.ala.org/ala/alcts/divisiongroups/membershipdiv/businessplan0205.doc.

Association of Specialized and Cooperative Library Agencies. "Surviving and Thriving on Your Own: Your Business Plan." Chicago: American Library Association (April

24, 2007). Available: www.ala.org/ala/ascla/asclapubs/surviving/yourbusinessplan/yourbusiness.cfm.

Abbott, C. 2006. "Mission Statement." Ontario, Canada: Aurora Public Library Board, Town of Aurora. Available: www.library.aurora.on.ca/dynamic/.

Bishoff, Liz and Nancy Allen. 2004. "Executive Summary: A Summary of a Report Published by the Council on Library and Information Resources. Business Planning for Cultural Heritage Institutions." Washington, DC: CLIR. Available: www.clir.org/pubs/execsum/sum124.html.

Brigevich, L. 2004. "Business Plan, Franklin Templeton Global Research Library." Fort Lauderdale, FL: Franklin Templeton Global Research Library; Franklin Templeton Investments.

Brook, Nigel. 2007. "Library Services: Business Plan and Library Strategy 2007–2010." Warwickshire, UK: William Harvey Library, George Eliot Hospital NHS Trust.

Budler, J. 2006. "Minutes, State Library Board Meeting, Sept. 26, 2006." Columbus, OH: State Library Board, pp.3-6. Available: http://winslo.state.oh.us/06septbrd2.doc.

Calgary Public Library. 2006. "Building Community, Building Capacity Business Plan 2006–2008." Calgary, AB: Calgary Public Library. Available: http://calgarypublic library.com/library/pdf/businessplan06.pdf.

Fifth Circuit Court of Appeals Library. 2005–2006. "Internet Home of the Fifth Circuit Library—Library Publications; the Circuit Library System 02/07/06." New Orleans, LA: Fifth Circuit Court of Appeals. Available: www.lb5.uscourts.gov/Publications/Netrep/.

Horan, Jim. 2004. *The One Page Business Plan*. 3rd ed. Berkeley, CA: The One Page Business Plan Company.

Horan, Jim. 2007. *The One Page Business Plan for Non-Profit Organizations*. Berkeley, CA: The One Page Business Plan Company.

International Federation of Accountants. 2006. "Business Planning Guide: Practical Applications for SMES." New York: IFAC. Available: www.cpaireland.ie/UserFiles/File/Technical%20Resources/SME%20Resource/Business%20Planning%20Guide %20-%20Practical%20Application%20for%20SMEspdf.pdf.

Kaplan, Robert S. 2007. "What To Ask the Person in the Mirror." *Harvard Business Review* (January): 86–95.

Kenosha Public Library. 2007. "The Kenosha Public Library 2007 Business Plan." Kenosha, WI: Kenosha Public Library.

Kott, Katherine. 2006. "DLF Aquifer Business Plan 2006." May 25. Washington, DC: Digital Library Federation. Available: www.diglib.org/aquifer/AquiferBusiness Plan.pdf.

London Health Libraries Strategic Development Group (LHLSDG) and electronic Knowledge Access Team (eKAT). 2005. "Business Plan Agreement 2005–2006." London: London Health Libraries.

London Health Libraries Strategic Development Group (LHLSDG) and London Workforce Development Group. 2006. "Business Plan Agreement, 2006–2007." London: London Health Libraries.

McKenna, Ray. 2004. "The Oconomowoc Public Library Annual Report 2004." Oconomowoc, WI: Oconomowoc Public Library. Available: www.wcfls.lib.wi.us/opl/business%20plan%202005.pdf.

Montana State Library. 2006. "Montana State Library Business Plan 2006–2010." Helena, MT: Montana State Library.

Oakville Public Library. 2007. "Oakville Public Library Business Plan, 2007–2009." Oakville, ON: Oakville Public Library.

Online Computer Library Center. n.d. "Mission and Vision." Dublin, OH: OCLC. Available: www.oclc.org/about/mission/default.htm.

Ontario Digital Library. 2003. "The Ontario Digital Library Business Plan: Connecting Ontarians." Guelph, ON: Ontario Digital Library. Available: www.accessola2.com/odl/pdf/ODL_BusinessPlan_Full.pdf.

Pope, K. "Second Life Library Business Plan." East Peoria, IL: Alliance Library System. 2006. Available: www.alliancelibraries.info/secondlife.htm.

Port Stephens Library. 2004. "Port Stephens Library Business Plan 2004–2005." Port Stephens, Australia: Port Stephens Library.

Sandwell Metropolitan Borough Council. 2005. "Library and Information Service Business Plan 2005–2006." West Midlands, UK: Sandwell Metropolitan Borough Council.

Society of Competitive Information Professionals. 2004. "About SCIP." Available: www.scip.org.

Special Libraries Association. "SLA Vision, Mission and Core Value Statements (Adopted October 2003)." Alexandria, VA: Special Libraries Association (April 15, 2004). Available: www.sla.org/content/SLA/AssnProfile/slanplan/index.cfm.

University of Otago Library. 2004. "Business Plan 2004." Dunedin, New Zealand: University of Otago Library. Available: www.library.otago.ac.nz/pdf/2004_business_plan.pdf.

University of Wollongong Library. 2006. "2006 Professional Unit Business Plan Library." New South Wales, Australia: University of Wollongong Library.

U.S. Environmental Protection Agency. 2004. "Business Case for Information Services: EPA's Regional Libraries and Centers." Washington, DC: U.S. EPA. Available: www.epa.gov/natlibra/epa260r04001.pdf.

U.S. Small Business Administration. 2007. "Small Business Planner: Write a Business Plan." Washington, DC: U.S. Small Business Administration. Available: www.sba.gov/smallbusinessplanner/plan/writeabusinessplan/serv_bp_compdesc.html.

Weingand, Darlene E. 1999. *Marketing/Planning Library and Information Services.* Englewood, CO: Libraries Unlimited.

4 CONDUCTING ASSESSMENTS AND CREATING A SWOT CHART

DESIGNING SERVICE TO MEET CLIENT NEEDS

Environmental scans and assessments identify gaps or problems in your services and trends in the information environment. Having this information will help you choose the best service for your library to offer. Only after determining what is needed can you design a service to meet your client's needs. The information from the environmental scan is placed into a SWOT chart. The evaluation of the SWOT chart helps provide a clearer picture of what options you have when choosing and designing a service. Scans and evaluations are highly subjective, so you will have to steel yourself to critically appraise the real situation and not one you wish you could have.

An internal assessment provides an unemotional look inside the library organization. It will illustrate your competitive advantages, key success factors, and value to clients. This will help you determine what needs to be done to strengthen your internal capabilities or to highlight existing skills and abilities that help you outshine competitors in the marketplace.

An external assessment provides actionable information about your competition, how they're meeting your clients' needs, and how their services compare to yours. Understanding your competitors' strategies is fundamental to understanding how you fit into the community as well as how you might go about attracting more clients. Once the competition and the environment in which you operate are known, it is easier to build a better service than what the competition offers.

LIBRARY ASSESSMENTS

Building successful services is a process in choosing how to compete. The first step in the process identifies a client or market problem and creates a solution. A common mistake is reversing the process by inventing a service and then looking for a market opportunity. Comparable to hammering a round peg into a square hole, this is not a viable option. You can't expect those offering support or funding to get behind a poorly planned solution.

Problem identification is achieved through a library assessment or usability study. This is "a structured process to learn about communities and evaluate how well the library supports them. The information acquired through library assessment is used in an iterative manner to improve library programs and services and make libraries responsive to the needs of their communities" (Storey, 2006).

One method of assessment is the environmental scan, which is divided into an internal assessment and an external assessment. These are designed to find out as much as you can about everything that affects the library and its offerings. Using the information gained during the scan enables you to develop a plan suitable to your organization. Following this step, the plan is implemented and monitored, progress is assessed, and appropriate changes are made to keep it on course. The altered plan is then implemented and monitored; based on further assessment, changes are again made to keep it on course. These iterative changes may be incremental or may encompass a large portion of the plan. Regardless, the plan is in a constant state of evolution in order to stay current with the changes in the environment. It is a living document that is reviewed often and modified as necessary.

In order to identify a problem and create a solution, you'll have to know your target client inside and out. Client knowledge is the starting point for every library and service. The assessments described in this chapter help determine services that are viable to your clients. Design your services *only* after learning what your clients value and balancing those values against what the library can afford to offer, the mission, and the trends of the information industry. "Just because it can be produced doesn't mean anyone will have a need for it or want to pay the price to buy" (MacKintosh, 1999: 54).

Regardless of the services you choose, you will need to consider all possible points along the competitive continuum:

- Do you know your clients (the market) well enough to find a particular niche to focus on?
- Can you find a unique strategy?
- Can you identify your services as different from competitors in your client's mind? Can you use a different sales or marketing technique? (Inc.com, 2000)

For many involved in day-to-day activities, it can be difficult to view a service as part of a broader picture. You may find it tough to step back and determine why a service is succeeding or what it will take to become successful. Committing to the structure of conducting the internal and external assessments of an environmental scan will provide the perspective and clarity required to determine viable services.

Assessment is a core function of library management. For example, more than 1,000 libraries worldwide have used LibQUAL+, a service-quality evaluation survey developed by the Association of Research Libraries, which is relatively inexpensive and easy for libraries to implement (Storey, 2006). LibQUAL+ is a diagnostic tool for measuring library users' perceptions of service quality. The user identifies gaps between desired, perceived, and minimum service expectations through predefined survey questions. Other commonly used methods to identify current issues and factors affecting libraries include formal surveys, focus groups, informal interviews, questionnaires, self-assessments, and simply calling other librarians to learn what they're doing.

INTERNAL ASSESSMENT

BASIC DEFINITIONS

An internal assessment focuses on the library organization itself. It identifies strengths and weaknesses—the first half of the SWOT formula—in the forms of competitive advantages, key success factors, and value to clients. Competitive advantage is the ability to outperform competitors or other organizations that provide similar goods and services (George and Jones, 2004). Competitive advantages are unique skills, abilities, or services that enable your service to deliver the same benefits as competitors but at a lower cost, or to deliver benefits that exceed those of competing products.

Key success factors are the three to five truly major determinants for financial and competitive success, which, if performed well, will almost always deliver higher-than-average results, helping you reach success. They are the milestones that can tell you when you've moved toward your goals and objectives. Identifying your key success factors allows for focus on the essential. Key success factors are divided into two broad categories: business processes and human processes. The factors could be a specific skill or talent, a competitive capability, or something a library must do to satisfy clients.

Offering value to clients is why your library exists. Your task when conducting an internal assessment is to identify the value your clients place on a service or product. Focus on the client and the client's needs or problems. You want to be in the position of meeting that need *as determined from the client's perspective*. Find out and document how you know that the need or problem exists. Your success in asking for support, funding, or permission for a new service will be based largely on the facts as the client sees them and how you plan to satisfy that need or solve that problem.

KEY POINTS TO INCLUDE

The internal assessment reviews the current situation only (see Worksheet 4-1 ⓒⓓ). (*Discussion continues on page 57.*)

Worksheet 4-1. Internal Assessment
The Mission
State the reason the service exists.
Role and Purpose
Identify the role of the library.
Identify the purpose of the library.
Staff
How many people, including volunteers, work for the library?
How many unpaid staff work for the library?
Name the strengths and weaknesses of the staff.
What special areas of expertise does the library staff possess?
What types of training and education does the staff need?
Identify training and education resources available and accessible.
What do the individual staff members need to accomplish each objective?
Does your staff focus on activities or do they focus on results?
(Cont'd.)

Worksheet 4-1. Internal Assessment *(Continued)*
Staff (Continued)
Identify technical and specialized expertise available to the library.
Does the library have access to adequate technical support and training/education? If not, then specifically what is lacking?
Services and Programs
Briefly list and describe all services and programs, include individuals responsible and resources dedicated for each activity.
Briefly list and describe the library's marketing activities, including public relations, promotion, and advertising.
Does the library maintain circulation and in-house use statistics? Are they itemized (subject, client type, etc.)? Are they useful? What do they indicate?
Identify the unique qualities of the library or the service.
What sets it apart from its competitors?
Identify its competitive advantages.
Why is the library uniquely qualified to provide the proposed service?
Managerial Structure
Describe the library's managerial structure: hierarchical (authoritarian) or vertical (participatory). How will this impact the planning process? For example, a fast-changing economy demands a management style that's capable of changing and making decisions. How will your current managerial structure impact your planning process?
How are decisions and policies made?
(Cont'd.)

Worksheet 4-1. Internal Assessment *(Continued)*
Managerial Structure (Continued)
Identify the staffing patterns and lines of communication.
Describe how the staff works together and communicates.
Describe the library's lines of communication.
Describe the library's technical structure (processes, procedures, and techniques).
Describe the library's informal staff structure (leadership style, politics, status, rewards, and ideologies).
Budget
Describe the library's annual budget.
Identify specific funding sources for your service.
Describe the process for creating the budget.
Who creates the budget?
Identify any potential funding sources not listed above.
Identify the library's expenses.
Does the library budget accommodate growth?
(Cont'd.)

Worksheet 4-1. Internal Assessment *(Continued)*
Physical Plant
Describe the conditions of the library's buildings and facilities, equipment, space allocation, furnishing, and other material effects owned or leased by the library.
Do the library's materials and programs have adequate space and appropriate configuration?
How would you rearrange the library's physical facilities to enrich the library's internal environment?
Does the library have the necessary wiring, telephone lines, and electrical outlets to provide for this service? If not, then specifically what are you missing?
Are there enough furnishings and are they comfortable and attractive to your clients?
What technology and equipment does the library have? Is it updated and adequate for the needs of the service?
Other thoughts, ideas, or considerations identified during the internal assessment:

Internal assessments generally cover:

- A description of your service
- Clients
- Marketing
- Use or sales of your service
- Staff structure and communication
- Management and human resources teams

EXTERNAL ASSESSMENT

BASIC DEFINITIONS

New issues, trends, and technologies are constantly emerging, and current ones are constantly evolving. With these factors all changing at an accelerated pace, it is essential that the planning *and* marketing processes feature assessment as a major component (Marcus, 2006). External assessment is a key to operating proactively.

Knowing your competition and their strategies is fundamental to understanding how you fit into the community and how you're going to get more clients. Once the competition and the environment in which you operate are known, it is easier to anticipate changes and, in essence, to build a better mousetrap. Describing in the business plan why competitors are successful or unsuccessful demonstrates that you understand your market, and provides insights into how you might copy others' successes or avoid their failures (Digital Federal Credit Union, 2006).

An external assessment identifies opportunities and threats—the second half of the SWOT formula—in the form of industry overviews, trends, growth rates, outlooks for the future, and an overall market assessment. It will help focus advertising and marketing on areas that will afford a competitive advantage. The external assessment incorporates scanning, which looks into the future and attempts to identify trends. The information collected and analyzed gives the background necessary when considering what kinds of services, programs, or products can be provided or developed.

KEY POINTS TO INCLUDE

The external assessment reviews only today's situation with a focus on identifying market trends. It covers:

- The economy and business environment
- The marketplace
- Competition—who are they and what do they offer?
- Market share—in each key market
- E-commerce and technology
- Regulatory—accreditation, licensing, or copyright requirements
- Organizational review and budgets
- Social—demographic
- Political—elections, policies, and laws (Albright, 2004: 41–42)

EXTERNAL ASSESSMENT WORKSHEET

When you've identified answers to the appropriate questions (for your situation) on the worksheet, the resulting picture of your service can be compared with your competitors' services—an external assessment (see Worksheet 4-2 ⊙).

Worksheet 4-2. External Assessment
Identifying Your Target Clients
Describe or identify your market (divide your market into groups).
Who is going to use the service?
Describe their most important needs.
Describe the overall needs of your clients, both present and projected.
What benefits do they seek? What benefits do they receive?
How does your library meet those needs?
What would the client say about how well those needs are being met?
Is there a gap? Can you describe it?
Why aren't you meeting that need? Is it important enough to fix? Why?
What products or services might meet the need?
Describe the size of your market for the project, service, or plan at hand.
Quantify the market segment in use or sales or units (what you choose to measure).
What portion of it do you hope to get?
How much of the service will each client use?
(Cont'd.)

Worksheet 4-2. External Assessment *(Continued)*
Identifying Your Target Clients (Continued)
Why will they use your service rather than another one?
Describe the anticipated market developments over the next 5 to 10 years.
How will these developments influence library operations?
How can the library respond to potential changes?
What perceptions and attitudes do members of your market groups hold toward your service?
Describe the image of the library within the community.
What do the library's clients feel about the library?
What do clients see when they visit the library?
Describe the staff, volunteers, and board members' perceptions of the library.
Describe the decision factors put into play by your market group regarding when to use or not to use the service.
Describe the information-seeking behavior of your market group's members.
Describe the tendency of each group to adapt to change.
What has caused the market for the service to exist?
Describe the key barriers to entry into your market. Describe the difficulties in introducing a library, service, or product.
(Cont'd.)

Worksheet 4-2. External Assessment *(Continued)*
Identifying Your Target Clients (Continued)
Describe the important information industry trends.
Describe the important variables in the information industry distribution or access system.
Describe the anticipated information industry developments over the next 5 to 10 years.
How will these developments influence your library's operations?
What changes have occurred in the industry over the past 5 years?
Regulatory Restrictions
What regulatory factors, economic, government regulations, new technology licensing, etc., will affect the information industry in the future?
What regulatory agencies will you have to deal with to receive approval to engage in this service?
Describe their requirements.
How can the library be better prepared for potential changes?
Competition

Who or what are your competing entities? Competitors may include:
    Independent information brokers
    Potential clients
    Corporate libraries
    Business consultants
    The public library
    The Internet
    Your clients' co-workers
    Bookstores
    Clients' lack of understanding that they even need the type of services provided
    Others

Who offers the same or similar service?
(Cont'd.)

Worksheet 4-2. External Assessment *(Continued)*
Competition (Continued)
Explain what you will do to exceed or stay ahead of the competition.
How long have they been in business?
Describe their strengths and weaknesses.
How will you take advantage of their weaknesses?
Approximately how much market share does each of your competitors have?
Describe how the competition promotes their services.
Describe their marketing strategies that seem to work.
What clients have you lost to your competitors?
Can you identify any areas of service duplication between you and your competition?
What are the possibilities for cooperation with competitors or parallel organizations?
Describe any future trends with regard to the competition, the targeted client-market(s), the service(s), and the opportunities for cooperation.
Given the reality of identified competition, is there a sufficient market to support both or all service providers?
What is the potential for carving out a unique market share?
Other thoughts, ideas, or considerations identified during the external assessment:

The comparison helps identify areas for potential niche service selection and development, possible growth areas, and duplication, cooperation, or collaboration of services. Answering the questions will also help determine:

1. Where the service is in its development
2. How the service is used
3. What is important to your clients and how the library meets those needs
4. Future needs

The questions presented are designed to help you gather your thoughts and information. Responses to the questions are also used in Chapter 7 to construct a marketing and promotional strategy.

EXAMPLES OF ASSESSMENTS

Maroochy Shire Council ⓒⒹ
Source: Maroochy Shire Council, 2006: 2; reprinted courtesy of Maroochy Libraries, Maroochy Shire Council.

Market research and consultation identified the following broad outcomes for Maroochy residents:

- Appropriate attractive and accessible library spaces (both virtual and physical in strategic locations
    - To ensure that people have good access to virtual and physical points of presence
    - To plan and develop social infrastructure to meet the needs of our growing community
    - To provide library spaces that meet the needs of communities and a range of target groups and ages
    - To provide libraries that are destination points or hubs in the community
- Services delivered in a cost-efficient manner with a focus on customer needs
    - To streamline processes for maximum efficiency and best value for the dollar
    - To maximize enabling technology in the delivery of service
- More flexible and innovative service delivery
    - To ensure that service delivery is adapted to meet changing needs
    - To apply models of best practice and successful library delivery identified

- Cohesive and inclusive communities
  - To facilitate an inclusive and cohesive community through effective community partnerships and targeted programming
- Learning and informed communities
  - To promote learning and access to information in the community
  - To develop and maximize learning partnerships in the shire and across the region
- Integrated service delivery and sustainable partnerships for mutual benefit
  - To provide a more integrated and sustainable model of service delivery across Maroochy Shire
  - To develop and maintain partnerships and cooperative activity within Maroochy Shire
  - To develop and maintain partnerships and cooperative activity with libraries within and outside the shire
- Libraries well used and highly visible
  - To increase the awareness of residents of the services and facilities offered by the library
  - To maximize usage of services and facilities

Halifax Public Libraries
Source: Halifax Public Libraries, 2006: 13–14; reprinted courtesy of Halifax Public Libraries.

Challenges with Service Delivery/Business Unit Impact
These are issues that affect the business unit's ability to deliver services (both internally and externally).

Opportunities:
- Business collaborations: In today's business savvy world, collaboration is critical. Tools such as calendaring, file sharing, and e-mail have become so ingrained in day-to-day operations that it is hard to imagine how a business could run without them. In fact, according to a recent survey, 80 percent of all intellectual property flows through e-mail every day.

The business of running a world-class library system is no different. With 14 locations across HRM [Halifax Regional Municipality], the need to collaborate effectively and efficiently is paramount. A system-wide unified collaboration solution at the Library will have clear and far-reaching benefits. It will allow us to seamlessly schedule meetings with colleagues, work on current version documents, allow for a library of organized information providing knowledge management, and, of course, it is vital for internal communication with employees as well as external communications with patrons and partners. The Library plans to improve internal and external communications and productivity through business collaboration with HRM to expand GroupWise access throughout the system.

Business collaboration knows no bounds. The Library must be able to share ideas, critical information, and perspectives with virtually anyone, anytime, anywhere.

Challenges:

- **Erosion of financial base:** Municipal funding has not kept pace with service development and public demand. At amalgamation in 1996, the Library operating budget represented 2.1 percent of the total HRM budget. After declining to a low of 1.9 percent in 1999–2000, funding was restored to 2.2 percent in 2002–03 and has remained constant for four consecutive fiscal years. At the same time, two new branches were opened and the automated system was replaced without an injection of sufficient budget and staffing, placing additional stress on an overtaxed system.

- **Budget planning framework:** The Library cannot meaningfully develop strategic plans in an atmosphere of funding uncertainty. Rather than implementing the recommended provincial funding formula, the Province has opted to provide "one-time only" sporadic payments that are not carried forward in base per capital funding. When coupled with municipal funding patterns, it is challenging to advance service.

- **Succession planning/training and development:** Current funding for staff training and development is inadequate to ensure skill development and preparation of employees to take on more senior responsibilities. HRM provides $595 per employee for training and development; the Library's budget provides $131 per employee. Funds cannot be reallocated internally without reducing public service.

While succession planning is a corporate priority, the Library is making little progress in this important area. Similarly, external competitiveness is necessary for recruitment, but funds are not available to conduct a compensation study and implement results.

The staff complement has experienced little growth despite the addition of new branches, making it difficult to maintain service levels.

- **Grants and partnerships:** The Library is unable to apply for grant funding, employment and internship opportunities, and other programs since matching funding is typically required.

Port Stephens Library
**Source: Port Stephens Library, 2004: 17; reprinted with thanks
  and acknowledgment to Port Stephens Library, NSW, Australia.**

Analysis of benchmarks

Expenditure on library services in Port Stephens is 46 percent lower than the NSW average. This is reflected in the lower than average expenditure on library materials and a comparatively small collection. The Library has difficulty in developing collections that adequately meet the demands of the community, particularly in new formats, such as DVDs. The average cost of library material for Port Stephens also reflects the purchase of a high proportion of paperback and economically priced material. The amount of funding available to purchase library resources restricts the opportunities to invest in more comprehensive, in-depth resources, such as reference items and online databases. The number of items acquired in a 12-month period represents only half of the NSW average.

While circulation levels are high in comparison with other libraries, staffing levels are low. Circulation per staff member is 101 percent higher than the NSW average. Since the number of items physically handled by each staff member is so high, there are reduced opportunities to offer quality customer assistance and programs. There has also been a negative impact on staff well-being. Although pressures on staff are being addressed through examination of work practices and use of technology, there is definite need for additional staffing. Expenditure on salaries per capita is 38.48 percent lower than the NSW average.

The Port Stephens community makes good use of limited library resources. Almost half of the community are registered library users, with circulation of materials at 10.07 per capita. This indicates reasonable heavy usage of library resources at a rate that is 39.28 percent higher than the state average.

In summary, the Library is a high performer in terms of circulation. However, overall performance is threatened by low levels of expenditure on staffing and resources.

George Eliot Hospital
Source: Brook, 2007: Appendix 2; reprinted courtesy of Nigel Brook, Library Services Manager, William Harvey Library, George Eliot Hospital NHS Trust.

Appendix 2: Client base and user statistics 2005–2006

Membership

Current Library membership is 1,202 registered users. While this is lower than figures published in the previous library strategy, in late 2005 the library deleted its entire membership and forced all users to reregister. This was done partially for data protection reasons, but also to rationalize existing membership and reconfigure the Library Management System [LMS] to facilitate a reduction in the number of unnecessary category distinctions and circulation rules.

Composition of membership [in descending order]:
Hospital Doctors
Hospital Nurses
Students
PCT Staff
Trust Staff
Allied Health Professionals
Midwives

SERVICES
Book loans: 6,222 loans
Interlibrary: 823 items
Training sessions: 291 staff trained
Induction sessions: 241 induction attendances
Mediated searches: 162 searches
Photocopies supplied: 1,021 articles provided

Despite the retrogressive work needed to bring the Library up to modern standards, removing old-fashioned manual systems and replacing them with integrated electronic systems, and the heavy recovery schedule imposed by service slippage incurred since June 2004, performance statistics when compared to the previous Library strategy document are increased.

Torbay Council Library Services ⒸⒹ
**Source: Torbay Council, 2005: 11; reprinted courtesy of Torbay Council
  Library Services.**

2.5   Customer, staff and stakeholders views

Torbay Library Services has a range of communication and consultative processes in relation to its staff, and outcomes from these exert a significant influence on the way the service is managed. In addition, feedback from staff is an essential element in service
planning, and the service benefits significantly from the opinions of staff resulting from
informal and formal customer feedback and their own views of what changes and developments are needed. Specific examples of this are:

- Proposed levels of fees and charges (Fees and Charges Working
  Group)
- Staff forum meetings—the March 2004 meetings concentrated on perceived barriers to library usage as a contribution to the work being
  undertaken in pursuit of LPSA Target 4.

The service has a program of public consultation, and key results from those undertaken during 2003 and 2004 are as follows:

Paignton Street Survey 2003

Key findings were as follows:

- As about 65 percent of nonusers are unlikely ever to have a desire to
  use a library, the next survey should concentrate on ways of improving
  the library experience for existing customers and lapsed users.
- There is a significant lack of knowledge about a number of the services we offer. Accordingly, these areas of poor awareness should be
  the focus of future marketing work.
- The service needs to learn more about contemporary attitudes to
  buying, reading, and possessing books.
- We need to know if the threat of fines is a significant barrier to the
  borrowing of books.
- Consideration should be given to relaxing and simplifying our joining
  procedures.

An equivalent survey was carried out in Brixham during October 2004, the findings of
which are currently awaited.

Viewpoint 7 on Library Opening Hours 2003

This survey yielded a wealth of information, from both users and nonusers of the library
service, which has been used to inform the way forward on opening hours. The overall initial conclusion was that, bearing in mind the high proportion of elderly people in Torbay
who have few problems with current opening hours, any change—as opposed to an
increase—in hours, would present a real danger of upsetting as many people as pleasing
others. Accordingly, the idea of simply "rearranging the deckchairs" should be approached
with great caution. The alternative of increasing hours, particularly evenings and Satur-
days, would be particularly popular with those in full-time employment or education.

The priority order that emerged for both reorganizing and increasing opening hours was
as follows:

(i) Later evening openings—the clear favorite

(ii) Extending Saturday opening

(iii) Opening all day on the current half-day

(iv) Opening earlier in the mornings, e.g., 9:00 or earlier.

Cariboo Regional District
Source: Cariboo Regional District Library, 2004: 3; reprinted courtesy of Cariboo Regional District Library, Williams Lake, BC, Canada.

Significant issues and trends:

- Meeting the increasing demand for interlibrary loan services and to handle more effectively the present Support Services workload. The increasing popularity of interlibrary loan service has placed considerable pressure on Support Services staff. To ensure all Support Services responsibilities are undertaken, restrictions have been place in interlibrary loan service. This is an important service to all of our clients, particularly those in rural areas. In addition staff are facing increasing inability to meet some of our regular support services such as:
  - Fulfilling all acquisitions procedures, including adding orders to the acquisitions database and sending those orders to various publishers and vendors, receiving ordered materials through the acquisitions database, and preparing invoice information for payment purposes
  - Maintaining and revising policies and procedures for continued efficiency
  - Staff training, especially respecting new procedures requirements
  - Increased opportunity to complete cataloguing procedures
- Strategy:
  - Review, with Manager and Treasurer, opportunities within current requisition, or impacts or amending requisition to address expressed needs.
- Provincial Public Library Service Strategic Plan could impact regional library service.
- Results of Quesnel/CRD Electoral Areas Library Service Review could impact regional library service.
- Continued high demand for Internet access and more demand for access to Office programs.
  - Library to install new public access workstations at each branch, resulting in improved public access to both the Internet and to Office software
  - Main issue—Need for sufficient space in our library facilities for additional computer stations
- Extension of circulation function to community branch libraries:
  - Identify circulation status of community branch libraries
  - To track items borrowed from community branch libraries

- To place holds on community branch items
- To allow patrons to place their own holds

Calgary Public Library

Assessment of Organizational Capacity

The Calgary Public Library has emerged from its previous planning cycle with many substantive accomplishments. During this period, the Library has introduced new service initiatives, completed a number of large-scale projects, experienced major increases in use, and managed significant growth in the complexity and scale of its operations. At the same time, changes have continued to occur in the external environment in which the Library operates, placing additional demands on available resources and adding new accountability and reporting requirements.

The Calgary Public Library has managed these developments well. However, as an organization already stretched in terms of its capacity, it will need to continue to streamline operations, manage its resources very carefully, and leverage these resources at every opportunity. The organization will also need to implement and maximize the appropriate infrastructure to ensure responsiveness to key stakeholders needs while managing an increasingly demanding workload.

Throughout this planning cycle and beyond, it will be necessary to develop additional depth and expertise throughout the organization by adding resources in key operational areas. This will allow us to strengthen organizational capacity and ensure that essential skill sets are in place to carry out required activities.

Growth in both the complexity and scale of library planning and operations is expected to continue during the next three-year period. The preparations for a new downtown Central Library will be a sizeable undertaking, with significant impact on operations and existing staff workloads. For the project to be successful, it must be appropriately resourced from the outset. Additional and experienced project staff with specialized skills will be required to support this major new initiative even beyond this planning cycle.

Other changes will continue to occur in the broader environment in which the Library operates. Sufficient organizational breadth, depth, and flexibility must be developed and maintained to ensure that the Calgary Public Library has the ability to respond in a timely manner to these changes and to other opportunities that present themselves.

Forces of Change

The Calgary Public Library will be operating in a changing and increasingly complex environment over the next three years. The following trends have been identified as major shaping influences that will impact the Library during this period.

Continuing Population Growth

With the population expected to hit the one million mark by 2008, rapid growth in the City of Calgary will continue. Much of this growth will occur in new suburban communities located at the edge of the city. The result will be increased community demand for additional library services, larger collections, and supplementary library service points.

Ongoing Demographic Change

As the overall population will continue to increase, significant demographic shifts within the population will also be experienced. In order to remain relevant, the Library must continue to anticipate and adapt to these changes in demographics to ensure its services, programs, and collections reflect the increasing diversity within Calgary.

Rising Customer Service Expectations

Fueled by a continuous stream of competitive new products and services in the marketplace, customer expectations have risen dramatically in recent years and will only continue to do so in the future. Convenience, choice, flexibility, perceived value, and cost continually drive service expectations, and therefore the Library will need to define and communicate its position in this more competitive context.

Changing Patterns of Library Use

Library use patterns are beginning to change in a number of significant ways. This is reflected in the growing popularity of the self-service and virtual-service options now available. A second emerging pattern is that customers are increasingly using the Library more for recreational and leisure pursuits and relying more on the Internet as their first source for information.

Collections and Electronic Resources

The volume of book publishing and number of book publishing companies in Canada is declining in general. The current emphasis on the bestseller market means less variety is available to purchase for the Library's collections. The cost of materials is also increasing and publishing is shifting from traditional print to electronic or combined formats. Maintaining strong print-based collections while integrating new electronic means and formats will be a significant challenge.

Human Resources Transitions

The next few years will bring significant staffing changes as a number of Library managers and other staff become eligible for retirement. This has the potential to have considerable future impact on the organization, and preparations for the transition will need to be carefully made. The organization's need for flexibility and depth in some key staffing areas must also be addressed.

Municipal Developments

Changes are continuing to occur at the municipal level with particular respect to governance for autonomous civic entities, ongoing process review, and organizational structure. The introduction of multiyear budgeting at the City of Calgary, its aim for a new business plan, and other developments will have major impacts on the Library over the course of this planning period.

Increasing Requirements for Accountability and Transparency

The number and complexity of accountability standards and reporting requirements are increasing. There is also a growing expectation that all decision making will be carried out in an open and transparent manner. The result will be increased workload demands for all public sector organizations, including the Library.

Funding Challenges

Funding for all public sector organizations is expected to remain severely constrained over the next three years. Meanwhile, the costs of providing library service continues to increase, particularly in the areas of collections, technology, human resources, building construction, and infrastructure maintenance. Limited funding increases will restrict the Library's ability to respond in a timely manner to emerging needs and priorities.

Sandwell Metropolitan Borough Library Council
Source: Sandwell Metropolitan Borough Library Council, 2005: 9–11; Sandwell Metropolitan Borough Library.

Section 4: Challenges and Ambitions

What are the key future challenges and ambitions for the Library and Information Service?

4.1   Known major challenges and ambitions for 2005/06—what are the drivers?

- Contributing to the corporate priorities for service improvement: raising educational attainment; safer, cleaner, stronger communities; and supporting vulnerable children

- Ensuring that the Library Service is clearly aligned to framework for the future and achieving the Public Library Service standards

- Ensuring that CHAS [Community History and Archives Service] has a robust ten-year plan to meet the ambitions for archive services set out in the Archive Task Force report and TNA standards for Archive repositories

- Contributing to the corporate lifelong learning and cultural strategies and the Education Strategic Plan

- Potential inspections by Audit Commission, IAG, Chartermark, and report to the National Archive and continuing to make progress on the improvement plan from the pilot inspection of cultural services

- Maintaining successful partnerships with learning engages learners in a Borough where basic skills levels are well below the national average and participation in Adult Community Learning is low, and, in particular, improving basic skills when 45.8 percent of adults had no qualifications at the 2001 census

- Developing the right balance of stock for the 21st century library and improving the overall quality of the stock at the same time as carrying a wider range of media, including electronic resources. Staff have highlighted the need to improve rate of supply of bestsellers, increased number of DVDs (including Asian language), respond more quickly to local needs, and overhaul the stock transfer system

- Responding to opportunities created by the national expansion of Bookstart and development of Children's Centers

- Maintaining and updating a quality of ICT and developing the 24-hour library with range of Web-based resources and services in order to achieve national target of 100 percent of possible transactions available online; urgent need to improve the speed of Internet access in response to customer and staff comments

- Contributing to social inclusion by targeting and reaching disadvantaged groups in a Borough where high deprivation is spread widely, car ownership is low, and there is strong but very local sense of identity

- Addressing the accommodation problems for CHAS—lack of space (public services and storage) and poor quality of environment as well as the long-term collections management issues arising from the lack of a Borough Archivist

- Need to increase outreach actively by CHAS to ensure reaching all communities in Sandwell, especially to black and minority ethnic groups, which make up 20.3 percent of the population
- Improving against national standards and local targets—Best Value indicators, Public Library Standards, CPA [comprehensive performance assessment] self-assessments, LPSA [local public service agreement] target, and establishing baselines for new standards and targets (e.g., Impact Public Library Standards, Cultural Strategy indicators).
- Concentrating on improving the customer's experience of the library service (addressing issues raised by formal and informal customer comments, for instance, reviewing opening hours, moving to DVDs, improving quality of IT [information technology]) in order to improve both satisfaction with and use of the service
- Marketing services and improvements more effectively in response to staff comments and the 2004 Cultural Services review
- Making sure there are enough staff who reflect local communities and who have the opportunity to acquire the skills to deliver rapidly changing frontline service
- Identifying the opportunities created through IT and customer service developments to simplify administrative procedures for staff so that they are able to concentrate on the public service
- Continuing highly productive Black Country partnerships for libraries and archives
- Responding to Children's Trust and the reconfiguration of Council

4.2   Major challenges and ambitions for 2006/07
- As above
- Additional challenges will be managing the end of NRF [National Retail Federation] Basic Skills, SPRinT, and the Arcade/Central Library/CHAS relocation

Potential activities identified through the planning process for 2006/07
- Implement changes in opening hours
- Review effectiveness of changes to staffing structures and progress towards staffing profile to reflect Sandwell community
- Single status
- Marketing program to include:
  - Develop bank of off the peg promotional ideas for use by local managers
  - Update library leaflets and customer information
  - Targeted marketing with clear product and target audience
  - Promotion of resources on Web site
- Work on Central/CHAS—The Arcade and Discovery Store
- Build up methods of consulting with service users including Friends/user groups for specific groups (e.g., young people)
- Program of Library inquiry points for Council information and to link to One Stop Shops

- Hold Black Country Book Festival
- Improve standards of homework clubs and secure new investment
- Introduce electronic information and learning resources available via Web site
- Develop different types of Learning Center branding—Game Zones, quiet times—to cater for different customers
- Investigate self-issue systems
- Building improvements
- Investigate feasibility of library services on school sites through Extended Schools and Building Schools for the Future (CS 3.3.1)

4.3   Major challenges and ambitions for 2007/08

- As above
- Additional challenges will be managing the end of Bookstart funding

Potential activities identified through the planning process for 2007/08

- Prepare for Chartermark renewal by reviewing procedures and customer involvement
- Implement results of Single Status
- The Arcade and Discovery Store
- E-books
- Wi-Fi hotspots in libraries
- Space on Web site for community groups (e.g., local history societies)
- Review provision for young people

Sandwell Metropolitan Borough Library
Source: Sandwell Metropolitan Borough Library Council, 2005: 22; reprinted courtesy of Sandwell Metropolitan Borough Library.

Part 1 [Internal Assessment]

5.3   What does this mean for our work?

The underlying assumptions behind the figures above are that there will be no growth in the overall budget. 88.6 percent of staff already work in public service points, ensuring that opening hours are achieved. There is no capacity to release further staffing for the front line. The priority will be to look at ways of freeing frontline staff from administrative work by using IT more effectively so that an even higher percentage of their time can be focused on direct service delivery.

Staffing strengths:

- Loyal, adaptable, and hardworking staff
- Relatively low levels of sickness for a service that is largely frontline (7.33 days compared to Council target of 5)
- Additional frontline staffing (L60,000 redistributed) in 2004–5 by deleting management posts
- Support for training (e.g., Training Hour, Post Entry Training)

- Use of short-term working groups/library visits by LMT to ensure staff expertise and knowledge influences plans
- Progressing toward 2006 target for 20 percent staff from black and minority ethnic groups
- Share and gain access to expertise through partnerships working

Challenges are:

- Fewer staff than our CIPFA [Chartered Institute of Public Finance and Accountancy] comparators, and this impacts our ability to deliver additional services or respond to changing need
- On average Sandwell staffs are paid less than staff in comparator authorities, affecting our ability to recruit key positions
- Maintaining services must take precedence, but this leaves limited capacity for service development—responding to changes in customer expectations
- Capacity issues in HR to support service that delay recruitment and add to the administrative burden of local managers (Sandwell Metropolitan Borough Library Council, 2005: 14)

Analysis

Buildings

Low floor space, poor condition, listed status inhibits delivery of modern service. Particularly crucial for CHAS and Central Evidence of past refurbishments shows that this is followed by increase in use that in many cases is sustained over a number of years. Considerable progress in past five years to improve buildings—plan now needs revisiting and updating

ICT [information and communications technology]

Achieved ODPM [Office of the Deputy Prime Minister] targets for priority public interactions, now progressing toward compliance with BVPI [best value performance indicator] 157.

High number of PCs [personal computers], but require investment to maintain quality and usefulness—new operating systems, hardware refreshment, speed of access to Internet.

Use of ICT to improve processes and productivity—slow but steady progress—PC bookings, Liberate—future developments are new server for whole service

Stock

- Additional investment over past few years but impact has been patchy
- Increased demand for multimedia identified by staff
- Stock transfer system has not been effective so on hold for 12 months to review and carry out other activities to improve stock
- Need identified to improve purchase of Asian DVDs as priority, black interest material generally
- Major priority for 2005–06 to improve quality and establish processes and skills to maintain high quality stock

George Eliot Hospital NHS [National Health Service] Trust
Source: Brook, 2007: 13; reprinted courtesy of Nigel Brook, Library Services
Manager, William Harvey Library, George Eliot Hospital NHS Trust.

Internal Analysis
Client and Customer-Base Analysis

The Library is multidisciplinary and provides services to all George Eliot Hospital staff, to North Warwickshire PCT [Primary Care Trust] staff [both those Trust based and those working in the community], local General Practitioners and Medical/Allied Health students on placement at the hospital. It also has an Associate membership scheme for those who wish to join the Library but who do not fall into any other membership category. Associate members pay an annual joining fee and must provide evidence of home address prior to acceptance.

In 2006 the Library introduced a full access facility for nursing students upon placement. In addition, a discounted associate membership for non placement nursing students was also introduced. This is a growing area of the service, and one that will be carefully monitored throughout 2007.

In addition the library allows "Reference Use" to anyone with a legitimate reason for using the service but who falls outside of all of the above categories.

The Library has a high number of service users, with 1,202 registered members. This has reduced from the 1,500 users stated in the Library Strategy & Business Plan 2002; however, we have recently performed a full system audit to bring us into line with data protection policy and legislation.

The Library was withdrawn from the Trust Induction program in 2005, along with several other departments, at the direction of the Induction program managers. The Trust's efforts to reduce the time and cost incurred by the induction staff resulted in reduction of the program and exclusion for many of the "nonessential" speakers. We still supply copies of the Library's marketing leaflet Multidisciplinary Health Information at your Fingertips and our user registration form. We have also arranged to be mentioned in the section on learning support delivered by Human Resources.

While this has impacted the Library service by removing access to a valuable marketing channel, we have endeavored to counter this by exploring electronic methods of marketing and being much more proactive in our approach to publicity.

The number of registered users is expected to develop dramatically over the next 12 months. With the move in to a new, larger, better-resourced building that is more central to the hospital we expect to see rapid increases in our user-base. This will be underpinned in the longer term by increases in the numbers of medical students on placement, with future growth of PCT staff based in the Trust, greater involvement in Patient Information issues, increased use by social sector staff, and the potential demands of KSF on the service.

George Eliot Hospital NHS
Source: Brook, 2007: 10–12; reprinted courtesy of Nigel Brook, Library
Services Manager, William Harvey Library, George Eliot Hospital NHS Trust.

External Assessment
Specific Dimensions
Health Information Environment

For the Library Services to be successful it must respond to developments at three distinct levels.

- Trust Level: We are committed to providing a quality library service to Trust staff that reflects the Trust's priorities.
- Local Level: At a local level there are opportunities for services to continue working together to improve access to resources and provide value for money to the regional health community. For example, the SAL and North Warwickshire PCTs and through closer working relationships with UHCW and Warwick hospital library services.
- National Level: There are opportunities to integrate with developments such as National Service Framework for Library Services, CNST standards, and widening participation in education.

Some tensions may arise as a result of demands from these different levels. To deal with these, the demands will be viewed within the context of the strategy's aims and underlying values.

As a matter of urgency, the Library Service must be ready to respond to developments in education within the NHS, including:

- Clinical governance
- Evidence-based practice
- Evidence-based librarianship
- Technological development within the field of point-of-care delivery of information
- A 24-hour culture and the on-the-spot requirement of information
- Seamless access to information across organization and locations
- Joint purchasing to extend the range of available resources and improve cost-efficiency
- Longer working hours and flexible working patterns
- Staff mobility and reconfiguration of workforce
- Development of primary care trusts and SHA [Strategic Health Authority] reconfiguration
- Increasing numbers of staff engaged in education
- Increasing numbers of students on clinical placement
- Interdisciplinary training and education
- Lifelong learning and unlocking skills of all staff
- Changes in the delivery of learning resources with an emphasis on e-learning
- Single education levy
- Development of an NHS University/NHS central training agency
- Emphasis on knowledge management
- Involvement of patients in health care and the development of a patient-led NHS
- Packaged or targeted information requirements
- Changes in copyright and licensing agreement
- Changes in the availability of national core content resources

This has led to a change in philosophy within the Library service:

- Library Services to cut red tape around its administrative tasks
- Library to be viewed as a function rather than a physical location

- Services to be user-focused rather than resource-centered
- Library staff to provide value-added information and services
- Resources tailored for the needs of specific users, groups, and teams
- Further development of electronic services and resources
- Development of point-of-care services and resources
- Training program that is multidisciplinary and underpins evidence-based practice

The Library Service must support key local and national policies. The Library Strategy 1998–2002 tackled issues raised by Guidance for Library and Information Services HSG(97)47 and was successful in developing an efficient, effective, and improved performance. The Library service will continue to improve the quality of its service and provide the high-quality infrastructure needed to support the development of evidence-based practice.

The NEW NHS: Modern and Dependable and A First Class Service documents both emphasized the need for quality, increased efficiency, and improved performance. The Library Service will continue to improve the quality of its services and provide the high-quality infrastructure needed to support the development of evidence-based practice.

The Library also has a role to play in the implementation of Connecting for Health: Business plan 2005/06. We will continue to support the principles outlined in this document through improving access to electronic formats. We shall continue to link Web services to the National Library for Health and contribute to best practice by training users in the correct, timely uses of cores clinical information services.

We will continue to support the central government modernization agenda as outlined in the NHS Plan 2000 and The NHS Improvement Plan by:

- Providing access to quality information to tackle health inequalities and improve clinical effectiveness
- Working with others at a local, regional, and national level to maximize access to resources and services
- Supporting patient information services by identifying quality consumer health information and liaising directly with PALS [Patient Advice and Liaison Service]
- Providing resources and training programs to support lifelong learning and CPD [Corporate Property Department] at the Trust
- Promoting and disseminating the NSF's [National Service Framework] and work done by NICE

Building the Information Core emphasized the need for a knowledge management approach in the NHS. It also highlighted e-learning requirements as does Learning for everyone: a development plan for the NHSU. While the future of the NHSU has been open to debate, Library staff shall continue to support the outlined principles. Library staff possesses skills in selecting, organizing, storing, retrieving, and disseminating explicit knowledge and so play a central role in supporting the development of knowledge networks. We shall continue to support the development of e-learning by provision of adequate resources, development of a new Library Web portal, investigation and construction of in-house electronic resources, and the provision of suitable for self-study.

The Library Service shall contribute directly to delivery on three of the five domains outlined in Standards for Better Health by ensuring that clinicians have access to high-quality information literacy training and have access to the highest quality of available evidence or mechanisms underpinning CPD and accessing current awareness information for better patient care.

Coordination of local learning and education facilities is now part of the remit of the SHA. The mission of the West Midlands SHA knowledge management strategy as expressed in mobilizing knowledge for patient care 2003 is:

> To provide easy and equitable access to current, relevant, and accredited knowledge in order to support the day-to-day and lifelong learning needs of the entire workforce from any location across organizational and sector boundaries to inform high quality patient care.

The Library Strategy will place a heavy emphasis on partnership working with others to improve access to quality information by health and social care staff.

In June 2005, the Library joined the national INSPIRE project group. INSPIRE seeks to create a wide-area network of multisector libraries that are capable of referring their registered users to other INSPIRE members. While this also underpins the patient information agenda at George Eliot Hospital, it will prove to be useful in helping us to support increased demands for nonclinical information. We aim to build on our successful member shop of local networks and expand the range of information partners accessible to us.

It is important that the library strategy also supports Trust developments and priorities. It will do this by linking the strategy to the balanced scorecard approach used by the Trust and supporting priorities identified in the Trust's core service delivery documents.

SWOT CHART

BASIC DEFINITIONS

The results of your internal and external assessments are recorded in a strength, weakness, opportunity, threats (SWOT) chart, which provides a clearer picture of the service's capabilities. An honest and thorough internal and external assessment provides core information to generate a picture of the library's advantages, if any, over other information competitors available to your clients. The results of the assessment bolster better decisions by helping you choose a stronger match between the interests and needs of your clients and the capabilities of your library. The results will also determine whether a service or program that does not add value to clients should be retired.

By explicitly examining your library's strengths, weaknesses, opportunities, and threats, you can direct resources to developing competitive advantages over other information services available. The SWOT chart is a simple tool that is not too time-consuming or complicated. Its effectiveness lies in its simplicity. It is an excellent first method for exploring the possibility of service development. The analyses you will derive from the results of the SWOT Chart are based on somewhat subjective material and as such should be considered a guide rather than a prescription.

Filling in the four boxes and analyzing the results will also help formulate a viable marketing strategy. Be positive but realistic about the library's prospects, and respond honestly to shortcomings and risks. Write your responses as specifically and concisely as possible. Building on accurate information gained in the SWOT, the business plan will help identify how you will compensate for or capitalize on these issues.

The SWOT Chart will help you to:

- resources into services that take advantage of talents, abilities, and opportunities
- Uncover opportunities you can take advantage of
- Understand the weaknesses of your services, after which you can manage and eliminate those threats that may take you by surprise
- After seeing the results, begin to identify which factors differentiate your library from competitors and use that difference to help you carve a successful niche

SWOT ANALYSIS

Prioritize the SWOT chart lists, ranking them for impact on your library relative to your competition. As you discuss the entries in each of the four SWOT sections, review and prioritize the value of the final entries. Then create a ranked list to reflect your planning group's consensus. Review and discussion by a planning group is necessary since two people rarely come up with the same final version of a SWOT. Decide what steps should be taken next and work them into your action plans with realistic targets, assignment of responsibility, and implementation. For example: Have you identified a service with weaknesses that requires redesign? Or have you identified an unmet critical need of your clients? Is the unmet need a priority issue? If so, should it become a strategy under one of your objectives? If not, should it wait until a later date?

It is essential to communicate your assessments with staff and stakeholders to gain consensus, support, and understanding. While not everyone will agree with your results, thorough communication ensures that you know if anyone feels that an issue has been overlooked or overemphasized. This is valuable information, as the SWOT is a subjective tool and vulnerable to the vagaries of personal opinion unless all entries are supported by facts. By including the staff and stakeholders in these processes, you encourage all interested parties to work together, focusing on the library's objectives. In essence, they understand the library's goals and incorporate them into everyday activities.

The detailed analyses and SWOT chart do not require presentation within the business plan. They can be placed in an appendix for further review if a reader chooses. See the end of the examples section for descriptions of techniques used to express the assessment and proposed strategy resulting from the SWOT.

KEY POINTS TO INCLUDE IN THE SWOT CHART AND ANALYSIS

Core elements to include when creating your SWOT chart:

- Use the form to keep track of your answers
- Keep each of the four lists short: ten items max
- When assigning an issue to a category, it becomes either an S or a W, but not both
- Facts must support every entry to reduce the subjective nature of the tool
- Include all competitive factors, even if you don't compete directly for funding
- Keep your language clear and concise, simple and plan
- Be realistic
- Your service characteristics may be your strengths
- Think about your strengths in relation to competitors: if all of your competitors provide highly accurate information services, then a highly accurate information service is not a strength to your clients, it is a *necessity*.
- When considering your weaknesses, ask if others seem to perceive weaknesses that you do not see. Are competitors doing better? Why? In what areas?
- When considering your weaknesses, ask what you could you do better. What could be improved? What should you avoid doing? When you think about your clients and their priorities, what do you offer that is not up to their par?
- When considering your opportunities, will changes in local events affect your capabilities? Will changes in social patterns or population profiles affect your funding? Will changes in technology restrict or advance your capabilities? Why? How will you overcome these issues?
- When considering your opportunities, what are your core competencies? What does the library do better than anybody else?
- When considering threats, what will make people stop coming to the library for one of your services?
- In the threats area, changes in technology are already eliminating the idea that clients need to come into the library for service. How will you overcome this notion, or how will you change services to create new access routes?
- In the threats area, what will technology changes do to your measurements of use or of success?

- When balancing between what your clients want and what you can provide, what obstacles do you face in meeting their wants?
- What is going to make something your library is doing unprofitable? Or what is your library doing that is unprofitable?

SWOT CHART WORKSHEET

Place the results of these questions in the appropriate section of the SWOT chart (see Worksheet 4-3 ⓒⓓ). Add or delete questions to suit your unique situation. These questions are only suggestions designed to help you choose among your options.

EXAMPLES OF SWOT CHARTS

Port Stephens Library
Source: Port Stephens Library, 2004; reprinted with thanks and acknowledgment to Port Stephens Library, NSW, Australia.

Strengths:
- 49 percent of population are registered users
- Community are highly satisfied with library services
- Provide a range of services on a lean budget
- Provide friendly and responsive customer service
- Children's programs
- Increasing use of Raymond Terrace and Tomaree branches
- Facilities at Tomaree

Weaknesses:
- Low staff/loans ratio (loans higher than NSW average; staff lower than NSW average)
- Facilities at Raymond Terrace
- Decreasing usage of Mobile Library
- No marketing plan
- Access to technology
- Access to electronic resources
- Lack of Web presence
- Partnerships
- Use of volunteers
- Provision of training for staff
- Community programs (*Example continues on page 87.*)

Worksheet 4-3A. SWOT Chart Analysis
What are your strengths and how might you capitalize upon them?
What advantages does your library have?
What do you do better than anyone else?
What unique, low-cost, high-quality, or quickest delivered resources do you provide or offer access?
What do clients see as your strengths?
Do you have adequate financial resources?
Do clients think well of you?
Do you have experienced management?
Do you have multiple locations?
Name and identify the library's competitive advantages.
What are your weaknesses and how can you overcome them?
Is the library lacking strategic direction?
Does the library have unacceptable loss of clients?
Does the library have cash-flow difficulties?
Is your service line too narrow?
(Cont'd.)

Worksheet 4-3A. SWOT Chart Analysis *(Continued)*
Is the quality measurement system inadequate?
Is your staff perceived as valuable and knowledgeable?
What are clients most likely to see as weaknesses? How do you know this?
What are your opportunities?
Can you expand service lines?
Is the library's competition complacent?
What do your clients want?
Identify the library's expansion possibilities.
Can you improve the curb appeal?
Can you upgrade the IT systems?
Where are the good opportunities facing the library?
Identify the interesting trends.
What would allow the library to create new revenues?
What threats are faced?
What are competitors doing? Are new competitors thinking of providing services?
(Cont'd.)

Worksheet 4-3A. SWOT Chart Analysis *(Continued)*

Are the required specifications for jobs, products, or services changing?

Is the library's market's growth slowing?

What would happen to your library if technology costs increased?

Identify any bad debt or cash-flow problem.

Could any weaknesses seriously threaten your service?

Could your library's service or quality rates decline?

Could your clients' needs change?

Create your SWOT chart using the template provided, and then continue your analysis using the following.

Match your strengths to your opportunities.

Could any of your strengths open up any opportunities?

Discuss ways to reduce or improve your library's weaknesses.

Could eliminating a weakness open an opportunity?

Discuss ways to protect your library against the identified threats.

How will you defend against threats?

(Cont'd.)

Worksheet 4-3A. SWOT Chart Analysis *(Continued)*
Identify ways to transform threats into opportunities for service.
How can your strengths help take advantage of your opportunities?
What markets or client types can you pursue as opportunities?
How can your strengths overcome identified threats?
Could developing a strength reduce a threat?
What action will overcome your weakness in order to take advantage of the opportunity?
How will you minimize weaknesses to overcome threats?
Is it really a threat or could it become a new opportunity?
When you have completed the analysis, what do your findings suggest? Do you see any patterns or possibilities?
Can you identify a situation in which no service exists to fulfill a high-priority need?
Can you identify a situation in which services currently being offered fulfill a low-priority need?
From these insights can you identify a way to differentiate your service from the competition's service?
Can you create a niche for your service?
Can you see any other important developments?

Worksheet 4-3B. SWOT Chart Template	
Section 1 STRENGTHS *List positive characteristics of the library* 1. 2. 3. 4. 5. 6. 7. 8. 9. 10.	Section 2 WEAKNESSES *List negative characteristics of the library* 1. 2. 3. 4. 5. 6. 7. 8. 9. 10.
Section 3 OPPORTUNITIES *List Opportunities* 1. 2. 3. 4. 5. 6. 7. 8. 9. 10.	Section 4 THREATS *List Threats to library operations* 1. 2. 3. 4. 5. 6. 7. 8. 9. 10.

Opportunities:

- Partnerships
- Redevelopment of Raymond Terrace Library
- Maximize use of technology
- Develop a Web presence
- Review of Joint Library Agreement
- Community presence and programs
- Library environment-creation of appeal

Threats:

- Library rated as the least important of Council's services
- Image of library in the community and larger organization
- Low level of state government funding
- Current level of funding is the lowest per capita in the Hunter Region and one of the lowest in NSW
- Competition for Council funds
- Population growth and demographics
- Capacity to implement technology trends
- Library facilities
- Demands of stakeholders
- Staffing levels
- Marketing
- Training for staff
- Image/perception of the Library
- Sustainability

CPLA: Country Public Libraries Association of New South Wales
Source: Country Public Libraries Association of New South Wales, 2004: 1;
   reprinted courtesy of Public Libraries NSW—Country.

Table 4-1. CPLA Strengths and Weaknesses	
Strengths	**Weaknesses**
• Strong track record of effective lobbying, particularly at outset • Opportunity and willingness for change and improvement • Extensive goodwill throughout the organization • Strong cooperative culture and effective network of zones • Support from the NSW State Library	• Need for a strategic plan with clear direction and priorities • Need to adapt to changing environment (accountability, meeting needs of members) • Need for more consultative mechanisms for decision making • Need for more effective communication • Defects in the constitution • Need for broader involvement of Councilors and Council management, particularly at the local level • Geographic dislocation and spread
	(Cont'd.)

Table 4-1. CPLA Strengths and Weaknesses *(Continued)*

Opportunities	Threats
• To amend the constitution and provide a more effective structure • To adapt to the changing environment • More involvement by members • Strategic partnerships, networking, and opening up communications with other agencies • Higher visibility	• Decline in membership • Loss of enthusiasm • Lack of planning, leadership, and communication • Conflict and division within • Competition from other associations/bodies performing similar services • Being ineffectual (failing to add value)

Haldimand County Public Library
SWOT Analysis
Source: Haldimand County Public Library, 2005; reprinted courtesy of Haldimand County Public Library.

Strengths, Weaknesses, Opportunities, Threats (SWOT)

The Board and Library management staff undertook a SWOT analysis of the factors affecting the Haldimand County Public Library.

Table 4-2. Haldimand County Public Library SWOT Analysis

Strengths	Weaknesses
Strong, supportive board of trustees, which maintains a progressive and county-wide outlook toward library services, and exercises careful, yet flexible, processes in decision making and visioning	Some lingering public and staff apprehensions as a result of amalgamation and restructuring; some community rivalry
Restructured management team, facilitating system-wide coordination of key library functions	Inconsistent standards at facilities; Caledonia, Cayuga, and Hagersville in particular have become limited in terms of space to house collections, delivering services, and providing areas for in-house activities.
Access to county expertise and support, including finance, information systems, facilities, human resources, etc.	Lack of public awareness about who we are and what we do.
A good relationship with Haldimand County council, largely achieved through positive participation of Councilor on Library Board	Competition from other divisions and county priorities for funding
Implementation of an integrated state-of-the-art automation system at all six branches.	Inconsistent use of cataloging standards in the former three boards has created numerous and significant errors in our merged database, requiring additional funding for staff hours to do the required cleanup.
Appropriate geographic distribution of the six branches across the county	Geography, i.e., size of the county can pose problems

(Cont'd.)

Table 4-2. Haldimand County Public Library SWOT Analysis *(Continued)*

Strengths *(Cont'd.)*	Weaknesses *(Cont'd.)*
Friendly staff, many of whom have worked for many years for the Library, establishing good relationships with patrons	Staff training required to provide consistent service levels across the county
Opportunities	**Threats**
Through improved collections, services, programs, and facilities, the board and staff can position the library branches as community centers.	The need for staff and public training on new technologies will place demands on staffing flexibility
Changing demographics and a renewed focus on the importance of early childhood education will open up important partnership opportunities.	There is competition at all levels for government and private funding to maintain and expand services, programs, facilities.
Well-trained library service can offer value-added service by acting as navigators in a complex, information-rich environment.	A growing number of young people do not use or value the library.
The older population will present increasing opportunities for creative outreach services.	

George Eliot Hospital NHS Trust Library
SWOT Analysis
Source: Brook, 2007: Appendix 4; reprinted courtesy of Nigel Brook, Library
   Services Manager, William Harvey Library, George Eliot Hospital NHS Trust.

Table 4-3. Appendix 4: SWOT Analysis of Library Service

Strengths	Weaknesses
• 24-hour access • Expertise and experience of the staff • Links with key departments • Links with Trusts education providers • Networked resources with access via Internet to additional resources • New library Web presence, professionally designed and incorporating e-learning resources • Automated purchasing system • Automated financial records system • Formal links with NWPCT library service • Formal cooperative links with other West Midlands health libraries • Membership of the national INSPIRE scheme • User involvement in service development • Feedback from users • Quality assurance procedure • Funding for different user groups	• Complex funding mechanism • Funding levels not sufficient to cover all hospital staff population effectively • Funding does not match inflation; particularly in key areas such as journal pricing with rises annually • Internet connection often unreliable • Lack of funding for specific user-groups, nurse students, etc. • Stock limitations in some areas • Current accommodation is too small and unsuited to task • Lack of awareness among users of the areas where the library can provide support • No dedicated IT training facility • Not enough computer workstations • Limited outreach activities • Inherited a classification system totally unsuited to medical work • Lack of flexible space in the Library

(Cont'd.)

Table 4-3. Appendix 4: SWOT Analysis of Library Service *(Continued)*

Strengths *(Cont'd.)*	Weaknesses *(Cont'd.)*
• Multidisciplinary service • Most services free at point of need • Working agreements in IT Training Dept. for access to computer training room • Clinical Librarian service • Literature Search service • Full training program relaunch • Protected medical student loan collection • Full stock audit carried out • Restructure into a flatter organizational model • Full staff contribution toward service development, including contributory manual of procedures • Good quality computers	• No coherent staff manual that explains procedures practically • Some electronic resources accessible only from within the library • Library stock out of date in many areas, with insufficient funding to rectify stock problems in all areas.
Threats	**Opportunities**
• Internet development allowing potential users to bypass the Library • Google-syndrome increasing the potential for substandard information to affect practice • NCC resources are not the best-available evidence, encouraging the use of information because it is available and not because it is the best available • Increased competition from other services; NLH, NLM, and HE providers • Low profile of libraries and library staff • Rising cost of resources • Users lack time to use resources/services • Instability of regional library provision, threats to service by spiraling costs, and potential for incorporation into a larger organization, thus reducing the amount of dedicated Trust support time • No control over national procurement policies • Development of outreach services that are isolated from the Library • The Library is not formally included in all Trust education and training; there needs to be a seamless and inclusive process in which all staff are taught research skills prior to engaging on a course of studies • Growth of department collections that duplicate work/increased spending • No protected learning time for many staff groups • A fragmented Trust-wide approach to education and training, no comprehensive inclusive system • E-patients using poor quality sources of health information • No recognition of the skills needed to effectively search for high quality information	• Consortium purchasing to increase cost-effectiveness, specifically with regard to e-resources • Continued focus on Clinical Governance • Increased focus on lifelong learning • Pilot access for nursing students and observers; potential to increase our user-base • Formal involvement with PALS, support for web development and access to information for patients • Potential to pilot the book prescription scheme at GEH • New technology; potential of PDAs as a means of transmitting information • Expansion of the Clinical Librarian service • Move into new building with all the publicity it will generate • Training opportunities for Library staff increased due to regional partnerships • Development of Web services for Trust departments integrated through the Library site; Journal Club, PALS, etc. • Intranet/Internet • Outreach learning centers • On-the-ward training for entire staff groups • Increasing range of users • Directorate of Clinical Education • Directorate of Audit, Research, and Evidence-Based Practice • NHS copyright agreement and movement on electronic signatures provide opportunities for vastly improved document delivery service • Patient-led NHS • Patch-wide working to maximize resources and access • NSF for Health Libraries • Further development of NLH • Electronic resources • E-Learning as method of training and potential for income generation

Bedfordshire County
SWOT Analysis
Source: George, 2004: 7–9; Bedfordshire Libraries Business Plan 2004/05
to 2006/07, reprinted by kind permission of the Bedfordshire County
Council.

5. SWOT Analysis

Strengths

- Committed, hardworking staff delivering a professional service
- Highly developed Integrated Library Computer System with online access
- Effective online services through the Virtual Library, Virtual Homework Center, Infopoint, You & Your Community, Gateways, and inquiry service
- Free public access to the Internet e-mail and Word packages
- Strong community support with high satisfaction ratings
- Network of buildings and vehicles with good access

Weaknesses

- Uncertainty about sustainable funding for some developments
- Some staff uncertainty in the current climate of changing use of, and expectations of, the public library service
- Limited number of staff at middle management level to drive continuous change and improvement
- Poor condition of some buildings

Opportunities

- Recent publication of "Framework for the Future" and the emerging new Public Library Standards provide a basis for refocusing the service to meet future challenges
- Close links with the ESD [electronic service delivery] and POP [points of presence] developments to maintain the Library Service profile in e-government
- Further use of buildings for wider activities, including more homework centers, learning centers, POPs, and links with the Learning Communities
- Replacement mobiles will allow a refocusing of this service to meet changing needs, particularly with elderly people
- Further regional developments and cross-sectioned working with archives and museums
- Development of a cultural services policy

Threats

- Failing to meet the challenge of changing use patterns and perceptions of libraries
- No sustainable funding to maintain ICT developments
- Limited number of staff for research and development

- The need to meet the needs of the whole community means a careful balance is necessary
- Need to ensure a balance between maintenance and development
- Libraries, as with other cultural services, being low on the overall priorities of the County Council

---

Ontario Digital Library
Source: Ontario Digital Library, 2003: 26–27; reprinted courtesy of Ontario Library Association, the Ontario Digital Library Business Plan. Toronto.

5.2 SWOT Analysis

A SWOT (i.e., potential strengths, weaknesses, opportunities, and threats) is an important tool to help start prioritizing areas to concentrate on.

Strengths

- Puts into place in Ontario a concept proven successful in Canadian, American, British, and Australian jurisdictions
- Has strong support within all sectors of the library community in all regions and cities in Ontario
- Is a unique response to solving the problems of Ontario libraries to deliver digital products and services and to meet the needs of Ontarians
- Supports the Ontario government's strategies for education, training, and lifelong learning
- Builds on the key success factors in other jurisdictions (i.e., receives government support; implements an effective branding strategy; benefits all residents of Ontario, has leadership and commitment from all library sectors as well as the academic, education, municipal, training, and health care communities; has an effective governance structure; and adopts an evolutionary, phased-approach)

Weaknesses

- The ability to effectively foster partnerships and cooperation between the library sectors (public, academic, college, and K–12), library associations, and individual libraries themselves
- Ensuring sufficient resources, in terms of funding and knowledgeable staff, are available and committed to the success of the ODL over the long-term (this will be possible through strong provincial leadership and support)
- Several of the electronic databases and streaming media projects planned for the ODL will require high-speed Internet connections, however currently many rural and remote areas of the province have access to only (regular) dial-up Internet connections

Opportunities

- To be a *provincial leader* in Canada offering extensive, province-wide, quality electronic library services
- To be at the *forefront of technology*, offering new and leading-edge information services and products on a timely basis

- To provide *long-term cost savings* through economies of scale—savings through maximizing buying power (in a consortia)
- To *foster partnerships and cooperation* between the library sectors in Ontario, library associations, and individual libraries themselves
- To *learn and build on the numerous examples* of successfully implemented digital libraries in other jurisdictions

Threats

- Lack of government leadership and commitment to the ODL project and the coordination between various government ministries that will have a stake in the benefits of the proposed services offered (i.e., including the Ministries of Education; Culture; Health and Long-Term Care; Training, Colleges, and Universities; and Enterprise, Opportunity, and Innovation)
- Attracting adequate sustainable funding to maintain the services and products of the ODL
- Marketing effectively to the Ontario public that the ODL goes "beyond the Internet" and offers superior added value to the Internet (i.e., the ODL will provide full-text articles from journals that would normally cost money through a basic Internet service)
- Avoiding duplication of efforts of other Ontario library consortiums or associations offering similar services to their members

---

The SWOT analysis indicates that significant tangible strengths and opportunities are inherent in the ODL concept. The major impediments to the success of the ODL are ensuring strong government support and financing and are maintaining and fostering cooperation and commitment among the various sectors of the Ontario library community.

Note the analysis of the SWOT analysis in the box above. The ODL has reduced the size of the SWOT chart to a two-sentence report, which will be useful later when developing an executive summary or elevator pitch (see Chapter 10).

DEMOGRAPHIC ANALYSIS WORKSHEET

Worksheet 4-4 ⓒⅅ will help you define your target audience by describing its demographic characteristics. Answer all of the questions on the worksheet. When you are finished, compare your demographic customer profile against the geographic profile of your market area. This will help identify the number of clients in your market area that match your demographic profile, which will help you determine the viability of your services. If you are offering services to more than one demographic group, describe them on different worksheets.

Worksheet 4-4. Customer Profile
Customer Profile
1. Are your clients individuals or businesses?
2. If they are individuals, describe their gender, age, income level, professional level, specific information needs, and any other significant demographic variables. If they are businesses, describe the subject range, use levels, and any other relevant descriptors of the businesses you will target.
Geographic Profile
3. Where are your customers located physically and electronically?
4. How many customers are located in your market?
5. How many times during the year will the total market you've chosen use your services?
6. What is the dollar value (or your organization's value measurement) of the use that occurs in your market each year?
Source: Entrepreneur.com (2007). Copyright © 2007 Entrepreneur.com; all rights reserved. Reprinted with permission from Entrepreneur.com.

EXAMPLE OF A COMPETITIVE COMPARISON

Association for Library Collections & Technical Services ⓒⒹ
**Source: Association for Library Collections & Technical Services, 2004:
2–3; reprinted courtesy of Association for Library Collections &
Technical Services (ALCTS).**

I. Products, services, and member benefits

    A. Products and service description

        i. Scholarly journals (e.g., library resources and technical services)

        ii. Online newsletters (e.g., ALCTS Online Newsletter, AN2)

    iii. Professional and reference books

    iv. Section series publications

    v. Division promotional materials

    vi. Online products and services such as ALCTS Newsletter Online searchable archives, databases such as book and serial vendors for Eastern Europe and the former Soviet Union, e-books, and other formal Web publications

B. Competitive comparison

    i. Competition

- Other library associations and organizations with publishing programs, such as ARL (Association of Research Libraries), ULC (Urban Libraries Council), or the Charleston Conference
- Other ALA (American Library Association) Divisions, such as ACRL (Association of College and Research Libraries) and RUSA (Reference and User Services Association)
- Electronic content vendors
- Commercial publishers in the library market, such as Neal-Schuman (professional and reference books), Cahners (Library Journal, LJ Hotline, Publishers Weekly)

    ii. Advantages of competition

- Associations
  - Usually smaller organizations with a narrow focus
  - Ability to direct resources to smaller niches
  - Type of library versus functionality-driven
- Commercial publishing companies
  - For-profit orientation enabling ongoing access to profits for reinvestment in businesses
  - More resources directed to marketing, market research, and product development
  - Larger travel and entertainment budget for author prospecting
  - Ability to finance author honorarium
  - Better able to pursue smaller markets and ancillary markets due to overhead structure
  - More resources directed toward developing product lines and marketing spin-offs/promotions

    iii. Advantages of ALCTS

- Most comprehensive selection of library technical services professional information
- Ability to produce smaller niche-market products quickly
- Access to the experts
- Promotion/tenure outlet ability through industry authority, quick-to-market capabilities, and reoccurring publications
- Reputation of ALCTS as the authority in the fields of technical services, including cataloging and classification, acquisitions, collection management and development, serials, and preservation and reformatting
- Maintaining high visibility in the development of standards, policies, and procedures in technical services and related fields for the library community, nationally, and internationally

COMPETITIVE COMPARISON WORKSHEET

Worksheet 4-5 ⊙ will help identify your competitors more specifically and prepares you for designing a marketing strategy. Competitors include anyone offering a service or product similar to or superseding yours. Fill in the worksheet with information about your competitors. You may need to alter the worksheet to have enough room for all of your major competitors or their competitive points.

Worksheet 4-5. Competitor's Profile			
	Competitor #1	*Competitor #2*	*Competitor #3*
Where are they located?			
What are their annual use/sales?			
What are their strengths?			
What are their weaknesses?			
What do they offer?			
How does it compare to yours?			
What is their marketing strategy?			
What is their advertising strategy?			
How much do they charge?			
Are they expanding?			
What do they have that you want?			

REFERENCES

Albright, Kendra S. 2004. "Environmental Scanning: Radar for Success." *The Information Management Journal* (May/June): 41–42.

Association for Library Collections & Technical Services. 2004. "ALCTS Publishing Business Plan." Chicago: ALA.

Brook, Nigel. 2007. "Library Services: Business Plan and Library Strategy 2007–2010." Warwickshire, UK: William Harvey Library, George Eliot Hospital NHS Trust.

Calgary Public Library. 2006. "Building Community, Building Capacity: Business Plan 2006–2008." Calgary, AB: Calgary Public Library. Available: http://calgarypublic library.com/library/pdf/businessplan06.pdf.

Cariboo Regional District Library. 2004. "Building Communities Together: Business Plan 2004." Williams Lake, BC: Cariboo Regional District Library.

Country Public Libraries Association of New South Wales. 2004. "Business Plan. Conference 2004." New South Wales, Australia: Country Public Libraries Association of New South Wales.

Digital Federal Credit Union. 2006. "DCU Business Library—Business Plan Guideline." Marlborough, MA: Digital Federal Credit Union. Available: www.dcu.org/business_services/library/fw0065.html.

Entrepreneur.com. 2007. "Customer Profile, Geographic Profile Worksheets." Irvine, CA: Entrepreneur Media Inc. Available: www.entrepreneur.com/contact-us/index.html.

George, Barry. 2004. "Working in Partnership: Libraries Business Plan 2004/5 to 2006/7." Bedfordshire, UK: Bedfordshire County Council. Available: www.galaxy.bedfordshire.gov.uk/webingres/bedfordshire/vlib/0.beds_libraries/business_plan_04.pdf.

George, Jennifer and Gareth Jones. 2004. *Understanding and Managing Organizational Behavior*. Reading, MA: Addison-Wesley.

Haldimand County Public Library. 2005. "Business Plan." Cayauga, Ontario. Canada: Haldimand County. Available: www.haldimandcounty.on.ca/community/library.asp.

Halifax Public Libraries. 2006. "Halifax Public Libraries Business Plan 2006–2007." Halifax, NS: Halifax Public Libraries.

Inc.com. 2000. "Pointers on Putting Together Your Business Plan." BusinessTown.com (April). Available: www.inc.com/articles/2000/04/18474.html.

MacKintosh, Pamela J. 1999. "Writing an Effective Business Plan for Fee-Based Services." *Journal of Interlibrary Loan, Document Delivery and Information Supply*, 10, no. 1: 47–61.

Marcus, Bruce. 2006. "Ten Good Reasons (At Least) to Start Planning." *Of Council*, 25, no. 12 (December): 8–12.

Maroochy Shire Council. 2006. "Library Strategy 2006: Executive Summary with Outcomes and Recommendations." Queensland, Australia: Maroochy Shire Council. Available: www.maroochy.qld.gov.au/maroochylibraries/documents/Maroochy%20Strategy%20Executive%20Summary%20Internet.pdf.

Ontario Digital Library. 2003. "The Ontario Digital Library Business Plan: Connecting Ontarians." Guelph, ON: Ontario Digital Library. Available: www.accessola2.com/odl/pdf/ODL_BusinessPlan_Full.pdf.

Port Stephens Library. 2004. "Port Stephens Library Business Plan 2004–2005." Port Stephens, Australia: Port Stephens Library.

Sandwell Metropolitan Borough Library Council. 2005. "Library and Information Service Business Plan 2005–2006." West Midlands, UK: Sandwell Metropolitan Borough Council.

Storey, Tom. 2006. "Are You Asking the Ultimate Question? The Answer Could Determine Your Library's Future." *NextSpace: The OCLC Newsletter*, 5 (December). Available: www.oclc.org/nextspace/005/1.htm.

Torbay Council. 2005. Library Services Business Plan 2006/07. Devon, UK: Torbay Council.

5 CLARIFYING OBJECTIVES

COMPONENTS

BASIC DEFINITIONS

Business planning is simpler if you break it down into two components: end results and methods. First, identify the end results you wish to achieve. The end results stimulate and direct the focus and energy of all stakeholders. These end results become your *objectives*, goals, or outcomes. They provide the answer to "What will make you successful over time? What targets do you seek?"

Second, identify the methods for achieving the end results. These are your *strategies*, activities, or tactics. They are the courses of action needed to achieve your end results and build on internal and external opportunities. Create your plans, programs, and services around these opportunities, which, if performed well, allow you to overtake the competition. Quantify what you hope to accomplish, because what you choose to measure will be completed. These measurable strategic actions cause you to move toward your objectives. In this book, the end result you want to achieve is called the *objective* and the method for achieving the objective is called the *strategy*. They are directly connected.

Every library needs a map to reach a destination and, just as important, needs to know when that destination has been reached. Objectives focus on results that can be specifically described to your staff. As each objective is accomplished, measured, and evaluated, the whole organization moves in unison closer to the overall vision. Targeted toward the needs of your clients as determined in the environmental scan, they guide your actions and are core to the success of your plan.

At this point the question is, "What is it you want to do?" Some examples include:

- Increase library use
- Improve client service
- Introduce new services
- Gain a foothold in a new field
- Develop a service within our new technical capabilities
- Productivity

- Increase market growth
- Promote a specific product or service
- Improve safety
- Maintain library use during a down period
- Win new clients
- Build client loyalty
- Develop and maintain positive business-to-business relationships
- Client relations
- Recognize performance
- Boost morale
- Smooth out in-house operations ensuring compatibility with your mission
- Improve employee loyalty
- Foster teamwork
- Marketing
- Management or staff structures
- Fee structures
- Improving recruiting
- Increasing retention
- Staff development
- Improve processes

Setting objectives involves a unified and continuous process of research and decision making throughout the year. Each step requires refining on a regular basis. Business plans are ongoing cyclic tools that help you simplify and clarify your objectives and strategies. Current knowledge of your clients—your market—is the vital starting point when setting objectives.

Objectives provide both a sense of direction and the action against which all performance gets measured. Results-oriented objectives form the basis for performance management. Good objectives place you in a position to do two things: create an evaluation program directly connected to performance, and create specific plans for coordinated action to reach the objectives.

Determining objectives cannot be performed in a vacuum. Staff relationships and communication are interrelated, and are fundamental to moving the organization forward and delivering a quality product. The individuals responsible for carrying out the objectives have to have a role in creating them. They will have the best ideas for determining what is achievable, and their commitment to reaching an objective is much stronger when themselves have established desirable levels of achievement. Every person needs to understand clearly his or her purpose and contribution to the overall effort (Granger, 1970: 3).

Because objectives reflect the end result to be sought and accomplished, senior management should participate in setting them. Senior management will have a stronger grasp of the larger picture; their task is to use this information to coordinate objectives to prevent confusion or operating at cross-purposes. Objectives are updated from past plans and evaluated with current information from the environmental scan. These issues of intent must be kept in balance with other key performance areas. The impact of accomplished objectives on one another will have to be considered in advance. The objectives in different units of the library and those of external organizational relationships should be reviewed to determine whether they are mutually consistent across the organization. For example, the collection development staff may try to simplify the collection to reduce electronic versus print costs while the reference staff may try to make it broader by offering services not key to the library's objectives.

The function of a given service is to support the parent organization or governing body as the service administers the policies of the parent. The mission of the parent organization identifies the function that the library intends to perform within its system. Once the basic mission is established, the specific objectives, strategies, programs, policies, and plans fall into place.

FORMULATING OBJECTIVES

The Bedfordshire County Council identifies how the Library contributes to the Council's vision and objectives.

The Bedfordshire County Council
Source: George, 2004: 5; reprinted by kind permission of Bedfordshire County Council.

Libraries contribute to the Council's vision and objectives in the following ways:
- Protecting the vulnerable: provision of services to elderly housebound people, people in residential care, looked-after children, excluded children
- Maintaining high standards of education: the Schools Library Service, Virtual Library, Virtual Homework Center, Homework Centers, Summer Reading Challenge, class visits
- Attracting new and increasing existing business: "You and Your Community," job-seekers information, free access to the Internet, e-mail, and word packages, business information

- Creating better transport infrastructures: making information and publicity available
- Protecting and enhancing a sustainable environment: making information and publicity available, recycling books and other material, revising mobile routes
- Promoting safer communities: provision of Homework Centers, provision of safe community spaces
- Fostering inclusive communities: revision of opening hours and mobile routes, improved access to buildings, People's Network, Virtual Library, Homework Centers, work with Basic Skills providers, material in community languages, staff with specific inclusion responsibilities. Specific targets relate to establishing the Virtual Homework Center and other e-services
- Managing an efficient and effective Council: closer involvement with the ESD developments; first point of presence to be established in Dunstable Library; links into the Learning Service Plan

The Board of Trustees and Library Administration of the Kenosha Public Library state a similar connection from a different perspective.

Kenosha Public Library (CD)
Source: Kenosha Public Library, 2006: 7; reprinted with thanks to the Kenosha Public Library in Wisconsin.

Library Governance

Kenosha Public Library Board of Trustees Goal

Acting under the authority of Chapter 43 of the Wisconsin Statutes, the KPL Board of Trustees carries out the Library's mission by authorizing the KPL business plan and operating policies, setting long-range goals and objectives, hiring and retaining a competent Library Director, monitoring Library operations, and providing accountability for the Library to the public.

Library Board Objectives

1. Participate in the formulation of and authorize KPL's mission and long range goals.
2. Participate in the formulation of and approve KPL operating policies.
3. Participate in the formulation of and approve the KPL annual business plan.
4. Adopt and monitor KPL's budget and fiscal management policies.
5. Evaluate the director's performance and approve his or her employment agreement.
6. Evaluate, review, and adopt KPL personnel policies and labor agreements.
7. Monitor and assess the achievement of KPL goals and objectives.
8. Advocate the mission of the Library throughout the community.

Library Administration

Library Administration Goal

Administration carries out the Library's mission by planning, organizing, directing, promoting, and controlling all KPL functions, operations, and activities, directly or through supervisory staff.

Library Administration Objectives

1. Administer the policies adopted by the KPL Board of Trustees.
2. Administer the Kenosha County Library System (KCLS).
3. Develop and manage the KPL business plan and budget.
4. Control the collection and deposit of all KPL revenues and the expenditure of all KPL funds according to generally accepted accounting practices.
5. Purchase and acquire all services, supplies, furniture, equipment, and library materials necessary for Library operations according to established rules and procedures.
6. Plan KPL service improvements, evaluate KPL service success, and anticipate KPL facilities and equipment needs.
7. Maintain the official KPL and KCLS records.
8. Develop and administer KPL personnel policies and practices.
9. Provide a comprehensive public information program to promote KPL and KCLS services and resources.
10. Promote communication among employees throughout the Library.
11. Develop and carry out an ongoing continuing education and in-service training program to upgrade KPL staff skills and promote employee productivity.
12. Work with the Friends of the Kenosha Public Library, the KPL Foundation, and other community organizations to promote better library service at KPL.

Prior to finalizing the objectives, factor into your mix the broad trends of the information community and industry identified during the external assessment. While there may be only four to six key trends, they will have a major impact on the kinds and levels of objectives set since they represent problems, opportunities, and issues requiring resolution.

Identified key functions or critical success factors may also be included with objectives. Be sure a timetable for each is included. These are issues that absolutely must be met to reach success. The environmental trends may suggest some key functional objectives. Examples might include:

1. New technologies
2. Hiring specific staff/personnel
3. Locations
4. Marketing strategies
5. Governmental regulation

6. Client focus

7. Evolving your operations into best practices

A good planning objective describes an end, not a means to an end. Objectives are results-driven, not activity-driven. The objective contains an action verb like "increase" or "improve" and is based on a problem or opportunity with an accompanying specific time for action. Verbs commonly used include:

Advance, adopt, begin, build, capitalize, compensate for, consult, continue, contribute, coordinate, create, control, define, deliver, develop, eliminate, empower, encourage, enhance, ensure, enforce, establish, evaluate, exchange, expand, gather, help, identify, implement, improve, include, install, integrate, invite, keep, maintain, make, manage, minimize, participate, plan, prepare, promote, provide, produce, protect, recognize, reduce, review, recover, re-create, repair, replace, restore, schedule, serve, strengthen, support, or test.

Objectives should meet the following seven criteria:

1. Well-defined, clearly stated targets; easy to recognize and follow

2. Measurable; countable

3. Realistic completion date; time-focused with timetables for action

4. Person responsible; identify each individual responsible for performing each function; name who will do what and when, even it it's an outsourced function

5. Challenging but attainable; they require work but they are doable

6. Written

7. Intermediate performance follow-up; perform progress checks to see how staff are doing, share praise and reinforcement for doing well, and counseling if the wrong track is taken

KEY POINTS TO INCLUDE

Structure your objectives to answer the following questions. These may assist in developing a critical view of the service and its competitive edge.

- Who are the most important groups of internal and external clients?

- What factors will influence their behavior toward the service?
- What service will be provided?
- Why will the service exist?
- What are you trying to accomplish in this measurable statement?
- What unique aspects of the service will differentiate us from other services?
- What is being sought or aimed for?
- What do you need to accomplish?
- What results will you measure?

Tips for formulating objectives (see also Worksheet 5-1 ⓒⒹ):

1. Be specific, identifying five or six issues or problems that really count and are of greatest concern (profitability, quality, customer relations, cost control, etc.)
2. Translate the problem into a challenging but achievable objective
3. Prioritize to determine the most important objectives
4. Narrow them down to precise terms
5. Be specific enough to either count, measure, or specifically describe what is to be done
6. Describe objectives as results-oriented, with a realistic deadline identifying where and how this objective will be met

---

Worksheet 5-1. Define Your Objectives

Write six clear and brief objectives. A common breakdown includes two for marketing, one for financial or use of revenue, one for operations, one for personnel, and one for any other important objective most critical to your success.

1. Marketing
2. Marketing
3. Financial or Use of Revenue
4. Operations
5. Personnel
6. Other

(Cont'd.)

Worksheet 5-1. Define Your Objectives *(Continued)*

Write the objectives, reviewing to make sure you have answered the following:

What current initiatives, services, and projects contribute directly to the achievement of the objective?

What specific and measurable objectives have you set for the next year?

What would the impact be on the overall success, if the year-one objectives are met?

What has to happen to achieve the overall objective?

Identify resources needed to achieve next year's objectives.

Identify risks and implementation issues associated with meeting objectives.

How can you reduce the impact of the risks and issues?

Further thoughts or ideas concerning your objectives:

EXAMPLES OF OBJECTIVES

Torbay Library Services ⓒⓓ
**Source: Torbay Council, 2005: 13; reprinted courtesy of Torbay Council
  Library Services.**

3. Looking to the Future

3.1 Service Objectives

The 11 policy aims of the library service are [shown in Table 5-1].

Table 5-1. Torbay Library Service Objectives	
Policy Aim	**Links to Corporate Themes**
1. "To provide a welcoming and stimulating environment that acts as a focal point for the whole community."	Creating sustainable communities Valuing our environment Placing learning at the heart of our community
2. "To provide and promote a wide range of services to meet both the current and future needs of library users."	Developing Torbay's culture Creating sustainable communities
3. "To provide and promote resources that enable all residents to fulfill their role as active citizens and participate in cultural, democratic, economic, social, and environmental activities."	Creating sustainable communities Equalities and social inclusion Developing Torbay's culture
4. "To promote social inclusion by developing equality of access to all library services and resources."	Equalities and social inclusion Creating sustainable communities Developing Torbay's culture
5. "To encourage a culture of lifelong learning in the community through the provision of appropriate services, including access to networked learning opportunities and resources."	Placing learning at the heart of our community Developing Torbay's culture
6. "To provide a wide range of materials and services for children and young people of a stimulating, informative, and enjoyable nature."	Developing Torbay's culture Placing learning at the heart of our community
7. "To encourage literacy and the love of reading and to contribute fully to local and national literacy strategies and initiatives	Placing learning at the heart of our community Developing Torbay's culture Creating sustainable communities Equalities and social inclusion
8. "To help sustain and develop the sense of local identity, culture, and heritage of the local community."	Developing Torbay's culture Valuing our environment
9. To consult with both library users and nonusers, of all ages, to ensure their views are fully considered in the provision and development of services."	Benchmarking and consultation Customer focus
	(Cont'd.)

Table 5-1. Torbay Library Service Objectives *(Continued)*	
Policy Aim	**Links to Corporate Themes**
10. "To keep work practices under review to maximize efficiency, economy, and effectiveness, and to monitor and improve performance, ensuring high-quality services and best value."	Performance management and best-value performance indicators
11. "To seek to nurture, support, and train staff so that they can develop and contribute fully to all aspects of the current and future nature of the library service."	Workforce planning and learning and development

Oakville Public Library Business Plan ⓒⓓ
Source: Oakville Public Library, 2007: 1; reprinted courtesy of Oakville Public Library.

Section 1: These strategies are delegated to Staff Teams.

Strategy: New residents/community information

> Hours of operation
> Outreach
> Web services
> Town services
> Digitization
> Online reference
> Increased awareness

Northeast Kansas Library System
Source: Hale, Butcher, and Hickey, 2003; reprinted from "New Pathways to Planning" created by Martha Hale, Patti Butcher, and Cindi Hickey.

Northeast Kansas Library System Objectives, Strategies and Action Plans

_____ Public Library

OBJECTIVE

In order to contribute to the quality of life in _____ community, the _____Public Library will provide information, materials, and services that will encourage healthy leisure and relaxation activities to all members of the community.

STRATEGY: _____ Public Library will offer recreational and leisure programming for children and adults.

PLAN

1. The children's department of _____ Public Library will offer three parent/child story hours during 2001.

> Person responsible: Children's Librarian
> Due date: December 31, 2001
> Evaluation: Action step completed: ___ Yes ___ No.

2. The _____ Public Library will spend 35 percent of its acquisitions budget on adult recreational reading materials in 2001.

> Person responsible: Adult Acquisitions Coordinator
>
> Due date: December 31, 2001
>
> Evaluation: ___ percentage of acquisitions budget spent on adult recreational materials by December 31 2001.

3. In 2001, the _____ Public Library Director will join with the _____ Arts Council to distribute materials about upcoming events in the community.

> Person responsible: Library Director
>
> Due date: December 31, 2001
>
> Evaluation: Action step completed: ___Yes ___No

OBJECTIVE

Free access to information, materials and services to all members of _____ community will be improved as a result of the _____ Public Library's participation in regional and statewide networks.

STRATEGY: Library staff will facilitate library customer access to and use of online databases.

PLAN

1. Library staff will receive training in using online databases available from the statewide network.

> Person responsible: Adult Services Coordinator
>
> Due date: March 31, 2001
>
> Evaluation: Action step completed: ___Yes ___No

2. The staff of _____ Public Library will enthusiastically teach library customers to use the statewide databases (SearchBank and FirstSearch) whenever trained staff is working and it appears the customer wants to learn.

> Person responsible: Adult Acquisitions Coordinator
>
> Due date: Continuing
>
> Evaluation: _____customer database training sessions by library staff conducted by December 31, 2001.

3. The staff of _____ Public Library will conduct searches of the online databases for the customer whenever it appears the best way to find free access to needed materials.

> Person responsible: Adult Acquisitions Coordinator
>
> Due date: Continuing
>
> Evaluation: _____database searches by library staff performed for customers by December 31, 2001.

4. During the first nine months of use, the staff of _____ Public Library will systematically study such use to help the staff decide what online reference services most needed by the public.

> Person responsible: Reference Services Staff
>
> Due date: October 1, 2001
>
> Evaluation: Report of suggested online information services presented to the Library Director by the references staff by December 31, 2001.

Strategic Alliance of Federal Science and Technology Libraries (SAFSTL) ⓒⓓ

Source: Strategic Alliance of Federal Science and Technology Libraries, 2005: 1; copyright Government of Canada; reproduced with permission of the Strategic Alliance of Federal Science and Technology Libraries.

Objective

The Federal Science eLibrary is an initiative to solicit government support for a proposal to deliver enhanced seamless and equitable access to full-text electronic journal content in STM [science, technology, medical] to the desktops of all federal government researchers. The eLibrary will be a new collaboration among the science-based departments and agencies to negotiate, license, and support access to STM electronic journals. The Government of Canada employs more than 22,000 professionals to support key activities in strategic research, environmental and health protection, regulatory activity, defense, and emergency preparedness. By helping federal government researchers do their work better, the eLibrary will serve the needs of the Canadian public.

The federal government lags behind the academic and many private sectors in providing access to a significant number of e-journals. STM journals cover the full spectrum of science from basic and applied research, technical analysis, product development, market assessment, product reviews, regulatory assessments, and product evaluations. Most major STM journals are available in electronic formats that provide convenient and timely access to information anywhere and at any time. Desktop access to e-journals is now a standard tool in universities and large private sector companies.

This initiative is in the best interests of all Canadians. With adequate information resources available conveniently and quickly, federal scientists will be prepared to face new health, environmental, and security threats. Policy analysts will be equipped with better information resources with which to define and evaluate policy. Federal STM professionals co-located in departments and researchers collaborating with scientists in university or private sectors will be equipped to participate fully in shared research.

Aurora Public Library

Source: Abott, 2006; reprinted with the permission of Aurora Public Library, Ontario, Canada.

Objectives

    A. Make the Library more welcoming and accessible

    B. Strengthen the Library's services to meet changing community needs

    C. Build enhanced awareness of the Library and what it has to offer

    D. Build the capacity of our organization to meet growing and changing needs

    E. Improve accountability

Jacaranda Public Library ⓒᴰ
Source: Sarasota County Libraries, 2005; reprinted courtesy of Jacaranda Public Library.

Objectives, Strategies, and Action Plans

Customer Service

Our customers come first, and we will strive to serve them in a friendly, fair, respectful, and cost-effective manner.

Objectives

A. Improve customer appreciation of library landscaping, interior environment, and way finding.
   1. Purchase and hang ALA graphical Dewey and numerical signs on nonfiction end panels by February 1, 2006.
   2. Collaborate with Kip Alexander and county landscaping contractor to complete large-scale landscape project by March 1, 2006.
   3. Add task lighting to art exhibit area and close ceiling around video screen by April 15, 2006.

B. Enhance physical access to materials and electronic access to records about library materials.
   1. Instruct at least 20 customers per month to use library catalog and electronic databases via computer class by March 30, 2006.
   2. Create featured book display for nonfiction collection by February 15, 2006.
   3. Outfit one workstation in computer lab for people with disabilities by March 15, 2006.
   4. Establish books-by-mail program and respite care collection via grant by August 1, 2006.

C. Expand methods of collecting data from customers on how to exceed their expectations.
   1. Produce action plan report from customer service advisory committee on data collection methodologies by April 1, 2006.
   2. Implement PLA [Public Library Association] New Planning for Results model for 07, which includes role for community members on planning team, by June 1, 2006.
   3. Create customer satisfaction survey instrument for respite care computer by August 1, 2006.

D. Empower customers to become confident, independent users of library collections and services.
   1. Move 50 percent of customer loans to express-check-through training, marketing, and adding third kiosk by June 1, 2006.
   2. Reduce number of customers who require reference staff intervention to troubleshoot library technology by May 1, 2006.

E. Promote lifelong learning and civic engagement opportunities.
   1. Establish dedicated tutoring area with moveable partitions in expanded wing by April 1, 2006.
   2. Schedule five public programs highlighting a community issue or need by September 30, 2006.

3. Market meeting room availability to all identified area neighborhood associations via mail invitation by March 15, 2006.

Business Processes

Business process efficiencies result in fiscal sustainability, competitive services, and increased productivity.

A. Develop comprehensive plan for cross-training all staff.
   1. Establish core competency list for reference, youth, and circulation teams by February 1, 2006.
   2. Implement cross training schedule by March 1, 2006.
   3. Test all staff members in at least one department other than their own—80 percent passing rate by September 1, 2006.

B. Equip staff members with tools and technologies that are cost-effective, reliable, ergonomically sound, right for the task.
   1. Purchase first wave of articulated keyboard trays for employee use by January 15, 2006.
   2. Train one staff member as functional expert in VTLS/TagSys by April 1, 2005.

C. Complete team process reviews and/or physical reorganizations.
   1. Install new shelving and re-site desks/furniture in circulation work area by February 1, 2006.
   2. Begin regularly scheduled equipment tests for public PCs, low-vision aids, and the like under reference team purview by January 15, 2006.
   3. Evaluate roles and responsibilities in youth department and rewrite job descriptions as warranted by April 1, 2006.

Financial Perspective

Control costs, increase revenue, leverage partnerships, and practice sound fiscal policies and procedures.

A. Reduce renovation/expansion CIP [capital improvement program] fund to $5,000 or less.
   1. Identify outstanding needs that are CIP eligible by March 1, 2006.
   2. Gather all quotes necessary to implement low vision room relocation by April 1, 2006.

B. Implement internal auditor recommendations following review of cash drawer, P-card, purchase order, and other financial records and procedures.

C. Begin planned giving initiative with Friends of the Library to exploit new donor options and opportunities.
   1. Include "Have you remembered the library in your will?" statement in Friends newsletter by spring 2006 issue.
   2. Establish Friends subcommittee to research planned giving and prepare action plan for Board by June 2006.

D. Capitalize on IFAs [independent financial advisors] and other tools for managing financial resources.
   1. Adopt regular schedule for reviewing all P-card and budget major expenditures by January 1, 2006.

    2. Coordinate with CIP liaison to track other agencies with CIP account access by January 15, 2006.

E. Improve resource allocation through team assessments of internal budget needs prior to adopting '07 business plan.
    1. Teams will submit line item budget projections for their FY 2007 needs by August 15, 2006.
    2. Teams will develop mechanisms to monitor and adjust purchasing during the year by August 15, 2006.

Continuous Learning and Growth

A high-performance organization depends on a knowledgeable workforce, a positive work environment, and a vision for the future.

  A. Prepare staff for serving a diverse population.
    1. Train staff in aspects of service to people with disabilities by June 1, 2006.
    2. Begin rotating staff members through respite care collection coverage responsibilities by September 1, 2006.

  B. Integrate enterprise knowledge and expertise into learning opportunities.
    1. Invite at least three guest speakers from other county agencies to address staff at monthly meetings by September 2006.
    2. Schedule time for all staff members to investigate GovMax as portal to county objectives and measures by July 1, 2006.

  C. Create and sustain a positive work environment.
    1. Review staff responses to motivations inventory at each IDP [individual development plan] and incorporate strategies for achieving at least one non-salary point throughout the FY.
    2. Build picnic area adjacent to staff entrance for enjoying meals and breaks outside by July 1, 2006.
    3. Recognize staff achievements on public BB by January 1, 2006.

NEYNL WDC Objectives, Strategies, and Evaluation Measurement
Source: North and East Yorkshire and Northern Lincolnshire Workforce Development Confederation, 2004: 15; reprinted courtesy of North and East Yorkshire and Northern Lincolnshire (NEYNL).

Table 5-2. NEYNL Objectives, Strategies, and Evaluation Criteria		
Objective	**Key Actions**	**Success Criteria**
1. Ensure compliance with the Working Time Directive Widen access to education and training	Continue to develop a collaborative approach to support hospital at Night Pilots developing longer than solutions to WTD requirments Development of a strategic approach to widening access to education and training Achieve effective involvement of NHSU	Indentified training, resource, and recruitment needs and started the HR process to support these needs Stragegy developed NHSU integral with local approaches to widening access
		(Cont'd.)

Table 5-2. NEYNL Objectives, Strategies, and Evaluation Criteria *(Continued)*		
Objective	**Key Actions**	**Success Criteria**
6. Establish robust working relationship with NHSU, Social Care, LSC, RDA, and allied learning organizations	Establish a shared learning and development agenda with NHSU Agree actions and responsibility to improve learning opportunities for staff within NEYNL area	Shared agenda developed and actions to improve learning agreed and implemented
9. Maintain and develop robust performance monitoring arrangements of HEIs contracts	Ensure routine exchange of key performance information	Robust contracts in place
9 Develop an evaluation mechanism to ensure learning is put into practice and contribute to the HE commissioning process	Agree evaluation tools and processes with NHS Trusts and HEIs	Successfully commission a number of evaluation studies
10. Work with all partner organizations to coordinate the provision and development of practice placements for students across all relevant training programs	Continue to work with HEI, NHS, and other partners to ensure the adequacy of placement support mechanisms and to facilitate the expansion of placement opportunities where necessary Develop a coordinated approach to the resourcing of practice placements across professions	Placement support arrangements developed in agreement with all relevant partners Local approach to resourcing of placements developed in context of national guidance
11. Develop a SHA/WDC approach to the patient and public involvement agenda	Identify current level of involvement Develop strategies to increase level of involvement in key areas	Strategic plan for public and patient involvement Increased level of involvement
12. Develop and introduce a modernized NHS Library and information service across the SHA/ WDC	Develop a Library Strategy for the next 3 to 5 years	Strategy and PID agreed and published. To include: a) A baseline survey of existing library and knowledge services offered across the SHA/WDC area, covering issues of access and funding b) Develop quality standards using the HeLICON framework c) A review of services against this framework d) A gap analysis with recommendations on a structured approach to improving services and consolidating funding
15. Active participation in the development of the Hull York Medical School through working closely with HYMS staff and with all relevant NHS organizations	Establishment of a robust model to support the provision of clinical placements	Robust clinical placement plans in place, both for provision of teaching and facilities

Kenosha Public Library ⓒⓓ
Source: Kenosha Public Library, 2007: 9; reprinted with thanks to the Kenosha Public Library in Wisconsin.

Public Services Department Objectives

Public Services Goal

The Public Services Department carries out the Library's mission by planning, coordinating, implementing, and evaluating the provision of the following high-quality direct services to the public: collections and circulation services, reference and readers' advisory services, services to adults, children's services, young adult services, special needs and outreach services, and topical programs for all ages. Public Services provide these services in a timely and cost-effective manner at the Southwest Library, Northside Library, Simmons Library, Uptown Library, and the Bookmobile.

Public Services Objectives

1. Promote KPL collections and services in cooperation with the Head of Administrative Services.
2. Evaluate, maintain, and improve KPL collections in cooperation with the Head of Collection Development.
3. Provide Public Services workshops to teach KPL staff improved and innovative service methods and techniques.
4. Train Public Services staff in circulation, reference, and children's services methods and techniques.
5. Continue to cooperate with the Literacy Council to deliver both library and literacy services at Uptown Library.
6. Provide programs to promote library use and educate the public.

Port Stephens Library
Source: Port Stephens Library, 2004: 24; reprinted with thanks and acknowledgment to Port Stephens Library, NSW, Australia.

Objectives, Strategies, Action Plans, and Evaluation Measure

Strategic focus: Customer-focused services
Objective: To provide a customer-focused approach to the provision of library services

Outcomes

- Diversity of programs available
- High levels of participation in programs
- High levels of customer satisfaction
- Increased usage of technology resources

Strategies

- Develop programs to educate and entertain Library users
- Establish customer service standards
- Improve access to collections and services
- Ascertain the needs and expectations of Library users and nonusers
- Ensure staff has up-to-date skills

Major Initiatives

- Deliver monthly Internet/e-mail training sessions for Library customers
- Deliver training sessions on advanced searching and specialist information
- Develop a customer education training module
- Schedule regular children's activities throughout the year
- Schedule author visits throughout the year
- Investigate the establishment of book clubs
- Investigate the establishment of an adult summer reading program
- Establish a liaison program with local schools regarding curriculum and assignment needs
- Implement a customer service charter
- Promote collections though retail standard displays
- Develop a survey instrument to ascertain community needs and expectations
- Develop a staff training program in customer service

Performance Indicators

- Number of programs offered
- Number of program participants
- Number of library visits
- Number of loans
- Number of bookings for technology resources

George Eliot Hospital NHS Trust
Source: Brook, 2007: 2–4; reprinted courtesy of Nigel Brook, Library Services Manager, William Harvey Library, George Eliot Hospital NHS Trust.

Objectives

Strategic Aims

The purpose of the library strategy 2007–2010 is to provide a plan that will move us toward reaching our vision and to enable us to respond to developments taking place in education and the National Health Service.

We will continue to work closely with all Trust departments and endeavor to plug in to key issues within; IMSAT, DARE, PALS, and IT training.

We will continue to develop local and regional working partnerships with other organizations, for example UHCW, North Warwickshire Partnership Trust, the NW PCT, and the SHA; seeking to improve services and resources and ensure coefficiency.

During 2007–2010, the Hybrid Library service already in existence will utilize Web technology to rapidly expand the range of online services and resources in place at George Eliot Hospital. We shall look toward group consortium purchasing and expanding the regional influence that the Library Service has in the West Midlands.

Our Strategic Aims

SA1: Knowledge Management

We aim to be a center of knowledge management activity by contributing to the development of a knowledge management organization, supporting staff in developing the skills they need to manage knowledge effectively and integrating with regional/national developments within the NHS—for example, the National Library for health and the NSF for Health Libraries.

SA2: Improved Patient Care/Clinical Governance

We aim to be a provider of high-quality resources and services that proactively support and promote the clinical governance agenda; we shall provide high-quality training opportunities to all of our registered users, assisting our user community to develop the skills needed to practice evidence-based health care.

SA3: Lifelong Learning

We aim to be a center of educational activity providing resources, services, and facilities that support, promote, and proactively encourage lifelong learning, continuous professional development, and educational developments such as e-learning. We shall build closer working relationships with the Training Department, IT training, the Postgraduate Education Center team, and IMSAT to facilitate a Trustwide unified approach to learning.

SA4: Health Priorities

We aim to provide resources and services needed to achieve national health priorities such as the National Service Frameworks and local priorities such as impact on patient care, CNST requirements, and the provision of new services within the Trust.

SA5: Equity

We aim to provide a truly multidisciplinary library service with equity of access and with resources, services, and facilities tailored to meet the needs of all types of health care staff.

SA6: Access

We aim to provide convenient, timely access to resources and services for our users and implement systems to increase their awareness of resources and services. We shall endeavor to take more services to the user at the point of need and to utilize Web technology to deliver services in the appropriate format at the appropriate time.

Business Aims

Working alongside our strategic aims, the William Harvey Library has adopted a framework of structured business aims.

BA1: Value

The William Harvey Library is committed to providing a high-quality service that provides value for money. Working within budgets and to financial imperatives, the service will provide a cost-effective information support service to all members of the Trust.

BA2: Income

Wherever possible, the Library will attempt to offset costs by adopting a structured system of charges. Value added services will be provided to the wider community and a range of income-generating services investigated for efficacy. Any income generated will be added to the library cost center by official channels and will be used to enhance services to George Eliot Hospital staff.

BA3: Financial Accountability

Library financial practice will be transparent, freely accessible, and reported regularly to the senior management team. All transactions will be open to the scrutiny of the user community. An Annual Financial Report will be produced at the end of each fiscal year to update stakeholders on progress toward achieving our business aims.

BA4: Fines

In line with existing library policy, and in support of BA2 and BA3, the Library will pursue an aggressive fines program. All outstanding fines, replacement fees, and uncollected interlibrary loan charges will be flagged and chased. The Library will also utilize a standard administration fee, to be levied upon accounts that cost the Trust financially and in terms of staff time.

Funding

(See Appendix 3 for details of library budget 2006)

Currently, staffing costs and library services to doctors are funded through MADEL. North Warwickshire PCT provides funding for library services for their users and George Eliot Hospital NHS Trust provides funding for Nursing, Midwifery, Allied Health staff in the hospital. SIFT [service increment for teaching] funding is available for resources for medical students.

Recurrent funding has always been based on the previous year's allocation with a 2.5 percent increase in MADEL funding each year but no increase in the Trust's contribution to revenue budgets. As a result, the budget cannot fully meet users' demands for new library resources. Annual increase in the cost of print and online journal publications coupled with rising book prices has meant that more of the available funding is required to maintain a position of status quo, with little left for forward planning.

The Library service has introduced the Blanket ILL charge to offset costs in this area and will be looking at the development of e-learning product and web services as a possible means of generating income in support of our business aims.

In 2005, SIFT supported a bid by the Library to upgrade the part time Senior Library Assistant post to a full time position. Funding for this was provided on a recurrent basis by the Trust.

The Library service will continue to work to attract additional funding for its resources and services as well as further investment in resource sharing across the region to maximize cost efficiency.

REFERENCES

Abbott, C. 2006. "2006 Business Plan and Budget." Ontario, Canada: Aurora Public Library Board, Town of Aurora. Available: www.library.aurora.on.ca/dynamic/.

Brook, Nigel. 2007. "Library Services: Business Plan and Library Strategy 2007–2010." Warwickshire, UK: William Harvey Library, George Eliot Hospital NHS Trust.

George, Barry. 2004. "Working in Partnership: Libraries Business Plan 2004/5 to 2006/7." Bedfordshire, UK: Bedfordshire County Council. Available: www.galaxy. bedfordshire.gov.uk/webingres/bedfordshire/vlib/0.beds_libraries/business_plan_04.pdf.

Granger, Charles H. 1970. "How to Set Company Objectives." *Management Review* (July): 3.

Hale, Martha, Patti Butcher, and Cindi Hickey. "New Pathways to Planning." Lawrence, KS: Northeast Kansas Library System (March 26, 2003). Available: http://skyways.lib.ks.us/pathway/wksht6b1.html.

Kenosha Public Library. 2006. "The Kenosha Public Library 2007 Business Plan." Kenosha, WI: Kenosha Public Library.

North and East Yorkshire and Northern Lincolnshire Workforce Development
    Confederation. 2004. "A Report on a Study Funded by the NEYNL Workforce
    Development Confederation for the NEYNL Knowledge Information and Libraries
    Services Strategy Group: NEYNL WDC Business Plan 2004–2005." York, UK:
    North and East Yorkshire and Northern Lincolnshire Workforce Development
    Confederation.
Oakville Public Library. 2007. "Oakville Public Library Business Plan, 2007–2009."
    Oakville, ON: Oakville Public Library.
Port Stephens Library. 2004. "Port Stephens Library Business Plan 2004–2005." Port
    Stephens, Australia: Port Stephens Library.
Sarasota County Libraries. 2005. "Jacaranda Public Library Business Plan, 2006."
    Sarasota, FL: Sarasota County Libraries. Available:
    http://suncat.co.sarasota.fl.us/Libraries/jacarandabusinessplan.aspx.
Strategic Alliance of Federal Science and Technology Libraries. 2005. "Service to
    Scientists in the Federal Government, Business Case." Ottawa, ON: Strategic
    Alliance of Federal Science and Technology Libraries.
Torbay Council. 2005. "Library Services Business Plan 2006/07." Devon, UK: Torbay
    Council.

6 DETERMINING STRATEGIES AND ACTION PLANS

STRATEGIES AND ACTION PLANS

Because they are so fundamental to success, strategies and action plans need to be known and clearly understood. Write them in a simple and easy-to-understand style. At a minimum, each individual accountable for the completion of the action plan needs to know how his or her actions fit into the whole picture. Ideally, each individual needs to be able to recall what has to be done without referring to notes or reviewing plans (Granger, 1970: 4).

STRATEGIES

BASIC DEFINITIONS

When you know where you are and where you want to go, then you can describe how to get there. Strategies set the direction and method to achieve your objectives. They establish guidelines and boundaries for evaluating important decisions and provide a technique for keeping your service on course. Quantify what you hope to accomplish, because these measurable actions move you toward your objectives.

Strategies address both internal and external influences that may affect the library. Every library must constantly monitor its environment and be alert to the threats or opportunities it faces. Strategies are created by building on strengths, overcoming weaknesses, exploiting opportunities, or avoiding threats. Successful libraries usually follow three broad choices of strategies.

Internal strategies address primary key function issues related to the *service's strengths and weaknesses*. Based on your objectives, they may include:

Library culture	Capabilities
Efficiency	Usability or profitability
Management	Staff
Service practices	Facilities
Service quality	Flexibility
Client service	Key clients

Location	Strategic alliances
Library image	Reputation
Time management	Technical knowledge
Employees	Service uniqueness
Referrals	Service cost

External strategies *capitalize on opportunities* to grow the service or to *overcome outside threats*. Based on the results of your external assessment, develop a plan to build on your opportunities. Identify ways to minimize your threats or turn them into opportunities. These strategies cover the library as a whole and may include:

Pricing and profit	Acquisition
New location or building plans	Markets
Use	Services
Technology	Management
Clients	Finance
Marketing	Increase staff competencies
Competition	Low-cost, efficient operations
Accurate information	Reliable, expert skills
Organizational Learning	Develop strong network of information resources

Focus on the unique qualities of your library that ensure you will provide better, faster, or less costly services than your competitors—your competitive advantage—and how you intend to grow those qualities. Developing and maintaining a competitive advantage is a large part of your strategy. Achieve this by developing current resources or creating new resources and capabilities in response to your changing environmental conditions (International Federation of Accountants, 2006: 16). Producing a competitive advantage may include any of the following:

Revenue	Keep high-value clients
Pricing techniques	Integrity
Adequate investment in services	Realistic targets of market share
Reduce overhead	Market growth
Reduce costs while providing services	Quality service culture
Actions	Ensure current teaching skills
Cost advantage	Provide superior connectivity
Positive quality control	Unique qualities
Social responsibility	

For example, the advantage of being innovative focuses on how you will keep up with changing client needs. Any of the following might apply in your plan:

- Create a more fluid management structure to increase responsiveness
- Increase awareness of client needs
- Design new products/services to replace old products/services
- All technical work is contracted out
- Creativity or innovation are a measurable portion of annual evaluations
- Internal cash flow funds all growth

Another example: the advantage of a training department represents an important value-creation asset of continuing to develop staff skills. Any of the following might apply in your plan:

- Expand staff skills to ensure well-developed core competencies
- Provide a positive, supportive, and innovative work environment
- Diversify approaches to ensure staff's motivation to provide suggestions for service improvement
- Invest in service development
- Provide a technically advanced facility
- Invest in a development specialist to connect staff training with library goals

KEY POINTS TO INCLUDE

If you can answer these questions, then you can describe your strategies:

- What do you want to do?
- What is your competitive advantage?
- What will it take to achieve your vision or what will it take to get "there"? What do you need to do to get what you want?
- Who are your clients?
- What currently works in the library?
- What currently does not work in the library?
- What are six issues limiting your growth or effectiveness?
- How will you make this service grow?
- What will make you successful over time?
- What specific practices will you employ in competing in your market?

BUILDING STRATEGY WORKSHEET

Create four to six strategies you want to achieve. Describe them so they are easy to understand, are measurable, and result in growth. To create a milestone or timetable, identify what you perceive as important times, dates, or events to manage the development of the strategy. (See Worksheet 6-1 ⓒⒹ.) Important events may include achievement of a certain number of users, a percentage of positive client evaluations, or a number of information services contracts signed. Upon completion, review your strategies to ensure they describe:

- How you will build and manage your service
- How you will incorporate and take advantage of opportunities
- How you will solve your critical problems

EXAMPLES OF STRATEGIES AND OBJECTIVES

Jacaranda Public Library ⓒⒹ
Source: Sarasota County Libraries, 2005: 1–2; reprinted courtesy of Jacaranda Public Library.

A. Improve customer appreciation of library landscaping, interior environment, and way finding
   1. Purchase and hang ALA graphical Dewey and numerical signs on nonfiction end panels by February 1, 2006.
   2. Collaborate with Kip Alexander and county landscaping contractor to complete large-scale landscape project by March 1, 2006.
   3. Add task lighting to art exhibit area and close ceiling around video screen by April 15, 2006.
B. Enhance physical access to materials and electronic access to records about library materials.
   1. Instruct at least 20 customers per month to use library catalog and electronic databases via computer class by March 30, 2006.
   2. Create featured book display for nonfiction collection by February 15, 2006.
   3. Outfit one workstation in computer lab for people with disabilities by March 15, 2006.
   4. Establish books-by-mail program and respite care collection via grant by August 1, 2006.
C. Expand methods of collecting data from customers on how to exceed their expectations.
   1. Produce action plan report from customer service advisory committee on data collection methodologies by April 1, 2006. (*Example continues on page 127.*)

Worksheet 6-1. Objectives and Strategies

Objective:

Strategy 1:

Milestone:

Milestone:

Objective:

Strategy 2:

Milestone:

Milestone:

Objective:

Strategy 3:

Milestone:

Milestone:

(Cont'd.)

Worksheet 6-1. Objectives and Strategies *(Continued)*	
Objective:	
Strategy 4:	
Milestone:	
Milestone:	
Objective:	
Strategy 5:	
Milestone:	
Milestone:	
Objective:	
Strategy 6:	
Milestone:	
Milestone:	

2. Implement PLA New Planning for Results model for '07, which includes role for community members on planning team, by June 1, 2006.

3. Create customer satisfaction survey instrument for respite care computer by August 1, 2006.

D. Empower customers to become confident, independent users of library collections and services.

1. Move 50 percent of customer loans to express-check-through training, marketing, and adding third kiosk by June 1, 2006.

2. Reduce number of customers who require reference staff intervention to troubleshoot library technology by May 1, 2006.

E. Promote lifelong learning and civic engagement opportunities.

1. Establish dedicated tutoring area with moveable partitions in expanded wing by April 1, 2006.

2. Schedule five public programs highlighting a community issue or need by September 30, 2006.

3. Market meeting room availability to all identified area neighborhood associations via mail invitation by March 15, 2006.

Torbay Council Library Services ⓒⅮ
Action Plan
Source: Torbay Council, 2005; reprinted courtesy of Torbay Council Library Services.

Table 6-1. Torbay Council Library Service Action Plan: Place Learning at the Heart of Our Community

Ref	Action	Thematic Cross Reference [Specific cross-reference to community plan/strategic plan/other strategy action]	Outcome/ Measure of Success	Current Risk Rating (1-24)	Deadline (Start on and achieve by)	Responsible Person	Financial Implications of Action and Budget Year (Grant/Additional/ Within current budget)	Other resource implications (HR, IT, Property)
1	LPSA Target 3 "To increase the life chances of children not in standard schooling by addressing their ICT learning needs"	Community Plan (Action Plan) Ref 7.1.5 Strategic Aim Ref: 3.2.3i Library Policy Aim 5	The overall target is achieved. 2005/06 targets are: No. of children: 1. Returning to mainstream education—24 2. Delivering their learning action plans—166 3. Achieving an externally accredited qualification—24	8	Already started Achieve 2005/6 targets by Mar 2006 Achieve overall target by Mar 2007	Librarian	L75k pump priming money being made available by ODPM over the 3 year life of the target	Within existing resources

(Cont'd.)

Table 6-1. Torbay Council Library Service Action Plan: Place Learning at the Heart of Our Community *(Continued)*

Ref	Action	Thematic Cross Reference [Specific cross-reference to community plan/strategic plan/other strategy action]	Outcome/ Measure of Success	Current Risk Rating (1-24)	Deadline (Start on and achieve by)	Responsible Person	Financial Implications of Action and Budget Year (Grant/Additional/ Within current budget)	Other resource implications (HR, IT, Property)
2	Develop the usage of the ICT Learning centres at Torquay and Paignton Libraries and, in partnership with local education providers, ensure their future sustainability	Community Plan (Action Plan) Ref 7.1.5 Strategic Aim Ref: 3.2.3ii Library Policy Aim 5	Enhanced usage of the ICT learning centres Future sustainability of the centres secured	12	Already started Achieve by Mar 2006	Librarian	Current provision within budget for 2005/6. Future sustainability to be secured through negotiation with local education providers	Within existing resources

Oakville Public Library ⓒ🄳
Service Strategies
Source: Oakville Public Library, 2007: 1; reprinted courtesy of Oakville
Public Library.

Table 6-2. Oakville Public Library Service Strategies

Section I. These strategies are delegated to staff teams.			Section II. These strategies are research in nature.		
Strategy Code	Strategy	Page No.	Strategy Code	Strategy	Page No.
01	New residents/community information	2	09	Residents 55 years of age and older	6
02	Hours of operation	2	10	New user groups	6
03	Outreach	3	11	Programming	6
04	Web services	3	12	Multilingual collections	6
05	Town services	4	13	Cataloguing	7
06	Digitization	4	14	Access for Town staff	7
07	Online reference	5			
08	Increased awareness	5			
					(Cont'd.)

Table 6-2. Oakville Public Library Service Strategies *(Continued)*					
Section III. These strategies are a focus of the Executive Team.			Section IV. These strategies are ongoing.		
Strategy Code	Strategy	Page No.	Strategy Code	Strategy	Page No.
15	Self-Checkout	8	22	Children and youth	11
16	New Library facilities	8	23	Childhood literacy	11
17	"Creativity and innovation"	9	24	Every Child Ready to Read	11
18	Advocacy	9	25	Teens	11
19	Customer service	9	26	Internal communication	12
20	Organization	10	27	Marketing and communication plan	12
21	Training and Development	10	28	Outreach venues	12
Section V. Town-dependent			Section VI. Performance measures		
29	Accessibility	13	31	Targets Based on Usage Statistics	14
30	Single user card	13	32	New Benchmark	14
			33	Qualitative Measures	14

Aurora Public Library
Source: Abbott, 2006; reprinted with the permission of Aurora Public Library, Ontario, Canada, 2006.

Goals 2006 (Strategies), Action Steps (Plans), and Planned Outcome (Goal)

A. Make the Library More Welcoming and Accessible

2006 Action Steps:

1. Enhance staff strategies to help patrons feel more welcome
2. Make the Library more user-friendly and accessible through the improved organization and display of collections as well as improved signage
3. Demystify access to the Library's technology and electronic services through the development of new training and information programs
4. Improve access to people of different abilities and investigate future service enhancements
5. Work with the Town to develop strategies to enhance parking and the exterior environment around the Library building

Planned Outcome (Goal)

B. Strengthen the Library's Services to Meet Changing Community Needs

2006 Action Steps:

1. Evaluate our current collections for currency and relevance
2. Develop an enhanced capacity to monitor and analyze current usage and satisfaction patterns
3. Enhance our collections by filling existing gaps and ensuring our ability to serve growing groups within the community—particularly youth and seniors
4. Develop new programs and targeted outreach initiatives consistent with the Library's mission
5. Enhance access to resources and collections through resource-sharing initiatives with other libraries and institutions
6. Continue to upgrade our technology and electronic resources to meet changing needs and realize efficiencies
7. Work with the Town to enhance public access to community information and e-government services

Planned Outcome (Goal)

C. Build Enhanced Awareness of the Library and What It Has to Offer

2006 Action Steps:

1. Develop a public relations strategy and implement to degree possible
2. Enhance our publicity
3. Foster and build community partnerships with partners whose interests are consistent with our mission (e.g., literacy organizations, educational organizations, and local heritage organizations)
4. Build our user base through outreach initiatives

Planned Outcome (Goal)

D. Build the Capacity of Our Organization to Meet Growing and Changing Needs

2006 Action Steps:

1. Complete implementation of the Library's Organization Review
2. Strengthen our staff development program
3. Continue enhancement of internal communications and teamwork
4. Assess and recommend to Council APL Library Board requirements for the next term of office

University of Otago Library ⓒⓓ
Source: University of Otago Library, 2004; reprinted courtesy of University of Otago Library.

Key strategies for the Library for 2004

In order to ensure that the "library dollar" is spent to optimal effect, the Library intends to undertake the following strategies through 2004:

Providing equitable, timely, and cost-effective access to information to teaching, learning, and research, independent of format and locations, using IT [information technology] to facilitate and enhance access.

Implementation:

Phase 4:1 of the implementation of the CONZULSys Shared Library System, involving the establishment of hosting services for the four universities and the implementation of the core Voyager modules at AUT [Auckland University of Technology], Otago, and Waikato, was completed in July 2003.

Phase 2, which is scheduled for October 2003 to February 2004, includes the implementation of the core Voyager modules at Victoria and the implementation of media scheduling, interlibrary loan, and the first of the ENCompass modules in the other three universities, together with the implementation of agreed software enhancements.

Phase 3 will include the implementation of universal borrowing and of ENCompass for digital collections during the remainder of 2004.

Time scale: 2003–2004

Budget implications: Capital and operating budgets approved by the Council in December 2002

Indicators: The University will have an information and resource access management system that will meet current and future needs. The collaborative initiatives being undertaken by CONZUL [Council of New Zealand University Librarians] will be facilitated. The delivery of library and information resources to the New Zealand tertiary and research community will be enhanced.

London Health Libraries ⓒ
Source: London Health Libraries Strategic Development Group and electronic Knowledge Access Team, 2005; London Health Libraries Strategic Development Group, 2006; reprinted courtesy of London Health Libraries Strategic Development Group (LHLSDG) and electronic Knowledge Access Team (eKAT).

WORKSTREAM 1: IMPROVING THE QUALITY OF DECISION MAKING

LHL staff will

- Increasingly deliver services at the point of care or in the workplace by extending the use of outreach/clinical librarian roles
- Design and deliver specialist targeted services that will meet diverse needs of different communities—clinicians, managers, networks, support services
- Work with those responsible for rolling out the care records service to develop links between the electronic patient record and evidence-based resources
- Bringing knowledge to bear: informing the commissioning process in primary care event planned for July 17
- Outreach trainer evaluation published on London Links
- Potential members of a focus group for this stream of work identified
- Have determined that research on the value of the mediated/facilitated search cannot be funded in 2006–7 London Health Libraries
- Set up a focus group to look at how this work stream can be better managed

WORKSTREAM 2: SUPPORTING THE DEVELOPMENT OF THE WHOLE WORKFORCE

- Encouraging staff to make the best use of new information and communication technologies

- Providing services and resources to enable staff to progress up the skills escalator
- Supporting staff in work-based learning
- Redesigning services to make them appropriate and attractive to non-registered and nonclinical staff
- Continuing working to overcome barriers between NHS [National Health Service] and higher education libraries to allow greater resource sharing
- Extending access to library services to all health and social care staff and students, regardless of their status, location, or time of day
- Working with the eKAT Promotion and Communications Manager, initiated an event for adult learners' week called London Health Libraries for ALL (Adult Learners in Libraries) Week; posters, designed by the Widening Access Group [WAG], were distributed to all LHL services together with suggestions for maximizing the effect of the week
- Designing an electronic questionnaire to assess the impact of London Health Libraries for ALL week
- Preparing a recommended book list for ESOL [English for speakers of other languages] and one for IT that will shortly appear on the WAG Web site
- Planning a follow-up event to the Widening Access event that took place in February this year; Bob Fryer and/or Richard Griffin of the DoH [Department of Health] have agreed to be keynote speakers
- WAG chair meeting with the deputy director of the DoH's Widening Participation Unit to discuss how the Unit and LHL can work together

Halifax Public Libraries
Source: Halifax Public Libraries, 2006: 15; reprinted courtesy of Halifax Public Libraries.

Anticipated Goals/Outcomes and Objectives (2006–2009):

O1.1. Halifax Regional Library provides a workplace environment that fosters employee and volunteer staff innovation, commitment, and competent service.

O1.1.1 Review core competencies and customize by position

O1.1.2 Develop a plan for workplace ergonomics

O1.1.3 Develop and implement a succession plan by December 31, 2006

O1.1.4 Conduct annual training and professional development assessment; maximize opportunities for professional development

O1.1.5 Complete job evaluation process audit and integrate results into JE program by December 31, 2006

O1.1.6 Evaluate effectiveness of recruitment process (core competencies, interview questions)

O1.1.7 Facilitate project planning sessions and training sessions for Management Team in alignment with implementation of project planning software

Direction 2: Goal-oriented, measurable performance through current and innovative practices.

- We are recognized as having best practices and exceeding industry benchmarks
- We measure outcomes and evaluate our progress and activities toward these
- Our continuous improvement culture—on small things and big things—is openly encouraged, recognized, and rewarded
- There is strong evidence of innovation and progression

O1.2. Halifax Regional Library uses current and appropriate information technology that is sustainable and effectively delivers service.

O1.1.1 Complete Strategic Technology Plan for 2006–09

O1.1.2 Develop and implement PC [personal computer] installation plan and configuration and install new PC profiles

O1.1.3 Review, update, and implement Information Security policies, procedures, and standards

O1.1.4 Implement new release of HIP/Horizon core updates and HIP/Horizon enhancements

O1.1.5 Review business intelligence to improve the timeliness and quality of decision making

O1.1.6 Determine the feasibility of unified word-processing solution

O1.1.7 Investigate use of social software (blogs, wikis, RSS [really simple syndication], IM [instant messager], Social Networks, etc.)

O1.1.8 Investigate feasibility of RFID [radio-frequency identification]

O1.1.9 Evaluate and implement fund-raising/donor software by June 2006

O1.1.10 Evaluate and implement room-booking software by March 2007

O1.1.11 Carry out annual In-House Use Count using PC Reliance software

O1.1.12 Complete Web site development plan and begin implementation

O1.1.13 Create a digital keyword searchable archive of Library-produced images for effective access to develop Library promotions

O1.1.14 Implement contact management database

O1.1.15 Implement Business Collaboration Solutions

O1.1.16 Review Overall Systems Architecture

O1.1.17 Upgrade graphics software available to C&M

O1.1.18 Implement e-mail notification

O2.2. Halifax Regional Library regularly assesses community needs and composition to ensure effective service delivery.

O2.2.1 Produce Branch Profiles and make accessible on the Intranet, the e-branch, and in print by the end of September 2006

O2.2.2 Complete use-trends study of people living in Eastern Passage area and present report in June 2006

Direction 3: Accountability and Stewardship ensuring sustainability while building our capacity

- Ample funding allowing us to achieve/fulfill our mission and vision

- Funders recognize the library as an essential service that is attractive to support and is a benefit and contribution to the community well-being and development
- We are always optimizing existing resources
- The community lobbies for and demands generous support and funding for their essential library service

O3.1. Halifax Regional Library ensures that the financial resources of the Library are managed and safeguarded and that assets are planned for, maintained, and replaced as necessary.

O3.1.1   Review organizational structure/team structure

O3.1.2   Complete the staff allocation review

O3.1.3   Evaluate effectiveness of Board operations and building an effective team

O3.1.4   Maximize DVD life expectancy

O3.1.5   Monitor and manage Operating and Capital Budgets while maintaining high quality, safe facilities by March 2007

O3.1.6   Implement Debt Collect to reduce delinquent accounts

O3.1.7   Conduct feasibility of a floating collection in which returns would remain in the branch to which they are returned rather than to an owning branch

O3.1.8   Investigate print management

O3.1.9   Review and recommend a solution for staff scheduling software

O3.1.10 Review design of Circulation areas; develop and implement model as appropriate

---

East Sussex County Library and Information Services
Source: East Sussex Public Libraries, 2005: 1; reprinted courtesy of East Sussex Public Libraries.

Table 6-3. Library and Information Services Business Plan 2006–2007					
AIM 1: To provide access to books, reading, and learning					
No.	**Target**	**Performance Measures**	**Budget/ Resources**	**Responsibility**	**By**
1.1	To provide high-quality stock in libraries				
	Ensure stock fund is deployed to meet Public Library Service Standards	Budget allocation produced Presented to Senior Management Team (SMT) and Libraries Management Team (LMT) for approval Budget summary produced monthly Monitoring meetings held	Stock fund	Reader Development Manager (RDM)	June '05
					(Cont'd.)

Table 6-3. Library and Information Services Business Plan 2006–2007 *(Continued)*					
AIM 1: To provide access to books, reading, and learning					
No.	**Target**	**Performance Measures**	**Budget/ Resources**	**Responsibility**	**By**
1.1 *(Cont'd.)*	Review the Stock Policy on an annual basis to include review of stock categorization	Stock days held Draft policy produced for consultation Policy approved and implemented	£1,000— service managers budget staff time	RDM	Dec. '05 Feb. '06 Mar. '06
	Continue stocktaking program	New technology piloted at Hastings Library Stock takes carried out as programmed	£5,000— income generation	RDM	Dec. '05 Mar. '06
	Identify, supply, and maintain core collections of hard-copy reference materials in all libraries	Core collections available and publicized	Existing book fund. Staff time.	Manager, Reference, and Information Services (MRIS)	Dec. '05
1.2	To promote reader development				
	Run a series of summer events for adults and children in support of the national initiative "Reading Voyage"	Publicity produced and distributed Fun book produced and distributed Events held Evaluation carried out and reported to LMT	Fun book: £4,000 Publicity: £1,000 Author events: £1,000	RDM/Manager Schools Library Service (MSLS)/Young People's Services (YPS)	June '05 July '05 July/Aug. '05 Sept. '05
	Promote BME literature	Black History Month events held Prospective reading groups identified	£2,000	RDM	Dec. '05
	Promote reading to inmates of HMP Lewes	Reading workshop held Participation in national promotions	Prison budget	Head of Professional Services	Mar. '06

ACTION PLANS AND IMPLEMENTATION

Action plans name the specific work done to achieve the strategies and reach your objectives. Each action plan is a small event contributing to the growth of the service. Each plan statement directly relates to an objective and a strategy by describing a specific task with a deadline (International Federation of Accountants, 2006: 14).

Implementation involves aligning your actions and resources with your objectives (Yukl, 2001). It involves managing the action plans, incorporating accountability, assessing results at predetermined stages, supporting changes, and either correcting goals if necessary or rewarding staff for achieving them. Make each action plan prioritized, specific, measurable, doable, and timed. It will have identified resources, metrics, or milestones. Identify how much each plan will cost to carry out and determine if you have enough cash to fund it. Identify a financial impact for each action. You will monitor these plans at least monthly to identify progress. Quantify each plan following its objective in relation to time and cost. For the sake of convenience, you might find a software application to assist. Many business-plan software programs incorporate budget worksheets to calculate the impact of each action plan on your cash flow.

The action plan section explains the timeline and specific steps required to move ahead. Measure the impact of each action routinely. Be realistic about the likely rate of progress and provide for slippages. Describe your contingency plans to cover shortfalls. The action plans are not just a to-do list. Prioritize and focus on *only* the most important tasks required to grow your service and reach the strategy and objective. Let the other items go. If they aren't high-priority items, they will probably not get done.

COMMUNICATION

Putting together an action plan of the main activities necessary to achieve the objectives and strategies of your business plan requires a great deal of communication. Make sure all stakeholders understand the reasons for change by providing as much information as possible and keeping the dialogue moving. Communication will always have to be tailored to the interests and understanding of the listener. Not every staff person comes to the table with the same background, experiences, or emotional awareness. Those factors must be taken into account and used to adapt messages.

All of those who will be responsible for actions must be involved in building the performance standards by which they will be judged in order to develop acceptance and a clear focus on the desired objective. Being involved in building the service creates a sense of ownership. It also develops an understanding of what is to be done and when. Keeping the lines of communication open and the dialogue flowing is core to success. While dialogue means creating alignment, openness, and trust with staff, it does not necessarily mean agreement.

As objectives are identified, it is important to discuss with each responsible party what is needed to reach the objective. Management should make sure that assistance or training is available if staff members do not have the tools, knowledge, or training to complete the job. Individual performance follow-up should be conducted at frequent intervals to determine if the plans are moving on course, if the individual requires coaching, or if the objective, goal, or plan requires adjustment.

Include information in the action plan about participation or support by leaders, strategic alliances, or partnering. This can be a strong signal of the library's significance and potential for success to anyone reading the business plan. If the plan is being used to apply for support, a grant, or funding, then explain how much support or money or is needed, how it will be used, or how you plan to meet the requirements.

KEY POINTS TO INCLUDE

Core elements to include in your action plans:

- If possible, each plan will have a stated impact
- Each plan is directly related to a strategy; the strategy is related to an objective
- As much as possible each plan has an identified budget; clarify how much support or money is needed for this project and how it will be used
- List each step in the action plan
- Each step is prioritized, specific, measurable (metrics or milestones), doable, and timed
- The individual responsible has direct involvement in creating the plan and has access to necessary resources
- Results are assessed at timed stages and according to budget
- Supervisors are aware of the timeline for which they need to support the work by either rewarding staff for completing them or correcting if necessary
- Timelines and specific steps are clearly communicated
- Allowances and contingency plans are built in
- Flexibility is a quality to be understood by all involved in the process
- The individual responsible is provided with adequate tools, knowledge, and training to complete the job
- Individual performance follow-up is conducted at frequent intervals to determine if the plans are moving on course or if coaching is required or if the objective, goal, or plan requires shifting

ACTION PLAN WORKSHEETS

List six to eight action plans or projects that would make a big difference in the service. Tie them to an objective and a strategy. Then answer the questions for each plan. (See Worksheets 6-2 and 6-3 ⓒⅅ .)

Worksheet 6-2. Action Plans
Objective:
Strategy 1:
Plan A:
What will be the result of completing the project?
How will you measure the result?
Who is responsible?
What is the completion date?
Objective:
Strategy 1:
Plan B:
What will be the result of completing the project?
How will you measure the result?
Who is responsible?
What is the completion date?

(Cont'd.)

Worksheet 6-2. Action Plans *(Continued)*
Objective:
Strategy 1:
Plan C:
What will be the result of completing the project?
How will you measure the result?
Who is responsible?
What is the completion date?

Objective:
Strategy 1:
Plan D:
What will be the result of completing the project?
How will you measure the result?
Who is responsible?
What is the completion date?
(Cont'd.)

Worksheet 6-2. Action Plans *(Continued)*
Objective:
Strategy 2:
Plan A:
What will be the result of completing the project?
How will you measure the result?
Who is responsible?
What is the completion date?

Objective:	
Strategy 2:	
Plan B:	
What will be the result of completing the project?	
How will you measure the result?	
Who is responsible?	
What is the completion date?	

(Cont'd.)

Worksheet 6-2. Action Plans *(Continued)*
Objective:
Strategy 2:
Plan C:
What will be the result of completing the project?
How will you measure the result?
Who is responsible?
What is the completion date?
Objective:
Strategy 2:
Plan D:
What will be the result of completing the project?
How will you measure the result?
Who is responsible?
What is the completion date?
(Cont'd.)

Worksheet 6-2. Action Plans *(Continued)*
Objective:
Strategy 3:
Plan A:
What will be the result of completing the project?
How will you measure the result?
Who is responsible?
What is the completion date?
Objective:
Strategy 3:
Plan B:
What will be the result of completing the project?
How will you measure the result?
Who is responsible?
What is the completion date?
(Cont'd.)

Worksheet 6-2. Action Plans *(Continued)*
Objective:
Strategy 3:
Plan C:
What will be the result of completing the project?
How will you measure the result?
Who is responsible?
What is the completion date?
Objective:
Strategy 3:
Plan D:
What will be the result of completing the project?
How will you measure the result?
Who is responsible?
What is the completion date?

Worksheet 6-3A. Action Plan Record Template				
Library's Business Plan				
Objectives:				
Strategy 1:				
Plan A (Action Steps)	Who	By When	$ Amount	Achievements
Objectives:				
Strategy 1:				
Plan B (Action Steps)	Who	By When	$ Amount	Achievements

(Cont'd.)

Worksheet 6-3A. Action Plan Record Template *(Continued)*				
Library's Business Plan				
Objectives:				
Strategy 1:				
Plan C (Action Steps)	Who	By When	$ Amount	Achievements
Objectives:				
Strategy 1:				
Plan D (Action Steps)	Who	By When	$ Amount	Achievements
				(Cont'd.)

Worksheet 6-3B. Action Plan Record Template				
Use this form to combine Goals, Strategies, and Action Plans.				
Strategy	Plan (Action Steps)	Responsibility	Time	Key Performance Indicator

EXAMPLES OF STRATEGIES AND ACTION PLANS

Franklin Templeton Global Research Library
Source: Brigevich, 2004; reprinted courtesy of Franklin Templeton Global Research Library.

Global Research Library Implementation Program Proposal (high level)

Option 1

Develop a global operation using the library in Ft. Lauderdale as a single location.

Option 2

In addition to the library in Ft. Lauderdale, develop satellite libraries/information centers in New York, San Mateo, Europe, and Asia. These satellites do not require a physical library facility and can be established by placing a library professional within a reach of the end users.

From the library's perspective the second option is best, as library staff needs to be embedded within research groups to add the most value to the research process. We also need to take time zones into consideration. Other options and ideas can be explored if the project gets approved.

Staff

Some of our competitors' model (50+ librarians) will not work for us due to cost consideration. Research portal and virtual library will automate routine requests for company, industry, and country related information. We would need one professional librarian for each satellite library, a total of four, to conduct complex ad hoc research requests, create effective information solutions for local groups, train research assistants, etc.

Implementation Plan

We are at a great advantage because we already have a model library as a foundation on which to build a global operation. The business relationships and reputation built by the library in the past seven years delivering information solutions to global community are a plus for a successful transition and acceptance. If this project gets approved, the transition process will involve the following aspects that will be detailed and refined upon approval (some of these steps can be taken simultaneously):

- Establish a new library department with global responsibilities and create new positions of Library Director and Research Librarians.
- Hire and train additional library staff.
- Conduct information-needs assessment of the research groups.
- Conduct an inventory and analysis of the external research systems and information sources used by these groups.
- Collaborate with Market Data Services on global content management issues to ensure each group gets required content and information services.
- Develop and implement service plan for each location and/or region.

Country Public Libraries Association of New South Wales
Source: Country Public Libraries Association of New South Wales, 2004;
reprinted courtesy of Public Libraries NSW—Country.

Table 6-4. Key Targets and Actions: Information Exchange and Communications

Targets	Actions
1. Provide a monthly newsletter on the Web	Monthly
2. Provide an annual conference relevant to the needs of members	Annually
3. Provide a feedback mechanism on CPLA performance, direction, and effectiveness	AGM
4. Provide mechanism for input and discussion on issues on Web site	Ongoing
5. Revise CPLA constitution through broad consultation with membership and with professional advice by July 2005	AGM
6. Have one member of the Executive and Zone meetings other than in their own zones	Coordinate with Zones
7. Provide a CPLA mailbox (e-mail, fax, and voice mail) and a home page by July 2000	Obtain est. costs by end of 1999
8. Encourage inter- and intrazone cooperation and information and resource sharing	Circulate minutes and use home page
9. Encourage Council senior officer and Councilor involvement in CPLA activities	Circulate minutes and reports to Councils
Lobbying and Advocacy	
10. Maximize funding opportunities from federal and state government bodies and other agencies on an ongoing basis	Ongoing
11. Executive to meet with the Minister annually where possible to discuss public library issues and funding.	Annually
Marketing	
12. Develop Public Libraries Marketing Plan in partnership with MPLA and SLNSW Professional Development	By AGM 2005
13. Maintain resources to support professional development in Public Libraries. Maintain an annual scholarship the "Colin Mills Scholarship"	Ongoing
Administration	
14. Implement a 2-year business planning and review process for the CPLA AGM 2006	AGM 2006

London Health Libraries electronic Knowledge Access Team (eKAT) ⓒⓓ

Source: London Health Libraries Strategic Development Group and electronic Knowledge Access Team, 2005: 3; reprinted courtesy of London Health Libraries Strategic Development Group (LHLSDG) and electronic Knowledge Access Team (eKAT).

Table 6-5. London Health Libraries eKAT Operational Objectives 2005–2006

Key objectives	Critical success factors	Lead + support	Delivery times/ key dates	Resource implications	Feasibility, risk factors, etc.
GOAL A: To ensure that London Health Libraries are positioned to take advantage of existing and developing electronic tools and technologies to enhance service delivery					
1. Explore new options for electronic service delivery and support integration into routine service delivery by LHL networks 1.1 Establish mechanism for horizon scanning 1.2 Audit services currently maintained by eKAT and recommendations made for those suitable for embedding in local service provision	eKAT is aware of developments in electronic service delivery and has capacity freed up to investigate these further	MS lead, CT support AR lead, MS, CT support	Sept 05 July–Sept 05		eKAT maintenance activities not suitable for embedding in local service provision with impact on eKAT capacity to explore developments
2. Contribute to national developments in electronic library services on behalf of London 2.1 London representative on LKDN Informatics Group 2.2 LHL representative on SCIE for the coordination of access to electronic resources for social care staff 2.3 Participate in the Health Libraries Group Online Directory Group to develop a national electronic directory of libraries	eKAT is in a position to influence decisions that reflect London priorities and provide services that meet the needs of London users	CT AR AN/LENDS	4/year 2/year Apr 05 - Mar 06		National view does not reflect London priorities and user needs

(Cont'd.)

Table 6-5. London Health Libraries eKAT Operational Objectives 2005–2006 *(Continued)*

Key objectives	Critical success factors	Lead + support	Delivery times/ key dates	Resource implications	Feasibility, risk factors, etc.
3. Negotiate best value electronic access models to complement national provision and ensure national and pan London resources meet the needs of users in London					
3.1 London representative on National Core Content (NCC) Service Delivery Board	NCC purchases reflect London priorities and users' needs	CT	May, Aug,, Nov 05, Feb 06	KA24 Budget 05–06	National view does not reflect London priorities and users' needs
3.2 KA24 top-up for 05-6 purchased including archival access		AR	Apr 05		May be insufficient funding to secure top-up and archival access
3.3 KA24 top-up for 06-7 negotiated with suppliers/ publishers following consultation with stakeholders	KA24 top-up is cost effective and reflects London priorities and users' requirements	AR	Jan–Mar 06		
3.4 Athens support, management and development including London Athens administrators' meetings, ad hoc Athens administrator training and advice on Athens related problems	Users in London have easy access to electronic resources	AR lead, MS, FL support	Apr 05–Mar 06		
3.5 London representation on National NHS Athens Administrators' Group		AR	2/year		
3.6 London representation on Nastional Core Content Technical Reference Group		AR	2-3/year		
3.7 Convene London KA214 Technical Reference Group		AR chair FL, MS support	2-3/year		
4. Work with the pan London Local Service Provider and other agencies to facilitate access to clinical evidence via the Electronic Patient Record					
4.1 Explore ways of engaging with the London cluster of NHS Connecting for Health (Formerly National Programme for IT, NPHT) and feedback to LHLSDG	Awareness by national IT and electronic resource programmes of London Health Libraries knowledge services	AN	Nov 05	Estimated l500 per SSE connection where software not in place	Difficulty of establishing dialogue with N HS Connecting for Health
4.2 Single Search Engine (SSE) connectors to local electronic resources maintained and updated		AR	Ongoing		

(Cont'd.)

Table 6-5. London Health Libraries eKAT Operational Objectives 2005–2006 *(Continued)*

Key objectives	Critical success factors	Lead + support	Delivery times/ key dates	Resource implications	Feasibility, risk factors, etc.
5. Co-ordinate access to expert advice on electronic service issues and ensure that knowledge and experience is shared					
5.1 pan-London communications plan developed	London Health Libraries' networks are aware of current programmes, services and developments	LG	Oct 05 April, Nov/Dec 05	Funding from eKAT budget 05–06	eKAT budget may be insufficient to support publicity
5.2 London Health Newsletter produced		LG			
5.3 publicity of eKAT and its services including network visits		LG	Bimonthly From June 05		
5.4 Support LHL induction programme:		LG	Jul–Sept 05		
5.4.1 induction packs		LG	May 05		
5.4.2 induction on web site		LG lead, AN Support	4/year		
5.5 email discussion lists reviewed and alternatives to current lists software explored		NR			
5.6 representation of SEL LMS Project Board		AN			

Bedfordshire County Council
Source: George, 2004: 20; reprinted by kind permission of Bedfordshire County Council.

Table 6-6. Bedfordshire County Council Action Plan

Action	Start Date	Finish Date	Accountability
1. Monitor the WiFi project at Potton Library to establish the potential of the system and report back to the Council, MLA, and the DTI next year; monitoring will be by statistical evidence and user feedback.	June 2004	June 2005	Andy Baker
2. Implement the Action Plan arising from the Access Review to revise opening hours and mobile routes to provide improved access; this will be achieved by further consultation with staff and citizens and the replacement of 2 vehicles next year.	July 2004	June 2005	Barry George and the Library Management Team

(Cont'd.)

Table 6-6. Bedfordshire County Council Action Plan *(Continued)*

Action	Start Date	Finish Date	Accountability
3. Develop 5-year future plan for Libraries to ensure the Service is positioned to meet the Council objectives, shared priorities, government agendas, and the needs of the community; this will be achieved by further consultation with staff, a review of current literature around public libraries, and production of a report.	July 2004	October 2004	Barry George and the Group Management Team
4. Develop "impact" measure for the service to demonstrate the role and impact of libraries against Council objectives and shared priorities; this will be achieved by working with colleagues in PMU to develop measures.	July 2004	March 2005	Barry George, the Library Management Team, and the PMU

Knowledge Information and Library Services in North and East Yorkshire and Northern Lincolnshire (NEYNL)

Source: North and East Yorkshire and Northern Lincolnshire Workforce Development Confederation, 2004: 15–16, 18; reprinted courtesy of North and East Yorkshire and Northern Lincolnshire (NEYNL).

Table 6-7. NEYNL Appendix Four Action Plan (with Identified Leads)

Strategic Driver	Action	Leads
Money and Funding	• Conduct an audit of funding of Knowledge Information and Library Services.	A.R. M.S.
Change Monitoring and Organizational Shift	• Evaluate the impact on organizations of a reduction in or withdrawal of funding by conducting a risk assessment. • Develop contingency plans to cope with change.	A.R. M.S.
Higher Education	• Develop support for students on placement from HYMS and other HEIs.	A.D. H.B. (in conjunction with HELP Committee)
Patient Centered NHS	• Evidence the case for Patient Information Liaison Librarians (PILLS).	J.S.
Workforce Training and Development	• Seek opportunities with the NHSU to develop access to course information and training. • Measure service against nationally accredited standards (HeLICON) to ensure that it meets the needs of the workforce.	J.T. V.C.
		(Cont'd.)

Table 6-7. NEYNL Appendix Four Action Plan (with Identified Leads) *(Continued)*		
Strategic Driver	**Action**	**Leads**
Modernization	• Develop mechanisms for remote 24/7 access. • Map existing roles to Agenda for Change and Knowledge and Skills Framework (refer to Agenda for Change). • Match training and development to job roles (refer to Agenda for Change). • Develop templates to describe job roles within NHS Knowledge Information and Library Services.	J.T. V.C.
Statutory Changes	• Plan service response to FOI. • Look at how Knowledge, Information, and Library Managers can support evidence-based patient choice. • Determine the implications for Knowledge, Information, and Library Services of the Disability Discrimination Act. • Address issues related to diversity. • Ensure compliance and awareness of the Data Protection Act, Caldicott, Information Governance and Copyright.	D.T. J.G.

REFERENCES

Abbott, C. 2006. "Goals 2006 (Strategies), Action Steps (Plans) & Planned Outcome (Goal)." Ontario, Canada: Aurora Public Library Board, Town of Aurora. Available: www.library.aurora.on.ca/dynamic/.

Brigevich, L. 2004. "Business Plan, Franklin Templeton Global Research Library." Fort Lauderdale, FL: Franklin Templeton Global Research Library, Franklin Templeton Investments.

Country Public Libraries Association of New South Wales. 2004. "Business Plan: CPLA Vision and Purpose." New South Wales, Australia: Country Public Libraries Association of New South Wales. Available: www.cpla.asn.au/agm/2k4/bplan.html.

East Sussex Public Libraries. 2005. "East Sussex County Council-Library and Information Services Business Plan 2005–2006."

George, Barry. 2004. "Working in Partnership: Libraries Business Plan 2004/5 to 2006/7." Bedfordshire, UK: Bedfordshire County Council. Available: http://www. galaxy.bedfordshire.gov.uk/webingres/bedfordshire/vlib/0.beds_libraries/business_plan_04.pdf.

Granger, Charles H. 1970. "How to Set Company Objectives." *Management Review* (July): 3.

Halifax Public Libraries. 2006. "Halifax Public Libraries: Business Plan 2006–2007." Halifax, NS: Halifax Public Libraries.

International Federation of Accountants. 2006. "Business Planning Guide: Practical Application for SMES." New York: IFAC. Available: www.cpaireland.ie/UserFiles/File/Technical%20Resources/SME%20Resource/Business%20Planning%20Guide%20-%20Practical%20Application%20for%20SMEspdf.pdf.

London Health Libraries Strategic Development Group. 2006. "Report on 2006–7 Business Plan 1st Quarter (April–June)." Paper 4. London: London Health Libraries.

London Health Libraries Strategic Development Group (LHLSDG) and electronic Knowledge Access Team (eKAT). 2005. "Business Plan Agreement 2005–2006." London: London Health Libraries.

North and East Yorkshire and Northern Lincolnshire Workforce Development Confederation. 2004. "A Report on a Study Funded by the NEYNL Workforce Development Confederation for the NEYNL Knowledge Information and Libraries Services Strategy Group: NEYNL WDC Business Plan 2004–2005." York, UK: North and East Yorkshire and Northern Lincolnshire Workforce Development Confederation.

Oakville Public Library. 2007. "Oakville Public Library Business Plan, 2007–2009." Oakville, ON: Oakville Public Library.

Sarasota County Libraries. 2005. "Jacaranda Public Library Business Plan, 2006." Sarasota, FL: Sarasota County Libraries. Available: http://suncat.co.sarasota.fl.us/Libraries/jacarandabusinessplan.aspx.

Torbay Council. 2005. Library Services Business Plan 2006/07. Devon, UK: Torbay Council.

University of Otago Library. 2004. "Business Plan 2004." Dunedin, New Zealand: University of Otago Library. Available: www.library.otago.ac.nz/pdf/2004_business_plan.pdf.

Yukl, Gary A. 2001. *Leadership in Organizations*, 5th ed. Upper Saddle River, NJ: Prentice Hall.

7 CREATING A MARKETING PLAN

MARKETING BASICS

Responsiveness to meeting its clients' needs should be at the core of any library's planning effort. This responsiveness depends largely on how well a library markets its services. A well-designed marketing strategy will create a competitive advantage, but the strategy requires creating the right tactics to make that happen. You must know what you're aiming for—define your market group—in order to hit the mark. A marketing strategy helps identify how to communicate the ways in which your library can fulfill your clients' needs. The goal here is not to just promote your services but to build relationships with clients who are using them (Davids and Newcomb, 2006). These relationships are the key to a successful plan. Keeping relationships strong is much harder than satisfying a one-time library user. They require daily effort.

Clients are sophisticated. To reach them, you will want to analyze various client groups and identify what benefits they receive from your service. If there are no benefits to the client, then no matter how good the service is on its own terms, it will not survive. Weingand (1999) states, "The client perception is critical: an excellent service must be perceived as excellent to actually achieve that status" (121). Your clients' perception may not be accurate, but it always needs to be addressed (Schultz, 1998). You might already provide exactly the services required by clients. But unless they perceive that it is exactly what they need and that they will benefit from an interaction with you, then there is little hope that they will even think of going to you for assistance (Booth, n.d.). Your aim is to develop a marketing strategy to explain how you will meet their needs (see Worksheet 7-1 ⊙). Moving in that direction will place your service in a stronger position.

The clients you serve—or want to serve—define your marketing strategy. The process of working through the business plan identifies your target clients and the areas most likely to need your services and products. It helps you understand how your clients behave and what they value. The analysis of your SWOT chart determines what threats (external and internal) might affect your ability to deliver. Using this information, the marketing strategy is written in terms of your clients' needs and your ability to meet those needs. Your intent is to inform your clients of the specific benefits they will purchase or use with the service—not to inform them of the features of the service (MacKintosh, 1999: 47). You provide benefits, not services, and your message communicates this clearly. Clients, just like everyone, are interested in what's important to

Worksheet 7-1. Define and Describe Your Service
How do you define your service in terms of your clients' needs?
Describe that service here:

them and how a service improves their life and their work—not what the service is. Keep your focus on the client (Kornik, 2007: 32).

Marketing distinguishes your offerings from those of the competition. Without your even knowing it, the first step in designing the marketing strategy is already completed: it was to create a mission statement, which sends a clear message about the library's unique role and contributions. The next step asks you to know what you want. Think through what you'd like to achieve. Start with the end in mind and work backward to develop a strategy.

Review the big picture: mission analysis, market analysis, external and internal scans, promotion capabilities, and evaluation. Identify what you do, who the clients are, which segments you will focus on first, what they want, who your competitors are, and what exactly you provide.

With that information in mind and knowing where you want to target your efforts, you can define your objectives. Later you will write one to five objectives only. More than five may dilute your focus. Each objective is doable. Then develop your strategies to support each objective. Each strategy is measurable, specific, and doable, directly linked with your objectives. If the strategy warrants further detail, then write an action or a series of action plans that identify responsibility, a milestone, or completion date, and the result sought to help you reach your strategy. The action plans may have multiple stages with different individuals accountable at different times. They can be as complex or as simple as you choose, but the core structure is: the actions complete the strategies that support your objectives. Strategies with clear and prioritized performance goals keep you on course. Staying focused helps gain and maintains a competitive advantage.

THE FIVE KEY ELEMENTS

1. Research 1 and 2: Market analysis and service design; identify target clients, their needs and wants and levels of satisfaction

2. Planning: Develop or refine the design of services suitable to client needs and wants

3. Objectives, Strategies, and Plans: Put into action effective ways to provide the service

4. Communication: Create awareness and convey the value of your offering

5. Evaluation: Monitor effectiveness (Wallace, 2004: 5)

RESEARCH 1—MARKET ANALYSIS AND SERVICE DESIGN

Review the results of the SWOT chart analysis discussed in Chapter 4 to either determine services offered or to refine their design. Design only after learning what your target client's values are and reconciling how those values balance against what the library can afford to offer, the mission, the trends of the information industry, and the community your library serves. Chapter 4 also included a competitive analysis and identified the target market, both of which are helpful in this and the next section, Research 2.

Generally, markets are large and diverse populations. Any attempt to attract every single member of a market to one service would probably fail. People bring too many variables in needs, preferences, and purchasing abilities. Instead, you will identify the factors that impact their usage decisions, then group those clients according to usage decision factors. Change marketing strategies to speak to the needs of each group. Segmentation itself does not guarantee success, but it is more effective than a generalized, scattershot approach.

Your target market is the specific segment of the community you serve that is most likely to use your services or purchase a product. When you have done your research and understand what makes the individuals in your target market use the library service, then you will have a better idea of what aspects of the service to emphasize; you will know how to promote the services that will bring the most possible benefit to the client. The information and analysis gathered through the entire market analysis and segmentation process allows you to assess the potential for achieving your objectives and to justify committing resources and efforts to develop that segment.

Review and answer these questions to design or redesign your service (Davids and Newcomb, 2006: 22–25; Shamel, 2002):

Strengths

- Identify the professional strengths of your library.
- Do you dominate a niche?
- Where do you outperform your competitors?
- What do clients like most about your services and your staff?
- Identify the greatest opportunities for success in the future.
- What do you provide that is the greatest value to your clients?
- How can you maximize the value of your activities to your clients?

Weaknesses

- Where does your competitor outperform you?
- Why do you have trouble keeping clients?
- Identify areas where you lack in providing value to clients that your competitors are meeting.
- Identify areas where you are not providing the value you could and where no one else does.

Opportunities

- Can you identify market niches that lack services you can provide?
- How can you build a stronger presence in existing markets?
- How can you focus more specifically on certain groups?
- Identify activities or services other libraries offer that might be applied to your target client groups.
- What activities or services need additional resources because their future looks strong?
- What services can be added?
- What products or services can you drop because other services look better?

Threats

- Discuss the long-term forecast for your library.
- Identify the threats that could affect your services in the months or years ahead.
- How will you deal with those threats?

Research 1 Worksheet

Describe your service here. Draw your description from your conclusions based on a combination of the SWOT analysis and the questions in the immediately preceding section. The intent is to identify a market gap or problem and to create a solution in the form of a viable library service. Ask yourself, "Now that you know what your clients value and have balanced those observations against what you can afford to offer, what service will you provide?" Describe that service in Worksheet 7-2 ⓒⓓ.

Worksheet 7-2. Target Marketing Plan for Your Service
1. Describe the idea or new service:
2. What are the benefits of this service?
3. Where are similar services used and sold?
4. What places do my clients go to for recreation?
5. Where do my clients go for education?
6. Where do my clients do their shopping?
7. What types of newspapers, magazines, and Web sites do my clients read?
8. What television and radio stations do my clients watch and listen to?

RESEARCH 2—DEFINING THE CLIENTS AND YOUR TARGET MARKET

Specifically identify your clients (MacKintosh, 1999: 52; Dow and Cook, 1996). For example, will your service target medium-sized corporate firms within the library's metropolitan area? Will you target chemists in pharmaceutical research and development-oriented companies in New Jersey, the New England region, or the entire United States? A successful marketing strategy identifies as much as you can about your clients. As you devise the marketing strategy, create a list naming which clients and which of their specific needs are to be addressed first in the marketing and advertising campaigns (Association of College and Research Libraries, 2003).

Generally, the group representing your top 20 to 30 percent of users is addressed first in the marketing and advertising campaign; the strategy is developed for them. Do you have clients outside this group who could move here if you offered new or expanded services? Identify your next top 20 percent of potential clients and view them as your best next market opportunity—your second group. Prioritize the second list to identify these clients and their needs.

Initially, target only those clients most likely to use your service. As your client base expands, modify the strategy to include the second group of clients. All other library service users belong to a third marketing group. Identifying your three markets makes it easier to appropriately divide your work and resources and to create a marketing budget.

In classic marketing, the first order of importance is to secure the most consistent or profitable business from a particular group; the second is to move more clients into the first group—the most profitable group—from the second group; the third is to make the middle or marginal group more profitable; and the fourth is to reduce the unprofitable business. However, in many libraries whose core competencies include altruism, this order of importance is counterproductive to the mission. Their goal is to identify users and their rate of use along with classifying the information they have been using. The value of the contribution of the information to the community supports its funding.

Geography also defines clients (MacKintosh, 1999: 52). In a large metropolitan area, the service may focus on local health care providers. For those in rural areas, the service focus moves to a geographically wider area. For example, does the University Health Sciences Center offer services to in-state health care providers or are alumni and university donors also considered primary clientele? Do they seek clients within the campus, county, state, nationwide, or around the world? Identify your clients in as much detail as possible.

When expanding an existing service, base the market on current and past experience. For a proposed service, identify who has asked for services and think about whether they would really become regular clients if such a service was created (MacKintosh, 1999: 52).

Determine how much of your service will be used or purchased, and which client groups would become repeat clients. Look at what your service can reasonably expect to sell or provide and how much of each service each client will use. Use figures as specific and current as your research can produce. Worksheet 7-3 ⊕ may be useful to help you list the current and future needs for each client group. To further identify your target groups fill out Worksheet 7-2 for each market group.

Research 2 Worksheet: Client Needs

List the current and future needs for each client group.

Worksheet 7-3. Define Client Needs				
Needs Categories				
Clients	Current Met Needs	Current Unmet Needs	Future Known Needs	Future Implied Needs

PLANNING: FOCUS ATTENTION ON THE PRODUCTS AND SERVICES

To expand the design of services you will need to know what services will allow you to fulfill the needs of each of your target markets. The product/services and benefits map (Worksheet 7-4 CD) will assist in identifying clients to address first, their most important needs, products or services offered to meet needs, and benefits received from the products or services. This will help link the products and services currently being offered or that will be offered to those most important client needs. Then, identify the benefits the clients receive from the products or services. The information on this worksheet summarizes the key elements of the strategic plan that are central to the development of the promotional campaign.

Worksheet 7-4. Products/Services Benefits Map			
Clients to Address First	Their Most Important Needs	Products/Services Offered to Meet Needs	Benefits Clients Receive from the Products/Services

Source: Association of College and Research Libraries (2003). Used with the express permission of the Association of College and Research Libraries 2003, owner of these materials. See Issues and Advocacy page at www.ala.org/acrl.

Laying out the information according to the worksheet allows you to:

- Identify obvious client needs—the gaps—not being met
- Determine whether the mix of products and services is complete or varied enough to satisfactorily meet client needs
- State specifically what benefits client's gain from the products and services
- Conclude whether the benefits gained by the clients truly meet their needs

OBJECTIVES AND ACTION STEPS

Previously, you established the business plan's objectives. Now, to identify marketing objectives, look at what action you want your clients to take. Do you want new clients, more repeat business from existing clients, or an increase of profits per client? Balance your resources, budget, and current skills available for the project. Then write your marketing objectives (see Worksheet 7-5 ⓒⓓ). These are usually lofty and long-term goals, and usually deal with difficult-to-measure perceptions such as positioning, changes in attitudes, or becoming the best in your business (Marvel, 2003). Write your quantifiable and doable strategies. Follow by identifying specific action steps or plans to be taken. Name the individuals responsible or accountable and specify milestones or dates for accomplishing the action.

Generally, you will want to select only up to five areas to build the success of your service. Consider focusing on:

- Function: How does the service meet their needs?
- Finances: How will the use affect their overall situation? What about their productivity?
- Freedom: How convenient is it to use? How will they gain more time and less worry?
- Feelings: How does the service make them feel about themselves? How does it relate to their self-image?
- Future: How will they deal with the service in the future? Will the library offer continued support? Will the service affect their lives in the future?

For example, if you want your clients to increase use of your services you might want a certain percentage of current clients to move from the lower 60 percent of users to the upper 20 percent. How will you entice them to use your services more? Through your SWOT chart and by identifying target markets you've begun to consider how to approach your marketing strategy. You've identified your client's needs as well as their criteria for satisfaction. The goal of promotion is to generate use or attitude changes. Which of the following tactical areas needs the most attention in your first client market in order for you to meet your objectives?

Increased awareness: By teaching clients what you do

Education: Determine what the client wants and then teach what you can do for them

Conviction: Your clients are certain you're the primary service to them

New clients: Brand new clients expect you to deliver what you promise

Repeat clients: They rely on you now

Additional questions designed to help develop objectives and strategies:

- Are some important client needs being underserved or not served at all?
- Are you delivering some services that are not high priorities to your clients?
- What service options should be considered?
- Are your objectives and measures clear enough to guide your daily decisions and actions?
- What should you add?
- What next steps should you take?
- How will the library entice clients to use the service?
- Can you identify the key market entry and/or development strategies?
- Can you identify the forecast costs for marketing and advertising?
- How will you present the service to clients?
- Can you identify the end-user prices?
- How will you respond to competitors?
- How will the competitors respond?
- Have you identified contingency plans in case the service's targeted levels of use are not met?
- What other opportunities exist?
- What threats exist?
- How can you minimize threats or turn them into opportunities?
- What are three critical issues preventing the library's success?
- What needs to change?
- How will you measure the results?

Worksheet 7-5. Identify Marketing Objectives
Identify Five Marketing Objectives:
1.
2.
3.
4.
5.

COMMUNICATION

All services need to be advertised and promoted in order to generate interest. First, you will want to identify the specific material you will use to communicate how the library will meet its clients' needs. The goal is to (1) educate or build awareness about your service and to (2) generate use.

The advertising portion of the marketing strategy focuses on what clients want and how to let them know you can meet their needs. In order to develop a message appropriate to your market area, you will want to address what the service or product does, completely focusing on the client: talk about what your clients want, and talk in their language.

The advertising devices will vary based on the specific services offered and could include any of the following:

- Personal calls to influential persons in your community
- Networking
- Direct mail
- Conferences
- Trade shows
- Training programs
- Talks at business clubs
- Advertising

- Press: articles for local media, professional journals, newsletters, television, or radio
- Exhibits
- Web pages
- Phone calls
- Face-to-face opportunities
- Brochures or flyers
- Web pages
- Referrals by other library units
- Staff education and in-house advertising
- Word of mouth

A promotion strategy could include any of the following:

- Refunds
- Sampling
- Coupons
- Price-of sales
- Contests
- Repeat-client offers

- Contests
- Bonus packs
- Premiums
- Trade discounts
- Special events

Note that promotions depend on incentives. This can be a price, a product, a gift, or an event—but make sure your incentive provides what your target clients want.

Collect a range of advertisements and messages that attract your attention. These can come from any source, library or nonlibrary. Analyze the advertisements that have an impact on your buying or information-use habits. Collect and review advertising campaigns from other libraries or similar institutions. Get accurate estimates of the costs of the advertisements or promotion. Check the requirements and resources of your organization—some require specific logos, clearance through a central department, files with proof of every statement, and so on. Also check into the funds and assistance available from your parent organization. If the service is available, collaborating with a public relations specialist, either within the library's system or outside, will enable you to develop a well-organized marketing strategy with clear objectives and plans (Bloedel, 2006). To ensure the best results, your method of advertising or promotion, the incentives, and the delivery methods must be reflective of your marketing objectives and your organization's culture.

Create a tentative marketing and advertising plan using the questions below. Then use Worksheet 7-6 ⓒⒹ to determine if you can afford your plans. If not, adjust and rework the plan and budget until you can balance objectives, costs and, capabilities.

Worksheet 7-6. Promotional Budget Template	
Mail Surveys	*Cost*
PRINTING ENVELOPES	
Envelopes	
Postage for mailing questionnaire and for return postage	
Incentives for questionnaire response	
Staff time and cost for analysis and presentation of results	
Independent researcher cost	
Other costs	
Total Costs	
Phone Survey	*Cost*
PREPARATION OF THE QUESTIONNAIRE	
Interviewer's fee	
Phone charges	
Staff time and cost for analysis and presentation of results	
Independent researcher cost	
Total Costs	
Personal Interviews	*Cost*
Printing of questionnaires and prompt cards	
Interviewer's fee and expenses	
Incentives for questionnaire response	
Staff time and cost for analysis and presentation of results	
Independent researcher cost, if any	
Other costs	
Total Costs	
(Cont'd.)	

Worksheet 7-6. Promotional Budget Template *(Continued)*	
Personal Interviews (Continued)	*Costs*
Interviewer's fee and expenses in recruiting and assembling the groups	
Renting the conference room or other facility and cost of recording media such as tapes, if used	
Incentives for group participation	
Staff time and cost for analysis and presentation of results	
Independent researcher cost, if any	
Other costs	
Total Group Discussion Costs	
Total Market Research Costs	

Key Points to Include

- How competitive is your service in terms of price, quality, features, and so on?
- How will your service enter the market?
- How will you advertise?
- Will you offer more service for a premium price or a simpler service for a lower price?
- How will your potential clients learn about your services?
- When will the use of your service actually occur?
- How much will packaging, physical or electronic access, and service support cost?
- Given the answers to the questions above, how will you differentiate your service in the market?
- Describe the method by which you will promote the service.

When writing advertising messages:

- Write short, descriptive text.
- Make sure the message clearly identifies your services, location, price, and contact points.

- Know your clients, your service, and learn the different media available to deliver your message.

- Check for approval from your parent organization for any material you develop.

- Make sure the advertisements created are consistent with the service image.

- Stick with your objectives.

- Be consistent.

EVALUATION

The marketing strategy continues to parallel the business plan. You are already aiming for your objectives by completing the strategies and action plans. Now establish a mechanism to measure which marketing methods work and which do not by reviewing periodically to see what has changed. Identify the successful features of your marketing strategy to determine which activity to try again and which to drop. Evaluation will include identifying the service's key clients and why they use your service. Evaluate the outcomes: determine what services these clients have used, their usage levels, and how price, delivery time, quality, and other measures affect their use. Your overall marketing plan may seem impressive on its own terms, but you must also show its effect on the targeted clients.

Creating measurable advertising strategies requires reflecting the marketing objectives. They are action-oriented, incorporating the information you've gathered about your target market and geography, and include specific issues of advertising. As an example, consider using Worksheet 7-7 ⓒ. As you consider various evaluation options, rank your options according to your perceptions and identify a consensus. Then, identify the next steps to take, clarify the sequence of the next best steps, and determine what it will take (time, effort and resources) to accomplish this strategy (Association of College and Research Libraries, 2003). Place the new plan in a chart or report and make it available to staff to consider, review, and implement.

Successful services are based on continuous improvement. Always try to improve your services before someone else does. Regardless of loyalty measurements, customer satisfaction, or performance benchmarking, continuous improvement keeps your programs or services fresh and alive. Focusing on the fundamentals of great client service, follow-up to develop strong relationships, offering a diverse range of services, concentrating to improve your knowledge of client needs and market segments, understanding the drivers of customer value (Oliva, 2004) utilizing a tracking system, employing regular review and evaluation, and using the most appropriate technologies will help create and sustain your marketing advantage.

Worksheet 7-7. Marketing Strategy Objectives Evaluation Template				
	Marketing Strategy Evaluation Objective #1			
Marketing Strategy Evaluation				
Used	**Location**	**Time/Budget**	**Target Group**	**Results**
Results: Services Used				_____
Use Levels				_____
Price				_____
Delivery				_____
Quality				_____
Comments?				_____
	Marketing Strategy Evaluation Objective #2			
Marketing Technique				
Used	**Location**	**Time/Budget**	**Target Group**	**Results**
Results: Services Used				_____
Use Levels				_____
Price				_____
Delivery				_____
Quality				_____
Comments?				_____
				(Cont'd.)

Worksheet 7-7. Marketing Strategy Objectives Evaluation Template *(Continued)*

	Marketing Strategy Evaluation Objective #3			

Marketing Technique

Used	Location	Time/Budget	Target Group	Results
Results: Services Used				_____
Use Levels				_____
Price				_____
Delivery				_____
Quality				_____
Comments?				_____

	Marketing Strategy Evaluation Objective #4			

Marketing Technique

Used	Location	Time/Budget	Target Group	Results
Results: Services Used				_____
Use Levels				_____
Price				_____
Delivery				_____
Quality				_____
Comments?				_____

(Cont'd.)

Worksheet 7-7. Marketing Strategy Objectives Evaluation Template *(Continued)*

		Marketing Strategy Evaluation Objective #5		
Marketing Technique				
Used	**Location**	**Time/Budget**	**Target Group**	**Results**
Results: Services Used				_____
Use Levels				_____
Price				_____
Delivery				_____
Quality				_____
Comments?				_____

MARKETING AND PROMOTION STRATEGY WORKSHEETS

Before launching a marketing campaign, it's important to answer a number of questions about your service. See Worksheet 7-8 ⓒ for a Market Planning Checklist that will help in evaluating your service.

Worksheet 7-8. Market Planning Checklist

☐ Have you analyzed the market for your service? Do you know which features will appeal to different market segments?

☐ In forming your marketing message, have you described how your service will benefit your clients?

☐ Have you prepared a pricing schedule? What kinds of discounts do you offer, and to whom are they offered?

(Cont'd.)

Worksheet 7-8. Market Planning Checklist *(Continued)*
☐ Have you prepared a sales forecast?
☐ What type of media will you use in your publicity campaign?
☐ Have you planned any promotions?
☐ Have you planned a publicity campaign?
☐ Do your publicity materials mention any optional accessories or added services that clients might want to use or purchase?
☐ When offering a service, have you prepared clear instructions? What kind of warranty do you provide? What type of client service or support do you offer?
☐ Do you need to have liability insurance?
☐ Is your style of packaging likely to appeal to your target market?
☐ If your product is one you can patent or copyright, have you done so?
☐ How will you distribute your product or service?
☐ Have you prepared job descriptions for all of the employees needed to carry out your marketing plans?
Source: Entrepreneur.com (2007). Copyright © 2007 Entrepreneur.com; all rights reserved. Reprinted with permission from Entrepreneur.com.

Using your five objectives from Worksheet 7-5, develop strategies and action plans for each (see Worksheet 7-9 ⊕). After crafting your marketing plan, insert the specific promotion or advertising material. Your strategy needs to answer the questions presented in Worksheet 7-10 ⊕. Use Worksheet 7-11 ⊕ to gain an overview of your marketing and promotion strategies.

Worksheet 7-9. Marketing and Promotion Strategy Planning Template
First Area Objective, Strategy, and Plan: Your Advertising Material:
Second Area Objective, Strategy, and Plan: Your Advertising Material:
(Cont'd.)

Worksheet 7-9. Marketing and Promotion Strategy Planning Template *(Continued)*

Third Area
    Objective, Strategy, and Plan:
 	
    Your Advertising Material:

Fourth Area
    Objective, Strategy, and Plan:
 	
    Your Advertising Material:

Fifth Area
    Objective, Strategy, and Plan:
 	
    Your Advertising Material:

Worksheet 7-10. Marketing and Promotion Strategy Considerations
How will you manage the service?
How will you capitalize on market opportunities?
How will you solve the service's critical problems?
Identify all unique characteristics of the service.
Identify three types of the best clients.

(Cont'd.)

Worksheet 7-10. Marketing and Promotion Strategy Considerations *(Continued)*
How or where do they get the service now?
How or where will they get it in the future?
How much will you charge for the service?
How will you accept payment?
When will use of this service begin?
How much use do you expect the service to experience?
Identify the costs of the service for the first month, quarter, and year.
Describe the packaging, access, support, etc.
How will you promote the service to the three types of best clients?
What does the service offer?
Identify its special advantages.
(Cont'd.)

Worksheet 7-10. Marketing and Promotion Strategy Considerations *(Continued)*
When will use of this service begin?
Name the benefits offered.
What will the service do for your client? (Consider writing a description of what jobs or problems the service eliminates for the client.)
Evaluate your competition (refer to SWOT and assessments).
Who else sells the service or product?
Who else can meet the market's needs (similar services or products)?
Name the competitors' strengths and weaknesses.
How will you deal with competitors?
What will you do if the price has to change due to technology advances or other competitive services?
Advertising focuses on tactical areas of importance and price, quality, features, etc.
Identify advertising for the service.
Source: Questions taken from Weingand (1999) and Booth (n.d.).

Worksheet 7-11. Marketing Strategy Overview Template				
Strategy	Plan (Action Steps)	Responsibility	Time	Key Performance Indicator

EXAMPLES OF MARKETING PLANS

George Eliot Hospital NHS Trust
Source: Brook, 2007: 7–8; reprinted courtesy of Nigel Brook, Library Services Manager, William Harvey Library, George Eliot Hospital NHS Trust.

User Groups

The library is interdisciplinary in approach and provides equitable service levels to all George Eliot Hospital staff.

In addition, the Library supports medical students on placement at he hospital, all PCT [Primary Care Trust] employees regardless of base of work, general practitioners in the Nuneaton area, nursing students on placement at the Trust [2006 pilot project], Allied Health students on placement, and paid external members. For a full breakdown of library user categories and service rights, please refer to the Membership Category Flowchart.

The number of registered users has decreased over the past year while the level of service uses has increased. The reasons behind this curious service anomaly lie with the Data Protection program instituted by the Library Services Manager.

The Library Service, prior to December 2004, retained a large number of active user accounts for persons who were no longer entitled to service access, had left the Trust, or moved on to another educational placement. This data had to be deleted in order to bring the library in line with data protection and storage policies. As a result, the number of actual service member declined. During the same period, full services were relaunched and the library began to market services more aggressively to clinical staff, resulting in a increased level of service use.

How do users find out about our services?

- The Library Service is advertised at all Trust inductions and attendees encouraged to visit the building.
- The Library provides 1–2–1 or small group inductions on demand; examples include the SHO [senior house officer] Induction, Medical Student Induction, and Nursing Student Sessions.
- Web presence is used to draw attention to Library Services; the Library Portal is marketed as the starting point for clinical research.
- E-mail. The Library Services Manager and Clinical Librarian use targeted, Trust-wide and manager e-mails to advertise training courses, the Literature Searches Services, and stakeholder-input, among other things.
- Library EJournal, to be launched in Summer 2007, will provide direct access to information, updates, and provide a place for internal research to be shared.
- Poster campaigns around the Trust.
- Articles in Bleep to reach a broader-based hospital population.
- Links with Trust educators to provide support to any member of staff studying for a qualification.
- Joint working projects with other Trust departments; e.g., books on prescription and integrated Web site with PALS [Patient Advice and Liaison Service].

Direct stakeholder input into services:

- Library User Group meets quarterly to discuss all issues around service provision, resourcing, and access to services in the Trust.
- Direct clinical/managerial input into the acquisitions process.
- E-mail and printed service suggestions and feedback questionnaires.

Association for Library Collections & Technical Services (ALCTS) ⓒⒹ
Source: Association for Library Collections & Technical Services, 2001: 3–5; reprinted courtesy of Association for Library Collections & Technical Services (ALCTS).

Plan Outline [Market Analysis]

1.0 Market Analysis Summary

1.1 Market Segmentation

ALCTS has a clearly defined market, assuming any library staff member who works in the technical services, collection management, serials, or preservation areas would benefit from an ALCTS membership. However, the number of professional librarians in this market is slowly decreasing as many positions in libraries previously held by librarians are now being filled by nonlibrarians.

1.2 Target Market Segment Strategy

1.2.1 Market Needs

Acquiring basic and higher level skills or updating skills and information on developments in the organization of information is the important need for library staff in ALCTS areas. This translates into identifying products and services that meet those needs and that would help this group improve in their job-related activities. This means continuing education in some format whether it is a workshop, course, program, or preconference. It also means high-quality and timely informational publications, best practices, and access to information resources in print or via the Web.

1.2.2 Market Trends

Technical services areas including cataloging, acquisitions, collection management, serials, and preservation are increasingly being staffed by nonlibrarians, many of who are professionals in different fields. Examples of this trend are evident in preservation where staff includes archivists and conservationists and in many libraries where heads of departments under the technical services umbrella are nonlibrarians. This can be seen in acquisitions, copy cataloging, serials, gift processing, and technology-based positions.

Fewer new library school graduates self-identify themselves as interested in technical services positions. An effort to "sell" technical services as a career path cannot be seen in isolation from membership in ALCTS.

ALCTS members move with some fluidity in and out of the for-profit library supplier market, for example, to companies providing outsourced cataloging or to utilities and back. Many vendor and publisher employees serve on ALCTS committees.

1.2.3 Market Growth

Market growth then is based on targeting the following areas:

- Retaining mid- and late-career and baby boomer ALCTS members, particularly when members move into others areas of responsibility such as administration and management
- Seeking new members from the growing ranks of the nonlibrarian, information professional in nontraditional settings, and librarian in ALCTS areas not now a member
- Working with new graduates and students to illustrate the benefits of careers in technical services, collection management, and preservation and hence how membership in ALCTS can further their career, enhance their job, and help them build a portfolio of skills
- Identifying those people working in nonlibrary settings having the same or similar needs for the products and services ALCTS can offer
- Expanding the interest of vendors in membership

The following five areas represent potential membership markets:

- Librarians working in traditionally ALCTS areas and are not now members
- Librarians who have moved into positions in which they cross over into ALCTS areas
- Nonlibrarians, many of whom consider themselves professionals
- New library school graduates and students many of who do not select technical services as a career path
- People who work in nontraditional information settings; the corporate or institutional knowledge manager is an example of a potential member ALCTS should consider
- Vendors with products and services of primary interest in ALCTS areas

1.3 Industry Analysis

Skills represented in the ALCTS membership are highly transferable to many other industry segments. The collection, organization, and preservation of information is a high priority in the "information age." This can be seen in the rise in positions such as chief information officer, knowledge manager, information manager, etc. These positions rise out of the need for companies and organizations to better deal with the vast amounts of information produced by and available to them. Organizations that are primarily technology-based continue to be established and to grow. An example of this is Web-based online learning, an industry that did not exist a few years ago.

Other associations have established a presence in ALCTS areas; however, they tend to cater to a specific market and do not reach out to the entire library community. Examples include the Medical Library Association for medical librarians and the Special Libraries Association for primarily corporate or special academic libraries.

1.3.1 Industry Participants

Participants include practically anyone in the business of collecting, organizing, and preserving information in whatever form. It also includes those organizations that provide support, products, services, and training in these areas. These include vendors, other professional and educational nonprofits, consortia, networks, and corporations outside of the library community.

1.3.2 Distribution Patterns

Services are delivered through a variety of outlets, including ALA [American Library Association] conferences, ALCTS–sponsored continuing education, and via the Web. Publications are distributed in paper and via the Web.

1.3.3 Competition and Buying Patterns

The competition providing continuing education offers opportunities in more venues, more frequently, and often at a lower cost. At the ALA Annual Conference, vendor user groups regularly compete with ALCTS programming. There are also several regular conferences that vie for ALCTS members' time and dollars, such as the Charleston Conference on Acquisitions. Members view these conferences as important subject resources.

Although the dues structure for ALCTS is comparable within ALA, outside of ALA many competing associations offer dues packages, which encourage participation in their divisions or sections.

1.3.4 Main Competitors

ALCTS as a functional division is not always the primary division of membership.

Within ALA: Type-of-library divisions such as ACRL [Association of College and Research Libraries], PLA [Public Library Association], and other functional divisions such as LAMA [Library Administration and Management Association] and LITA [Library and Technology Association]. As stated before, ALCTS members and potential members often are active in multiple venues as they relate to the member's interest.

Outside ALA: ARL [Association of Research Libraries], NASIG [North American Serials Interest Group], and other library associations such as MLA [Museum Libraries and Archives], ARLIS/NA [Art Libraries Society of North America], SLA [Special Libraries Association], and state and regional chapters, especially for the library support staff target market; vendor user groups: Society of American Archivists (SAA); other preservation groups; and regional, state, and local consortia and networks.

Orradre Library, Santa Clara University
Marketing Plan Outline with Executive Summary
Source: Orradre Library, Santa Clara University, 2003; reprinted courtesy of Orradre Library, Santa Clara University.

Executive Summary
Situation Analysis
    Market Summary
        Market Demographics
           Competition

Marketing Opportunities
    Market Needs
    Market Trends
    Market Growth
   SWOT Analysis
    Strengths
    Weaknesses
    Opportunities
    Threats
Critical Issues

Marketing Strategy
    Mission
        Marketing Vision Statement
    Marketing Objectives
        Marketing Programs
            Metrics
            Timelines
        Positioning
        Strategies

Web Plan
    Web Site Marketing Strategy
        Financials
        Expense Forecast
        ROI [return on investment]
Controls
    Marketing Organization
    Implementation Plan

American University Library
Communication Objectives
Source: American University Library, 2004: 52; reprinted courtesy of American University Library, Library Marketing Team, 2004—Members: Nick Banovetz; Julie Darnell; Mary Evangeliste; Mary Mintz; Jonathan Silberman; Diana Vogelsong; Treva Williams.

Objectives

The library has decided on five objectives that will change the attitude and increase the knowledge of the target audience by the end of the campaign.

- To create a cohesive visual identity for all new library publications, which includes a campaign tagline, campaign logo, key messages to create buzz among undergraduate students by September 2004.

- To create welcome kits that will be distributed to all incoming residents. These kits will include a library mug Post-it notes and a copy of fall workshops by August 15, 2004. These kits will also be available to students throughout the year.

- To actively pursue campus-related media exposure by creating press releases, submitting informational articles that will appear campus newspapers, and advertisements to generate positive news coverage about library services by June 1, 2005.

- To assess the library's current publications and communications outlets into an integrated communication plan.

- To market the marketing campaign to all library stations at a library-wide open house so that they can continue to communicate key messages and utilize visual identity.

Prospect Heights Public Library District
Marketing Plan SWOT Chart with Objectives
Source: Prospect Heights Public Library District, 2002: 1–2; reprinted courtesy of Prospect Heights Public Library District.

SWOT Analysis

Strengths
Personal service
Technology commitment

Unity of purpose from staff
Strong senior citizen program attendance
Community support through use of the Library
Library usage increasing
Record highs for both Youth and Adult/Young Adult Summer Reading Programs
Good program attendance for both youth and adults
Growing "Friends of the Library" group
Positive patron comments
Voluntary donations
Growing population and tax base
Building, environmental, organizational, and lighting improvements

Weaknesses

Staff technology knowledge
Library location; poor public visibility, not located at a main intersection
Lack of room to grow in shelving and parking space
Public perception of libraries in general; stereotypes
Media education of libraries
Young adult/high school (ages 12–18) programming

Opportunities

Neighboring libraries
Library Cable Network
Improvement of staff's technology knowledge
Public perception of libraries in general; overcoming stereotypes
Media education of libraries
Young adult/high school (ages 12–18) programming

Threats

Neighboring libraries with similar services
Computers, television, and other media compete for patrons' limited time
Technology/Internet—fast-paced changes overwhelm the nontechnical services
Bookstores
Tax caps limit library revenue
Nonprint media undermines reading
Changing political districts and responsibilities
Impact of potential new legislation

Marketing Action Goals

Based on the SWOT analysis, Department Head meetings, and the Board/Department Head meeting, our three main Action Goals were determined. Many individual Marketing Action Goals are already implemented and intend to be continued, maintained, or enhanced. The three main Action Goals consist of the following:

- To increase overall Library use, both in house and at remote locations
- To build electronic resources as well as staff and public knowledge to encourage more electronic use
- To build community involvement with young adult (ages 12–14) and high school (ages 15–18) programming, area agency, and library cosponsored programs.

George Eliot Hospital NHS Trust
Marketing Strategy with Objectives
Source: Brook, 2007: 8; reprinted courtesy of Nigel Brook, Library Services Manager, William Harvey Library, George Eliot Hospital NHS Trust.

Marketing Strategy Goals

In order to improve advertising and marketing procedure within the Library Service, we have set out some basic achievable targets to be assessed on an annual basis.

Raise awareness of services:

- Published article in Bleep twice per year
- Develop library e-journal and have quarterly issues
- Poster displays sent to wards/departments quarterly
- Redesign of library Web presence
- Develop in-house library branding and apply to all products
- Develop resource-update newsletter on a quarterly basis

Increase uptake of services:

- Initiate targeted-group surveys to evaluate current serve-levels and idealized service requirements
- Targeted training sessions provided for staff groups
- Maximize public/staff areas by advertising in Raveloes
- Maximize joint interdepartment projects, such as PALS project
- Generic e-mail advertising to ensure that all staff are made aware of services
- Attendance at induction and mandatory update days

EXAMPLES OF MARKETING STRATEGIES AND TACTICS (ACTION PLANS)

Association for Library Collections & Technical Services (ALCTS) ⓒⒹ
Marketing Assessment and Segmentation Strategy
Source: Association for Library Collections & Technical Services, 2001; reprinted courtesy of Association for Library Collections & Technical Services (ALCTS).

I. Market Analysis Summary

  A. Market Segmentation

    i. Primary markets include: public and academic librarians, nonlibrarians in technical services, librarians in nontraditional roles, information specialists in nonlibrary settings.

ii. Secondary markets include: school and special librarians;,public (for technical service awareness/advocacy), individuals, and vendors (for advertising space).

iii. Other markets include state library associations, teacher organizations, library and information science educators and students (working or enrolled in library and information science degree programs), institutions in the library profession such as corporations and international libraries, and bookstores.

B. Target Market Segment Strategy

  i. Market needs

* Staff development and continuing education materials that train and prepare librarians for change
* Online enhancements to print products: content experience packages
* Forward-looking products that take advantage of new media formats, platforms, and delivery/distribution streams
* Rapid-response products covering hot-topic trends and developments
* "Information packages" versus traditional professional monographs
* Straight-into-the job publications for paraprofessionals
* Application of technical services in nontraditional professionals
* Multiple language format
* Products that support industry principles, standards, and best practices for creating, collecting, organizing, delivering, and preserving information resources in all forms
* Quick production response schedules ensuring currency of information and quick turnover of manuscripts to publication
* Products supporting public awareness/advocacy of industry policies, principles, and standards for creating, collecting, organizing, delivering, and preserving information resources in all forms (specialty marketing)
* Full product line development stretching the reach and influence of every product subject

  ii. Market trends

* Increased spending on library technology is driving the need for support products.
* Library automation may be moving from bibliographical control to content management.
* Overall library market for print subscriptions continues to decline slightly.
* Changing skill sets/accountabilities.
* Higher level ("professional") staff positions replaced by lower level ("paraprofessional") positions.
* Multiple languages formats for library materials and patrons.
* Increased demand on librarians to train nonprofessionals, or paraprofessionals.
* Fewer MLS [master of library science] graduates.
* MLS graduates seeking work in nontraditional, nonlibrary settings.
* Boom in spending on electronic products in academic libraries and a lesser extent in public libraries.
* Copyright issues in electronic publications.
* The growth of the global economy and international markets.
* Faster production cycles to shorten the time it takes to get a product out.

American University Library
Marketing Campaign Strategies and Tactics
Source: American University, 2004: 52–54; reprinted courtesy of American University Library, Library Marketing Team, 2004—Members: Nick Banovetz; Julie Darnell; Mary Evangeliste; Mary Mintz; Jonathan Silberman; Diana Vogelsong; Treva Williams.

Campaign Goal

Our goal is to create an awareness campaign targeted toward undergraduate students. Once implemented, the campaign goal is to increase undergraduate satisfaction and use of library services by 20 percent over the 2004–2005 school year.

Objectives

The library has decided on five objectives that will change the attitude and increase the knowledge of the target audience by the end of the campaign.

- To create a cohesive visual identity for all new library publications, which includes a campaign tagline, campaign logo, and key messages to create buzz among undergraduate students by September 2004.
- To create welcome kits that will be distributed to all incoming residents. These kits will include a library mug, Post-it notes, and a copy of fall workshops by August 15, 2004. These kits will also be available to students throughout the year.
- To actively pursue campus-related media exposure by creating press releases, submitting informational articles that will appear campus newspapers, and advertisements to generate positive news coverage about library services by June 1, 2005.
- To assess the library's current publications and communications outlets into an integrated communication plan.
- To market the marketing campaign to all library staff at a library-wide open house so that they can continue to communicate key messages and utilize visual identity.

Campaign Strategies and Tactics

Strategy One: Consistency and repetition

Tactics: Create consistency and repetition using key campaign messages and the campaign themes, "Are You in the Know?" and "Ask @ Your library." The theme of the campaign will give students a sense of belonging and communicate the benefits the library has to offer.

- Create and distribute welcome materials including mugs and Post-it notes with a design that is consistent with the campaign theme.
- Campus posters will be created to hang around campus in high-traffic areas where students are waiting in line, hanging out with friends, or studying.
- Informational articles written for campus publications, press releases, and advertisements will highlight the new campaign, along with specific services that are underutilized by undergraduate students.
- Yearlong timeline includes additional tactics the library can implement to increase awareness of their services.

Key Messages:

1. Ask @ Your Library: We Can Find You the Books You Need
   (Speaks to the fact that we have books, and asking for assistance can aid in locating the materials they need.)
2. You Asked, We Listened.
   (Promotes improvements in the library and reinforces the benefits of asking.)
3. Ask @ Your Library: We Can Save You Time.
   (Encourages students to ask for help so they don't just get frustrated and leave.)
4. Ask @ Your Library: Librarians Can Make Your Research Simple.
   (Encourages students to ask for help so they don't just get frustrated and leave.)

Strategy Two: Use of salient information

Tactics: The use of salient information will address library misconceptions. This will enable undergraduate students to be exposed to new information that counters negative preexisting beliefs about the library. The library will be presented as inviting and helpful to overcome negative student assumptions. An additional strategy is to emphasize that librarians can show students how to use the library with ease and efficiency as well as teach them research skills they can use throughout their studies and their careers.

- Welcome kits highlight library services. These kits will be more task specific than most generic literature. This kit will include schedule of fall instruction sessions, a calendar of events, Post-it notes, library mugs, prize contest raffle ticket, and library bookmark.
- Campus posters will emphasize how librarians can teach students how to use the library more efficiently as well as research skills that will benefit them in their studies and their careers.
- Feature articles, press releases, and paid advertisements will highlight librarian services, book loan services, and e-resources; they will also address current questions and concerns from the students about the library and highlight library improvements.
- i-Pod prize contest raffle is an incentive for students to come in and experience all of the services that the library has to offer. It also encourages students to form relationships with library staff and faculty.

Strategy Three: Timing

Tactics: Timing of our welcome kit, on-campus posters, news articles, press releases, ads, and other tactics included in the timeline plays a critical role in planning the marketing campaign. We want to attract students early in the year while reinforcing our messages through repetition the entire year. Careful strategic planning will make certain that all campaign elements work together to deliver messages that appeal to students.

- Welcome kits will be passed out at new student orientations and in the library.
- Campus posters will be placed around campus and on shuttle buses at the beginning of the semester and will change frequently to influence students throughout in the school year.

- Feature article will be published at the beginning of the semester to attract students early in the year and press releases will be distributed to campus-wide publications to increase awareness of library instruction courses, events, and improvements.

Highlighted Dates

June 15:	Finalize visual identity and taglines, Present to University Librarian and Management Team
June 17:	Open house for staff, in staff lounge
June 22:	Order mugs and Post-its
July 1:	Have poster designs finalized and ready to place order
July 1 to August 13:	Welcome kits assembled
August 16:	Posters hung in library
August 23:	Information wall set up in library
August 26:	Submit articles to *AU Weekly* and the *Eagle* (American University Library, 2004: 52–53)

College of DuPage Library ⓒⒹ
Source: College of DuPage Library, 2002: 9; reprinted with permission from College of DuPage Library Marketing Plan.

Table 7-1. College of DuPage Marketing Plan 2002–2003 Theme: Your Library . . . Information to Go

Plan	Goal	Target Market	Product/Service	Vehicle/Strategy	Timeline	Assessment
Library slogan	Obtain a slogan for the Library	Current/pro-spective users of the Library	The Library	In-house Library "contest"	Spring/Summer '02—Use Fall Quarter '02	# of entries Slogan
First-week student marketing campaign	Help students personalize the Library	Students	The Library	Roving Library ambassadors	First week—Fall Quarter '02	Feedback from ambassadors # of handouts
First-week orientation for new faculty	Introduce new faculty to librarian	New faculty	Librarian Library services	Include Library in formal orientation program	Fall Quarter '02	Feedback from new faculty
First-week orientation for p-t faculty	Introduce p-t faculty to librarian	Part-time faculty	Librarian	P-T reception	Fall Quarter '02	# of attendees # of Library staff
Library brochure	Promote Library to students	All students	Library resources and services	Print brochure PDF format on Web site	Ready by Spring Quarter '03	Completed brochure
Marketing campaign to off-campus students/faculty	Promote Library services to off-campus students/faculty	Off-campus students/faculty	Library resources and services	Work with off-campus librarian	Winter '02/ Spring '03 Quarter	

(Cont'd.)

Table 7-1. College of DuPage Marketing Plan 2002–2003 Theme: Your Library . . . Information to Go *(Continued)*

Plan	Goal	Target Market	Product/Service	Vehicle/Strategy	Timeline	Assessment
Inform community about Library	Link to Library Web site from public libraries in COD District	Public libraries Community	Library Web site	Contact public libraries through DLS/SLS	Spring Quarter '03	# of links to COD Web site from public libraries
Focus groups	Solicit input from Library users to help in marketing efforts—what they know about products/services; what they use	On-campus students New faculty Part-time faculty	Knowledge and use of existing resources/ services	Outside facilitator One focus group for each target market	Spring or Summer Quarter '03	

Museums, Libraries and Archives (MLA) England
Action Plan and Timetable
Source: Museums, Libraries and Archives, 2005: 25; reproduced courtesy of the MLA Partnership.

Table 7-2. Improved Promotion: The Transformation of Public Libraries Story

Action	Deliverables	Dates	Partners
Recruitment-based PR campaign	• National news story • Follow on media coverage • Librarian of the Year • Radio campaign • Awards event	July 2005 July 2005 onwards Launched at PLA October 2005 January/February 2006 April 2006	Idea Generation, CILIP CILIP
Families with under 5s	• Partnership with 4Children • Roll out to libraries • Tommy Parent Friendly Awards entry	June 2005 September 2005 January to April 2006	4Children
Young adults 18 to 25	• Partnership with YouthNet • Survival guide for young adults • Public library at the Big Chill	July 2005 September 2005 August 2005	YouthNet Idea Generation Arts Council for England
Pre-retirement 55 to 65	• New report into "active mind, active body" • Media coverage	September 2005 September 2005	tbc
Adult literacy and reading	To be confirmed, connecting with BBC campaign	2006/07	
Adult learning	To be confirmed, connecting with BBC campaign	2006/07	

(Cont'd.)

Table 7-2. Improved Promotion: The Transformation of Public Libraries Story *(Continued)*

Action	Deliverables	Dates	Partners
Children and young people	To be confirmed, dependent on product improvement for young people based on *Fulfilling Their Potential*	2006/07	
Internal communications	• Twice yearly staff newsletter • Staff briefing information to download • Online staffroom, as part of the People's Network	July 2005 January 2006 July 2005 October 2005	

Association for Library Collections & Technical Services (ALCTS) ⓒⅅ
Membership Business Plan Outline
Source: Association for Library Collections & Technical Services, 2001: 6; reprinted courtesy of Association for Library Collections & Technical Services (ALCTS).

1.4 Marketing Strategy

1.4.1 Positioning Statements

As has been stated, the increased need for the expertise represented by ALCTS members is a substantial positioning prospect. What is needed is recognition of this expertise and the benefits that an ALCTS membership can provide to a potential member, as indicated in the six areas previously mentioned. The ALCTS position in any marketing strategy is to emphasize this expertise and the opportunities available to members to prosper from it. ALCTS, in another word, is the "expert" association in these areas. Any person who wishes to excel in ALCTS areas would definitely benefit from membership.

1.4.2 Pricing Strategy

ALCTS has a single priced personal membership rate of $45.00. This is within the range of dues other ALA divisions charge. The student dues for ALCTS are also in line with other divisions. There is an option that is available that ALCTS does not now have: a reduced price for new members of the division. This would follow the ALA model plus other divisions.

A new ALA dues pricing model has been proposed, combining three memberships into one price. This is being tested on an ALCTS target market, library support staff. No comparable dues structure exists in a quick search of other library associations.

1.4.3 Promotion Strategy

Once the ALCTS position is strongly enunciated (the Strategic Plan does this), this message should be contained in all ALCTS communications. It is a "branding" strategy. ALCTS is identified with specific positives. Along with this the message should be that without ALCTS membership, a potential member is missing a segment of their professional development.

1.4.4 Distribution Strategy

The strategy here would rely on traditional outlets. In addition, an increased Web presence and more emphasis on electronic communication would enhance the reach.

1.4.5 Marketing Programs

The Library Support Staff Membership Outreach Plan defines a new approach to marketing to a potential audience. This is a benefits-oriented approach, which suggests to the potential member the advantages of membership and what membership would bring to the person's job. This approach can be carried through to other segments of the potential market.

Museums, Libraries and Archives (MLA) England
Communication Strategies: Messages
Source: Museums, Libraries and Archives, 2005: 10–11; reproduced
  courtesy of the MLA Partnership.

Main messages

- Framework for the future set out the government's ten-year vision for public libraries. The realization of that vision will ensure that libraries continue to meet the needs of their communities in the 21st century.
- Public libraries are working together and with others to transform themselves, in response to the challenges of Framework for the Future. MLA is supporting and enabling that transformation.

Messages for government

- Libraries are a trusted and popular community resource. By developing and using them to their full potential, government can use them to deliver against key agenda, e.g., raising standards in schools, creating stronger communities, and promoting economic vitality.

Messages for the library sector and partners

- Framework for the future is a program that brings together local and national initiatives, some new, some existing, to drive the transformation of libraries.
- It gives libraries a common platform and therefore a more powerful voice with policymakers and the public.
- Opting out of Framework for the Future is not an option. Its themes underpin everything you do in libraries. Even the better performers cannot afford to be complacent.
- By engaging with Framework for the Future you can help protect and develop the future of public libraries.

Messages for the public and other stakeholders

- Public libraries are changing to meet the needs of 21st century users without losing sight of their heritage and place at the heart of the community.
- Rediscover your local library.

Methods and media [see Table 7-3]

Table 7-3. MLA Communication Strategies: Methods and Media		
Method	**Audience**	**Actioned by**
Face-to-face		
Regular contact with key influencers, e.g., CILIP, LGA	Local government, library sector, stakeholders	MLA, partners
Relationship-building in Whitehall	Government departments	MLA, DCMS, partners
Conferences and exhibitions, e.g., Skills for Life	Government, library sector, stakeholders	MLA, regional agencies, partners
Media		
Trade, professional, local government press	Library sector, stakeholders	MLA, partners
Consumer and special interest	Public, all audiences	PR agency
National press and online coverage	Public, all audiences	MLA, PR agency, partners
Regional and key local newspapers	Public, local government	MLA, PR agency, regional agencies, partners, libraries, local authority PRs
Broadcast media	Public, all audiences	MLA, PR agency, partners, local authority PRs
Publications and direct mail		
MLA publications	Government, library sector, stakeholders	MLA
Regional agency newsletters	Local government, library sector, stakeholders	Regional agencies
Partners publications	Library sector, stakeholders	Partners
Electronic		
MLA Web site	Library sector, stakeholders	MLA
Framework e-mail updates	Library sector, stakeholders	MLA
Regional agency Web sites	Library sector, stakeholders	Regional agencies
Local authority Web sites	Public	Local authorities
PN Web site	Public, library sector	PN team
MLA e-bulletin	Library sector, stakeholders	MLA
Partner Web sites	Library sector, stakeholders	Partners

Wombatta Public Library ⓒⒹ
**Source: Henshaw, n.d.: 14; reprinted courtesy of Roger L. Henshaw,
www.rhes.com.au.**

5.0 Controls

The implementation of our strategies and actions will be constantly monitored and reported to ensure WPL maintains control over all processes. This will allow us to constructively "fine tune" our actions and help avoid poor performance. It will also provide a means of reassessing our priorities and, importantly, help prevent wasting our limited resources.

Expected performance versus actual performance will be monitored and include:

Quantitative measures:

- Level of activity, including trending to determine growth or otherwise based on plan strategies and actions (i.e., increased attendance at programs, membership growth, turnover of stock, etc.)
- Staff time allocated versus staff actual
- Revenue and expenditure comparisons (where there is a revenue component our aim will be to be at least cost neutral)

Qualitative measures:

- Exit interviews and evaluations
- Surveys
- Comparative data from other library services
- Accountability monitoring (staff/team ability or inability to meet performance targets)
- Team meetings/feedback sessions

Sandwell Metropolitan Borough Library Council
**Source: Sandwell Metropolitan Borough Library Council, 2005: 42; reprinted
courtesy of Sandwell Metropolitan Borough Library.**

Table 7-4. Sandwell Metropolitan Borough Council Action Plans

Action to Address Functional or Priority Needs	Milestones to Achieve the Action	Timescale	Outcome Measure of Success	Resource Implication Including Funding Stream	Responsible Officer
Deliver a coordinated program of activities to promote core and traditional services (especially books and reading) to new users and excluded groups, including vulnerable and older adults (Unit Plan 3.1)	Identification of excluded groups. Promotional activity to address group impact evaluations	Mar. 2006 (quarterly review)	Visits by groups, people with disabilities, gender	Core budget 11,000 plus staff time	JF/DE/RD

(Cont'd.)

Table 7-4. Sandwell Metropolitan Borough Council Action Plans *(Continued)*

Action to Address Functional or Priority Needs	Milestones to Achieve the Action	Timescale	Outcome Measure of Success	Resource Implication Including Funding Stream	Responsible Officer
Attend key events to promote services to whole community (Unit Plan 3.2)	Sandwell show, Vaisakhi festival, Impact evaluation	Mar. 2006 (Sep. review)	Numbers at events, numbers joining at events	Staff time	JF/DE
Run annual program of minimum of six events in partnership with Central and for Black History Month (Unit Plan 4.6)	Timetable established	Mar. 2006 (Sep. Dec. Review)	Numbers at events	1,000	TN
Make contact with local groups and communities including faith groups, local history groups, friends groups (Unit Plan 4.13)		Sep. 2005		Staff time	TN

REFERENCES

American University Library. 2004. "F—Communication Plan." Ask @ your library. (May). Available: www.ala.org/ala/acrl/acrlissues/marketingyourlib/AU_application.pdf.

Association of College and Research Libraries (ACRL). 2003. "Facilitator Guide. Strategic Marketing for Academic and Research Libraries." Chicago: American Library Association.

Association for Library Collections & Technical Services. 2001. "Membership Business Plan Outline FY 2002–2005." (February 26). Chicago: American Library Association. Available: www.ala.org/ala/alcts/divisiongroups/membershipdiv/businessplan0205.doc.

Association of Specialized and Cooperative Library Agencies. 2007. "Surviving and Thriving on Your Own: Your Business Plan." (April 24). Chicago: American Library Association. Available: www.ala.org/ala/ascla/asclapubs/surviving/yourbusinessplan/yourbusiness.cfm.

Bloedel, Kimberly. 2006. "Not Just for Celebrities: Collaborating with a PR Representative to Market Library Education Services." *Medical Reference Services Quarterly*, 25, no. 3 (fall): 33–43.

Booth, Tracey. n.d. "Pre-Marketing: Analysis of Information Needs." Columbia, SC: University of South Carolina School of Library and Information Science. Available: www.libsci.sc.edu/bob/class/clis724/SpecialLibrariesHandbook/booth.htm.

Brook, Nigel. 2007. "Library Services: Marketing and Advertising Strategy." Warwickshire, UK: William Harvey Library, George Eliot Hospital NHS Trust.

College of DuPage Library. 2002. "College of DuPage Library Marketing Plan." Glen Ellyn, IL: College of Dupage Library.

Davids, Mike and Kelly Newcomb. 2006. "Turning the 'Wheel.'" *Debt* (July/August): 22–25. Available: www.clla.org/debt3.

Dow, Roger and S. Cook. 1996. *Turned On: Eight Vital Insights to Energize Your People, Customers, and Profits*. New York: HarperCollins.

Entrepreneur.com. 2007. "Startup Capital Requirements—Repeating Monthly Expenses." Irvine, CA: Entrepreneur Media Inc. Available: www.entrepreneur.com/contact-us/index.html.

Henshaw, Roger L. n.d. "Wombatta Public Library Service Marketing Plan." New South Wales, Australia: Wombatta Public Library.

Kornik, Joe. 2007. "Motivation Makeover." *Sales & Marketing Management*, 59, no. 2 (March): 32.

MacKintosh, Pamela J. 1999. "Writing an Effective Business Plan for Fee-based Services." *Journal of Interlibrary Loan, Document Delivery and Information Supply*, 10, no. 1: 47.

Marvel, Pat. 2003. "How 2003 Library of the Year Las Vegas-Clark County Effectively Uses Marketing and PR Planning." *The Gale Report* (August). Available: http://gale.cengage.com/enewsletters/gale_report/2003_08/voices.htm.

Museums, Libraries and Archives (MLA). 2005. "Marketing Plan for Public Libraries in England. April 2005–March 2008." London: MLA.

Oliva, Ralph A. 2004. "B2B for Sale." *Marketing Management*, 13, no. 5 (September/October): 48–49.

Orradre Library, Santa Clara University. 2003. "Orradre Library Marketing Plan." Santa Clara, CA: Santa Clara University.

Prospect Heights Public Library District. 2002. "Prospect Heights Public Library District Long-Term Marketing Plan." Prospect Heights, IL: Prospect Heights Public Library District. Available: www.phl.alibrary.com/board/2002_MarketingPlan.html.

Sandwell Metropolitan Borough Library Council. 2005. "Library and Information Service Business Plan 2005–2006." West Midlands, UK: Sandwell Metropolitan Burough Council.

Schultz, Lisa. 1998. "Strategic Planning in a University Library." *MLS: Marketing Library Services,* 12, no. 5 (July/August). Available: www.infotoday.com/mls/jul98/story.htm.

Shamel, Cynthia L. 2002. "Building a Brand: Got a Librarian?" *Searcher*, 10, no. 7 (July/August). Available: www.infotoday.com/searcher/jul02/shamel.htm.

Wallace, Linda K. 2004. *Libraries, Mission, and Marketing: Writing Mission Statements That Work*. Chicago: ALA Editions.

Weingand, Darlene. 1999. *Marketing/Planning Library and Information Services*. Englewood, CO: Libraries Unlimited.

8 EVALUATING YOUR BUSINESS PLAN'S SUCCESS

EVALUATIONS

BASIC DEFINITIONS

You cannot manage that which you do not measure. No matter how well your plan is designed, its implementation will require periodic reviews to make sure that you are moving along your chosen course. Evaluation is any systematic process designed to reduce uncertainty about the effectiveness of a particular service or portion of a service. Your library's internal and external environments are always changing and require follow-up, assessment, and measurement. As a living document, your business plan requires updating on a consistent basis as the service grows. The overall evaluation process shows how far you have come. Periodic reviews allow time to spot potential trouble and to either be ready for it or to alter the course of the plan to avoid it. This keeps your services or programs fresh, relevant, and vital in a rapidly changing environment.

Keeping services fresh, relevant, and vital also means continually striving to improve their quality. Quality measures do not aim for perfection; they aim for improving gradually and insisting on continually transforming yourself and your services. The ultimate evaluation measure is to see how your overall performance stacks up against your competitors' performances. Objective evaluative measures as well as perceptive measures apply to all issues inside and outside the library.

Evaluation provides the opportunity to reward those who are going in the right direction. Clearly communicated responsibilities, measurable criteria, and established timelines are the foundation for assessment and measurement. Involving library staff in setting self-goals, clearly communicating the team's overall goals, and consistently evaluating the team's success creates commitment and trust. These activities help staff by naming what every person, group, or unit needs to do and when. They demonstrate a beginning and an end to a process that is often interpreted as abstract, endless, and unfair by staff (Attard and Jones, 2005). However you plan to use the evaluation, you will still need to take an unemotional and honest look at your efforts to ensure that your expectations are realistic.

A major component of the implementation process is realistic evaluation. The results help fine-tune the business plan as you progress and establish the foundation for the next planning cycle. Measurements of results are integral to successful plan implementation. They require you to take into account alternatives that have been highlighted or noted through your continuous assessment of the need to continue, expand, or end the service. The nature of competition asks us to continuously adapt our strategy to the always-changing needs of clients. Evaluation is the key to understanding how to adapt.

Stay focused on what the target market needs and on the core competencies that you can provide to meet those needs. This will help your service keep ahead of the change curve. Measurements of client satisfaction and service value include process, outcome measures, and a balanced scorecard. With any evaluation tool, critical success factors include (Attard and Jones, 2005):

- Making sure your definitions, measures, and communication style match those of your stakeholders, other service organizations, nonprofits, and others in the local community
- Ensuring that your measures are communicated in a meaningful and understandable way for stakeholders

The mechanics put forward here are not the only approach to evaluation. Your choice of measurement instruments will be strongly influenced by your parent organization, and you will have to determine what it prefers when choosing tools. Each library and parent organization will have its own local techniques, but each technique will incorporate the issues mentioned here.

An evaluation:

- Ensures objectives are met
- Identifies problems and weakness
- Creates evidence of benefit and impact
- Validates budgeting or secures funding
- Gains support
- Guides future plans
- Develops guidelines useful in other projects
- Positions the library for success

The more detailed the plan, the more frequently you will want to review its progress. This needn't be difficult: the strategies and action plans described in previous chapters already include specific measurable criteria and performance timeline that must be met to achieve both short- and long-term goals. The action plan already outlines expectations for all staff. Employees' goals, key performance indicators, and individual contributions are already connected to the evaluation of the plan. Review and evaluate the entire business plan to identify what worked, what didn't, what got done, and what never got started (Hale, Butcher, and Hickey, 2003). Progress is monitored and tracked, and where the plan is found off course, you'll take remedial action during regularly scheduled meetings held to assess progress. Use the information gained from each periodic review to adjust your objectives.

One of the biggest reasons business plans don't work is the organization's inability to embrace change. The ability to change is fundamental to an effective business plan. The nature of planning and evaluation is to allow for review and revision, alteration and change. Those professionals entering the information industry after you will manage your library and institute their plans based on today's efforts. The environment will never be static. Allow for alterations in the plan and the library by realizing that the whole process is permanently transitional. Flexibility is achieved by building in an evaluation mechanism that allows making midcourse corrections. You want a plan that is adaptable enough to allow change as well as sophisticated enough to encourage the right kind of change, so the plan is continuously improving. There are any number of reasons why an evaluation will identify the need to shift objectives or strategies. It may be that more information is required to assess a situation, or that some portion of your target client market has changed. Technology may have evolved, which would require new staff skills and training. As your service evolves, review your business plan and update it with accurate information about changing market and economic conditions.

By conducting regular reviews of each strategy, objective, or plan, midcourse corrections are made without having to restart or resort to a long planning process. Take the time to define and discuss the basics of your library, outlining your new service, your markets, and the current financial situation. Regular review and assessment help you monitor costs and stay close to evolving needs in client service. Those factors will be of great help when it comes time to add value to your service. Determine what adds value for your local clients and stay on top of those drivers. Library staff can structure and update processes, shifting operations to focus directly on the results and away from the processes themselves. You can accomplish this with a business plan flexible enough to change as necessary.

Having the capability to measure allows you to be flexible, to shift your plans, strategies, or to focus as necessary. When reviewed in regular increments, the plan evolves with alterations in size, time, or focus. Each alteration relies on feedback from clients and staff to tell you how well objectives and plans have been met and what the next step will be. Within the bounds of your organization's requirements you can design and implement evaluation measurements that analyze your progress. Some measurements will be financial and measurable and some will be difficult to quantify, but they are all directly related to your efforts. The closer the evaluation measurements are set to your objectives, strategies, or action plans, the easier and more meaningful the results will be. No reason exists to have a business plan packed with meaningless figures: only the issues critical to success get evaluated. Critical issues gauge how to determine what changes, if any, are needed.

Regardless of the type of performance measurement or plan evaluation system you have, it is not uncommon for it to fall short in some regards. Often, evaluation systems do not provide the information management needs. Some potential problems are inaccuracy of data, too much complexity, measures that are not tied to organization goals, or the lack of a link between measures and individual performance (Institute of Management and Administration, 2004). Measure those things that are current and relevant—only the *five or six* things on which you want to stay focused. Having decided on what is important, stay close to the results of the critical factors and achieve the important things. There will always be more things to measure or do. Prioritize for importance to your objectives and stay focused.

Every aspect of library operations is aligned with your strategy. For example, human resources, especially the compensation and benefits, are aligned with the plan. Your staff are compensated for achieving the type of behaviors the plan encourages. The more your organization connects everything they're doing with the plan, the more likely you will achieve positive results.

Align the individual performance measures with the plan. This will go a long way in developing the support and understanding necessary for a positive result. Maintaining an ongoing evaluation tool in this manner allows staff and management to focus on results, changing personnel skills, responding to the impact of new technology, and developing better service plans.

KEY POINTS TO INCLUDE

When adding the evaluation tool to the business plan, you will want to include:

- The specific metrics chosen that reflect the parent organization's thinking, leadership style, or values; the information chosen to measure success must be information that will be appreciated, heard, and understood by members of the group to whom you report
- How the evaluation data were gathered
- Who evaluated the work, their objectivity (are they neutral?), and expertise in the area being evaluated
- How you propose to continuously monitor the plans (by date, events, etc.)
- The reporting system
- The sequential procedure for planning and implementing internal adjustments (by committee, team leader, board approval, etc.)

The evaluation section of your business plan will give a sense of what you expect to accomplish in two to five years. It will explain in quantitative and qualitative terms the benefit to the user of the library's products or services. You will present evidence of the marketability of the services and financially justify how you choose to promote the services. The plan will contain believable financial projections, with the key data explained and documented. It will enable you to evaluate performance and the proposal of the service. The clarity you develop by working through the steps of the business plan process will show in the commitment to produce high-quality information services and products.

EVALUATION WORKSHEETS

The main goal of an evaluation tool is to make sure that the library "makes plans in full awareness of the current competitive and strategic environment and ensures the plans are credible, deliverable and monitorable" (Davidson, 1994: 18). To monitor and evaluate progress, create a tool based on the measures and timelines already established and aligned with the plan's objectives, strategies, and action plans (see Worksheet 8-1 ⓒⓓ. Include any outsourced or contracted work. The evaluation tool includes:

- The specific measurements stated in the action steps
- The dates or times for milestones, completion, or key performance indicators
- The individual responsible for the work

Worksheet 8-1. Evaluation Tool Template				
Strategy	Plan (Action Steps)	Responsibility	By When	Key Performance Indicator *(When this is finished, we move forward.)*
1.	1			
	2			
	3			
	4			
	5			
				(Cont'd.)

Worksheet 8-1. Evaluation Tool Template *(Continued)*				
Strategy	Plan (Action Steps)	Responsibility	By When	Key Performance Indicator *(When this is finished, we move forward.)*
2.	1			
	2			
	3			
	4			
	5			
3.	1			
	2			
	3			
	4			
	5			
				(Cont'd.)

Worksheet 8-1. Evaluation Tool Template *(Continued)*				
Strategy	Plan (Action Steps)	Responsibility	By When	Key Performance Indicator *(When this is finished, we move forward.)*
4.	1			
	2			
	3			
	4			
	5			
Etc.				

Express the issues most valuable to your purpose and your organization.
Use a form for each objective (see Worksheet 8-2 (CD)).

Worksheet 8-2. Evaluation of Objectives Template				
Objective #:				
Strategy	Plan (Action Steps)	Responsibility	Time	Key Performance Indicator
				(Cont'd.)

Worksheet 8-2. Evaluation of Objectives Template *(Continued)*

Objective #:

Strategy	Plan (Action Steps)	Responsibility	Time	Key Performance Indicator

EXAMPLES OF EVALUATIONS

Red Deer Public Library ⓒⒹ
Source: Red Deer Public Library, 2006; reprinted courtesy of Red Deer Public Library.

Performance Measures

1. We continue to compare RDPL with other public libraries in Canada, based on annual national survey information.
2. We strive to provide services in the most cost-efficient manner possible and to measure the costs of providing key library services.
3. We continue to gather quantitative and qualitative information from stakeholders, regular surveys, interviews, focus groups, questionnaires, and online forms.

Output Measures

Table 8-1. Red Deer Public Library Output Measures			
Performance Measure	**2004 Actual**	**2005 Projected**	**2006 Targets**
Customer Visits	592,768	610,000	620,000
Web site Visits	126,929	200,000	220,000
Circulation of Items	680,160	682,000	685,000
Program Attendance	19,159	18,000	19,000
Volunteer Hours	9,237	9,000	9,000
Reference Questions	92,636	96,000	97,000
Public Internet Computers	40	44	47
Internet Research Sessions at Public Access Workstations in the Library	54,072	60,000	75,000

Oakville Public Library 2007–2009 ⓒⒹ
Source: Oakville Public Library, 2007: 14; reprinted courtesy of Oakville Public Library.

Section VI: Performance Measures

A. Targets Based on Usage Statistics (reported quarterly and annually) [see Table 8-2]

B. New Benchmarks to Measure Business Plan Outcomes

Several new benchmarks will be established in 2007 for specific Business Plan initiatives. Targets for 2008–2009 will be established once 2007 levels are known.

Table 8-2. Oakville Public Library Performance Measures: Targets Based on Usage Statistics				
	Benchmark*	**2007 Target**	**2008 Target**	**2009 Target**
Circulation	2,192,979 ('04)	2,302,600	2,417,800	2,538,650
Cardholders per Capita	112,664 ('04)	118,297	124,212	130,423
Program and Outreach Attendance	59,812 ('04)	62,803	65,943	73,020
*Benchmark used is 2004 due to 9-month closure of Glen Abbey in 2005–2006.				

a) Number of Web site searches on local history images (launch will take place in February 2007)
b) Circulation of adult and children's multilingual materials
c) Number of new resident kits distributed

C. Qualitative Measures

The detailed business plans include the following qualitative measures for specific Business Plan projects. These include:
a) Library ranking in 2007 Citizen Survey
b) Feedback from Town staff on their knowledge of library services
c) Impact of enhancements to the online catalogue

London Health Libraries Strategic Development Group and electronic Knowledge Access Team Performance Measures 2005–2008 ⓒ
Team Performance Measures 2005–2008
Source: London Health Libraries Strategic Development Group and electronic Knowledge Access Team, 2005: 1; reprinted courtesy of London Health Libraries Strategic Development Group (LHLSDG) and electronic Knowledge Access Team (eKAT).

Table 8-3. Team Performance Measures 2005–2008				
Performance area Performance areas 1–4 inform the library networks, 1-5 inform the LHLSDG and 1-6 line manager	**Measurements**	**Method of Monitoring**	**Monitored by whom**	**Timing**
1. Business planning and development	• The eKAT service specification is reviewed annually and revised if necessary	eKAT annual report and business plan	Team leader's line manager	May
	• Annual eKAT business plans are developed which are fully integrated into policy setting and the business planning process of LHLSDG and based on consultation with relevant stakeholders, e.g., eKAT reference Group, LHLSDG, library networks, users	Drafts of business plan	Team leader's line manager LHLSDG eKAT Reference Group	February–April
				(Cont'd.)

Table 8-3. Team Performance Measures 2005–2008 *(Continued)*				
Performance area Performance areas 1–4 inform the library networks, 1-5 inform the LHLSDG and 1-6 line manager	**Measurements**	**Method of Monitoring**	**Monitored by whom**	**Timing**
1. Business planning and development *(Cont'd.)*	• Business plan objectives are regularly tested for relevance and feasibility	Quarterly reports	Team leader's line manager	August, October, February, May
	• Horizon scanning, e.g., new relevant developments in e-resources provision and technologies are identified and prioritized with networks and working groups	Business plan Quarterly reports	eKAT Reference Group LHLSDG	August, October, February, May
2. Consultation and communications	• Library networks are consulted on national developments in electronic library issues where eKAT contributes	Quarterly reports	eKAT Reference Group	August, October, February, May
	• Library networks are kept up to date on developments in electronic services and technologies through briefings and workshops	Business plan Quarterly reports	eKAT Reference Group	August, October, February, May
	• eKAT managed web sites are kept up to date and library networks are involved in maintaining relevancy and identifying improvements	Business plan Quarterly reports	Web Development Group	August, October, February, May
3. Delivery of services	• Performance report through 3 x quarterly monitoring reports and an annual report which identify achievement against business plan objectives, slippage and remedial action	Quarterly reports Annual report	Team leader's line manager LHLSDG	August, October, February, May
	• Library networks are involved in prioritizing eKAT activities and understand how they should work with eKAT to ensure delivery of shared objectives	Business planning meetings (conventional or virtual) and feedback from library networks	eKAT Reference Group	September, January
	• User and usage statistical reports produced 2 x year and published on Web site	Reports to LHLSDG	LHLSDG eKAT Reference Group	May/June, November
4. Value for money	• eKAT achieves the annual business plan objectives within budget	Annual report	Team leader's line manager LHLSDG	May
	• Resources purchased or produced meet user needs (library service or direct user need) and show savings on individual or SHA-wide purchasing	Statistical reports Annual report	LHLSDG eKAT Reference Group	May/June, November
				(Cont'd.)

Table 8-3. Team Performance Measures 2005–2008 *(Continued)*

Performance area Performance areas 1–4 inform the library networks, 1-5 inform the LHLSDG and 1-6 line manager	Measurements	Method of Monitoring	Monitored by whom	Timing
5. Budget management	• Quarterly/end of year income and expenditure reports (global report for staff; budget headings for non-staff costs) showing actual against predicted expenditure and any action proposed to achieve balance	Finance reports Annual report	Team leader's line manager SHA eKAT finance lead LHLSDG	July, October, January, May
6. Staff performance and development	• Individual performance plans for each team member are agreed by line manager by the end of June each year and are reviewed quarterly	Business plan Quarterly report	Team leader's line manager	August, October, February, May
	• Each member of eKAT has an annual appraisal and 6 monthly review	Business plan Quarterly report	Team leader's line manager	June/July, December/January
	• Each member of the team is supported in achieving a personal development plan which identifies the skills development required to fulfill their current role and which helps prepare them for future roles	Business plan Quarterly report	Team leader's line manager	August, October, February, May

Calgary Public Library
Evaluation of Outcomes
Source: Calgary Public Library, 2006: 20; © Calgary Public Library, All
    Rights Reserved.

9. Outcomes

In the course of this planning cycle, the Calgary Public Library will assess its performance in each area of strategic focus by establishing outcomes and performance targets and applying a range of measurement techniques. Specific and quantifiable targets will be incorporated into the plans developed for each key action and results will be reported on a regular basis to the Calgary Public Library Board and other key stakeholders.

Many of the measurement techniques are already in place. The Library has recently updated its benchmarking program and will continue to conduct annual surveys of both users and nonusers. These surveys measure satisfaction, awareness, and perceived value to individuals and to the community at large. A variety of techniques will also continue to be used to measure the many ways Calgarians use the public library. Number of materials borrowed, in-person and remote visits to library facilities and the Web site, questions asked and answered, programs and program attendance, use of materials in-house, use of library seating, and use of computer work stations are all measured. Market penetration will be measured by the number of new and renewing cardholders. Other appropriate measures will be used to evaluate the success of actions undertaken to build internal capacity.

The Library will continue to be an active contributor to the Canadian Urban Libraries Council initiative, which permits the comparison of the performance of public libraries across Canada. Finally, it will seek new and cost-effective techniques for measuring all aspects of its performance, including those related to the increasing applications of technology to library services and service delivery.

University of Wollongong Library ⓒⒹ
Performance Evaluation
Source: University of Wollongong Library, 2006; reprinted courtesy of University of Wollongong Library.

2.2.   Evaluation of performance [1–2 pages]

2.2.1   Overview

Discussion to include achievements and milestones, awards, challenges, and constraints

The Library continues to evaluate its performance, based on its Performance Indicator Framework, through regular reviews, surveys, focus groups, and the client feedback database. Internally, performance data is regularly monitored by the Library's Executive Committee. Performance is also tested through surveys and external evaluation. Key 2005 results are outlined below.

Client Satisfaction

- Clients indicated they received excellent service at the Research Help desk, with 72 percent rating the service as excellent and 85 percent rating the service as good to excellent.
- 87 percent of document delivery clients surveyed agreed that they were satisfied with the print quality of articles received via desktop delivery.
- 85 percent of document delivery clients surveyed rated the Document Delivery as helpful

Materials Availability

- Using the CAUL [Council of Australian University Librarians] Performance Indicator: Materials Availability, client success in locating materials was evaluated. Materials immediately available was recorded at 77 percent—a 5 percent improvement compared to the previous evaluation in 2003 and a 29 percent overall improvement from the original benchmark recorded in 1997.
- Library ranked first for Materials Availability in CAUL Best Practices Performance Indicator Database
- 88 percent of document delivery clients surveyed agreed that they received materials in time to meet their needs

Skilled and Knowledgeable Staff who Responded Creatively to Change

- The Library won a Gold Award from the Investors in People accrediting agency in the category Best IiP Government Agency or Institution.
- The Library established a new national benchmark across best practices categories within the Rodski Survey Research database for staff satisfaction.

2.2.2 Effectiveness of strategies in achieving Unit and institutional objectives

Refer to "UOW Strategic Objectives—Roles of Professional Units in Attachment A. In the interests of brevity, if results have been reported against unit goals (above), in most cases they are not repeated below.

1.1 Apply a quality process (PARI) in all teaching programs and practices, including course development and assessment

- New performance indicators and measures for information literacy established, aligned with the ANZIL [Australia and New Zealand Institute for Information Literacy] standard

1.2 Continue to invest in staff development, mentoring, and reward

- Successful professional development seminar series introduced by the Information Literacy Coordinator focusing on improvement in teaching practice and assessment of information literacy by faculty librarians
- Information Literacy Forum initiated to revitalize teaching staff knowledge of information literacy and the Graduate Attributes. Has resulted in improved collaboration between the Library, CEDIR [Center for Educational Development and Interactive Resources], and Learning Development in the design and delivery of assessable components to support the attainment of the Graduate Attributes
- Two Library staff were seconded to CEDIR to contribute to the development and implementation of the Learning Management System
- Two Library Professional Cadets have been appointed; one cadet commenced in September and the other has commenced in February 2006
- A staff member has commenced the pilot Certificate IV—Workplace Certification

1.3 Promote innovative services and resources

- An offshore student guide on CD-ROM titled "Getting Connected: Your Guide to Online Learning" has been produced with input from ARD [Academic Registrar's Division], CEDIR, ITS [Information Technology Services], Learning Development, the Library, and several faculties. The project was funded by the University Internationalization Committee and was coordinated by the Remote Services Manager. The guide is designed to introduce students to the University's online learning environment, including SOLS [Student Online Services], Webmail, WebCT, and Library resources. Copies of the CD have been sent to the University's offshore teaching locations for distribution to all students
- A new training video for EndNote was developed as an alternative to face-to-face classes. Library component completed and with CEDIR for final editing
- E-books featured in satellite site promotional activities, highlighting hints and tips to make the best available use of these resources
- "What's New for My Faculty" online newsletters were introduced resulting in over 6,500 hits during Autumn and Spring sessions

2.1   Build and develop areas of research strength

Significant Acquisitions

- Electronic access to the following journals, identified during the 2004 Library Support for Research Strengths Review, were activated:
  - ○ *Current Medicinal Chemistry*
  - ○ *Journal of Bacteriology*
  - ○ *Marine Ecology Progress Series*
  - ○ *Medical Care*
  - ○ *Proceedings of the Royal Society of London B: Biological Sciences* (including print)
  - ○ *Superconductor Science and Technology*
  - ○ *Synlett* (including print)
  - ○ Australian University Indicators database
- Successfully negotiated an upgrade in access to the ScienceDirect database to include all Elsevier journal titles on the database from 1995 onward

2.2   Raise the international profile of UOW research

Collection Data on the University's Research Output:

- Number of unweighted DEST points awarded to UOW 2004 was 945.63, up from 779.37 in 2003— a 21.3 percent increase
- Number of DEST publications submitted by faculties was 1,219, up from 997 in 2003—a 22.2 percent increase
- Number of total publications submitted by faculties was 1,671 in 2004, up from 1,376 in 2003—a 21.4 percent increase
- Funding received for a Wollongong Research Archive digital repository project, which will support the forthcoming Research Quality Framework (RQF); this is an outcome of the work of the Content Management System Evaluation Team

2.3   Continue to improve the quality of the research experience for Higher Degree Research students

- Working with the Research Student Center, Library research skills were integrated with other training programs. All targeted classes were offered and included EndNote, Where do I publish? Finding theses.
- Contributed to the development and delivery of a Supervisor Training pilot program in collaboration with CDU [Center for Student Development]
- Developed and implemented tailored HDR [higher degree research] programs in collaboration with FRC [Faculty Research Committee] for the target faculties of Creative Arts, Education, Informatics. Evaluations were positive, with students indicating their knowledge and skills improved as an outcome of participation. Remaining faculties to be targeted in 2006

3.1   Cultivate, within all students, the attributes of a Wollongong graduate

- ILIP100 online modules and assessment tasks developed for students at offshore locations. Planned implementation due in 2006.

- To promulgate the principles and practices of information literacy, an Information Literacy Forum was held inviting guests from CEDIR, Learning Development, and faculty teaching staff. 56 academic staff engaged in energetic discussion of issues about integrating the Graduate Attributes into academic curricula and into collaborative relationships between academics and ASD staff.

3.2 Provide policies, services, and facilities that guide and encourage all students to participate and succeed in the University experience

- The eLearning@UOW Web site is designed to introduce students to the University's online learning environment and includes a Library Online component with content developed by the Remote Services Manager and Education Faculty Librarian.

3.3 Facilitate access to quality information resources, services and information skills development

- Materials Availability and Document Delivery Survey results in overview
- E-readings processing times reduced to a 5-day maximum (including the Book of Readings project) a 42 percent reduction in processing time as compared to 2004

5.2 Provide a supportive, equitable, and inclusive staff work environment

- A staff member has commenced the pilot Certificate IV—Workplace Certification
- See award and outcomes in overview
- Increased number of job enrichment opportunities

6.3 Improve educational opportunities

- 149 high school students participated in Library information literacy classes throughout the year
- 2 students from Dapto High School participated in a one-week research/work experience program
- 3 university and 6 TAFE library students were supported with work placements throughout the year

---

Jacaranda Public Library ⓒᴅ
Indicators
Source: Sarasota County Libraries, 2005; reprinted courtesy of Jacaranda Public Library.

Indicators (indications that we are moving toward or achieving desired outcomes)

Customer Service
Customer satisfaction responses
Express check kiosk transactions
Computer class attendance
Meeting room reservation statistics

Business Processes
VTLS/TagSys troubleshooting requests
Number of customers reporting equipment failures in reference area

Financial Perspective
IFAS reports
Cash drawer anomalies
Friend's revenues other than bookstore sales

Continuous Growth and Learning
Ecological footprint self-test scores
Recognition from disability organizations
Staff member comments on IDP forms

Hamilton Public Library
Business Planning Indicators: Customer Benefits/Impacts
Source: Hamilton Public Library, 2002: 3; reprinted courtesy of the Hamilton Public Library, Hamilton, Ontario.

Table 8-4. Community Services Department Planning Indicators with Budget

				Note: These are not dollars		
Customer Benefits/Impacts	**Indicators**	**Data Source**	**Report Freq.**	**2002 Budget Plan**	**2002 Projected Actual**	**2003 Budget Plan**
Accessible, sustainable collections, programs and services that anticipate and meet community need, demand and expectations	% of residents surveyed who express satisfaction with the library's collections (e.g., selection, quality of materials)	Exit/city survey	Annual	NA	NA	75% Satisfaction
	Physical measures of the collection • # of items held in the collections • Turnover rate • Age of collections	Internal	Bi-annual	• 1,484,681 • 1.3 • NA	• 1,475,000 • 1.3 • NA	• 1,475,000
	# of public access computers per 10,000 capita	Internal	Annual	6.8	6.8	6.8
	Number of people using public library computers	Internal	Annual	NA	NA	NA
	Transactions per capita—the total of • # of circulation • # in-house use • # visits in person • # information • # of visits electronically	Internal	Annual	21.2 • 4,555,845 • 1,442,217 • 3,247,050 • 598,272 • 559,566	21.2 • 4,500,000 • 1,400,000 • 3,247,000 • 600,000 • 1,100,000	21.2 • 4,500,000 • 1,400,000 • 3,247,000 • 600,000 • 1,100,000
						(Cont'd.)

Table 8-4. Community Services Department Planning Indicators with Budget *(Continued)*

				Note: These are not dollars		
Customer Benefits/Impacts	**Indicators**	**Data Source**	**Report Freq.**	**2002 Budget Plan**	**2002 Projected Actual**	**2003 Budget Plan**
	# of other library systems that Hamilton residents may use because of partnership agreements with eligible libraries	Internal	Annual	1:5	5:5	5:5
High quality and accessible library facilities	% of residents surveyed who express satisfaction with facilities (appearance, cleanliness, access, locations, hours)	Survey	Bi-annual	NA	NA	NA
	% of residents who are within 15 minutes of a library branch	Internal	Bi-annual	NA	NA	NA
	Size and number of locations • # of locations • Square metres of library space per capita	Internal	Annual	• 26 • NA	• 25 • NA	• 25 • NA
Learning opportunities (public)	% of schools participating in partnership opportunities with the public library	Internal	Annual	NA	NA	NA
	Number participating in core youth services and programs • # of Grade 4/Grade 7 class visits • # of programs for preschoolers • # participating in summer reading programs and related activities • # of teens participating in teen writing activities	Internal Annual		• 196 • 1090 • 7739 • 530	• 200 • 1090 • 7500 • 550	• 200 • 1200 • 7800 • 550
	Number of adults attending computer training courses	Internal	Annual	NA	NA	NA
Learning opportunities (staff)	# of staff training courses	Internal	Annual	119	120	150
	# of staff participating in training courses and educational opportunities	Internal	Annual	1000	1000	1000

George Eliot Hospital NHS
Quality Assurance and User Involvement
Source: Brook, 2007: 21; reprinted courtesy of Nigel Brook, Library Services Manager, William Harvey Library, George Eliot Hospital NHS Trust.

The Library Service uses a variety of mechanisms to ensure that it remains user-focused. Regular surveys are carried out to review aspects of the services and resources on offer. In 2005 a Journal Usage survey was carried out to isolate the level at which hardcopy journal stocks are utilized in the Trust. The findings of this survey supported the need for greater marketing of the Journal collection to departmental groups.

In 2008 the Library carried out a full staff survey. The results of this have been published in the Survey of Library and Information Services May 2006 document. In addition the Library undertakes regular sampling exercises to check the quality of diverse aspects of the service; for example, user records are checked for the quality of the data, its adherence to Library policy, and its status within existing Trust guidelines and legislation.

Survey information does not remain static, but is acted on by the Library staff. For example: Feedback from the medical students in 2006 resulted in the expansion of the student collections and the purchase of more duplicate copies.

The Librarian sits on the UMEC, PGMEC, Team Teaching, GETEC Management, Patient-Information Committee, and the Internet Group; in addition, we are members of regional library groups and sit nationally on the TRG; utilizing these links to involve clinicians, educators, and peers directly within the development of the service.

In 2006 the Library user group was relaunched on a quarterly basis. Extra care was taken while establishing this group to ensure that representatives from nonclinical, allied health and nursing were included as well as medical reps. The group is used as a two-way forum to report back and inform developments in library practice.

General user feedback forms are provided online, via the Library Web site and in hardcopy format in the library building.

Targeted feedback forms for specific service areas are dispatched after training events and literature searches in an effort to obtain feedback about the efficacy, possible improvements, and the impact that the service may have had upon education, audit, or patient care.

In order to measure the use of services, the Library collects hard information regarding users, number of loans, stock ILLs [interlibrary loans], training, etc. in addition regular samples of study spaces, service uptake, computer, spot-counts, etc. are carried out. In this way we are able to build up a collection of evidence to inform and direct services and monitor existing performance. A selection of these measures is produced in the Annual Library Report.

As part of its quality assurance process, the Library staff have access to an electronic copy of this folder via the shared network. All members of staff contribute directly to the content of this manual, with individual Library Assistants being responsible for leading on designated areas.

Stockport Metropolitan Borough ⓒⓓ
Evaluation and Outcomes Form
Source: Stockport Metropolitan Borough Council Adults and Communities Directorate, 2006; reprinted from Library and Information Service Business Plan 2006/06; courtesy of Metropolitan Borough of Stockport.

Business Area: Library and Information Service
Date: April 2006

1. Facilitation of access to accurate information and high quality advice

Table 8-5. Stockport Metropolitan Borough Evaluation of Library and Information Service

ACD key outcomes (1.1-7.5)	What do we want to achieve and links to PIs?	What actions need to be taken?	What is your measure of performance?	Who is Resp.?	Time scale?	(Column reserved for quarterly progress updates)
6.1, 6.3, 6.4, 7.3, 7.5	1.1 Seamless face-to-face access to Council services through Stockport Direct local centers in 9 libraries (BV220, 226;F4F 5,6)	1.1.1 Monitor service provided at each co-located SD local centre launched in April/May	Baseline data for satisfaction in answering enquiries collected (PLUS 2006)	DRM	March	
		1.1.2 Liaise with Adult Social Care to put systems in place for SD to be first line of contact on all social welfare issues	Systems in place at 9 libraries	DRM	Dec.	
		1.1.3 Liaise with Stockport Homes to provide frontline housing service in Brinnington	Provision agreed and procedures in place	DRM	Feb.	
		1.1.4 Carry out process mapping of all procedures common to all SD centers and Stopford House reception	Policies and procedures agreed and stored on a shared network drive/Internet site	DRM	Dec.	
		1.1.5 Agree management arrangements between Stockport Advice and 7 libraries	Systems in place for day-to-day management of the centers and line management of Advice staff within each center	DRM	April	
Etc.						

REFERENCES

Attard, Yvonne and Rebecca Jones. 2005. "Recognize Progress: Measuring Outcomes Not Output." PowerPoint presentation. Dysart Jones Associates and Oakville\Public Library. Available: www.accessola2.com/superconference2005/sat/docs/906/recognize.ppt.

Brook, Nigel. 2007. "Library Services: Business Strategy and Business Plan 2007–2010." Warwickshire, UK: William Harvey Library, George Eliot Hospital NHS Trust.

Calgary Public Library. 2006. "Building Community, Building Capacity: Business Plan 2006–2008." Calgary, AB: Calgary Public Library. Available: http://calgarypubliclibrary.com/library/pdf/businessplan06.pdf.

Davidson, A. B. 1994. "Planning and Performance Measurement." Management *Accounting: Magazine for Chartered Management Accountants*, 72, no. 5 (May): 18.

Hale, Martha, Patti Butcher, and Cindi Hickey. 2003. "New Pathways to Planning." (March 26). Lawrence, KS: Northeast Kansas Library System. Available: http://skyways.lib.ks.us/pathway/wksht6b1.html.

Hamilton Public Library. 2002. "Business Plan and Budget." Hamilton, ON: Hamilton Public Library.

Institute of Management and Administration. 2004. *2005 Yearbook: Financial Analysis, Planning, and Reporting*. New York: IOMA.

London Health Libraries Strategic Development Group (LHLSDG) and electronic Knowledge Access Team (eKAT). "Performance Measures, 2005-8." (August 2005). Available: www.londonlinks.ac.uk/ekat/ekat_performance_measures_2005-8.pdf.

Oakville Public Library. 2007. "Oakville Public Library Business Plan, 2007–2009." Oakville, ON: Oakville Public Library.

Red Deer Public Library. 2006. "Business Plan 2006–2008." Red Deer, Alberta, Canada: Red Deer Public Library.

Sarasota County Library System. 2005. "Jacaranda Public Library Business Plan, 2006." Sarasota, FL: Sarasota County Libraries. Available: http://suncat.co.sarasota.fl.us/Libraries/jacarandabusinessplan.aspx.

Stockport Metropolitan Borough Council Adults and Communities Directorate. 2006. "Library & Information Service Business Plan 2006/7." Stockport, UK: Stockport Metropolitan Borough Council. Available: www.stockport.gov.uk/content/leisureculture/libraries/pdfslib/librarybusplan0607?a=5441.

University of Wollongong Library. 2006. "2006 Professional Unit Business Plan Library." New South Wales, Australia: University of Wollongong Library.

9 FORMING A FINANCIAL PLAN

FINANCIAL PLANS

BASIC DEFINITIONS

A financial plan illustrates that the strategy, market, service, and predicted usage described in your business plan can actually come together to create something that will be economically viable. Here is where you can attach a precise cost to your plan and show how the figures add up. Historically, the financial description of a plan includes tried and true, conventional statements:

1. Income statement (or a profit/loss statement)
2. Balance sheet

It is wise to express your finances in the format required by your parent organization. Those methods of accounting, financial controls and auditing, purchasing records, payroll items, taxes, insurance, and the financial equations that express profit and loss, cash flow, and other necessary statements may be in a format that differs from the historical standard business plan. You will want to identify any support from outside your particular budget to include grants, foundation support, loans, special fund-raising efforts, behests, corporate sponsorships, or special forms of university backing.

To meet the needs of a very broad audience, this chapter will explain only a few techniques. Cash flow projections will not be addressed in depth because they are generally not applicable to a service start-up; when promoting a service within an organization, it is best to defer to the organization's preferred forms of reporting.

Prerequisites: If your library is part of a larger organization, identify your parent organization's

- accounting and financial reporting practices and guidelines;
- fiscal year schedule;
- established procedures (accounts payable and receivable, employee time sheets, etc., as well as policies relating to services and employees); and
- any other fiscal or bookkeeping preferences.

The financial description of the plan presents a picture of your marketing strategy and operational plans. If you aren't comfortable with your skill level when creating this, then secure professional services. Your choices range from hiring the services of a CPA (certified public accountant) to obtaining free consulting from the Small Business Development Centers (part of the U.S. Small Business Administration): both are able to review your efforts and assist in keeping you on track.

Even if you have hired a professional to verify that you have gathered the most accurate figures and data possible, you will still have to do the initial data-gathering work yourself. At the very least, ask your professional if all of the necessary issues have been adequately addressed and if the lines along which you've collected data apply to your situation. In this scenario, your first task is to teach the hired professional about your situation and issues; when your needs are clear, have the professional explain the implications of your financial statements.

Be sure you *clearly* understand all the numbers, figures, and reasoning behind your financial plan before incorporating it into the overall business plan. Hiring someone to review the financial section doesn't negate the need to understand financial tools well enough to make appropriate use of them and to explain their purpose to others (Association of Specialized and Cooperative Library Agencies, 2007). Most Small Business Development Centers are also available to review your efforts and help keep you on track.

RECORD KEEPING

Work to keep all financial statements as simple and uncomplicated as is appropriate to the service and its needs. Software applications can be extremely helpful in this regard. You will find numerous off-the-shelf software packages adaptable to the library's needs, but shop carefully and be sure your needs are met. There are many Web sites where you may download free business planning tools, calculators, forms for financial predictions, and expert advice in using those forms. Don't feel compelled to reinvent the wheel unless it's necessary.

As your service grows, it's best to use a comprehensive accounting program instead of relying on a simple spreadsheet application. An accounting program will integrate the balance sheet and income statement and will provide other reports such as a statement of cash flows, if needed. These programs also track sales on credit and integrate client accounts with the balance sheet. They capture client usage data that can be analyzed for service improvements, new service opportunities, and so on. You will not have to be concerned about overwriting a crucial formula or other piece of data. Your financial advisor should be able to help formulate a chart of accounts if required by your parent organization.

The option of hiring your own CPA may seem excessive, but it has solid merits:

- The depth of services will depend on the financial background of the librarians and the complexity of the library.
- If you have a financial background and some accounting experience to manage your three- to five-person library, you might need the CPA only for tax preparation.
- If you have a strong technical background but minimal financial experience, you might need the CPA to provide monthly financial statements.
- If you submit for outside financing, having CPA prepared statements is a definite advantage.

KEY POINTS TO INCLUDE

Your business plan's financial section begins with a summary overview: a brief review of the most important factors affecting the finances of your service. This requires only a few paragraphs, and should be designed to impart a good sense of the overall financial picture before moving on to a more thorough examination.

You have already created a description in an earlier chapter explaining what your service is and why it makes good sense for it to be supported. Use this information now to support the numbers in the financial statement. You can approach this from one of two directions:

1. To support a new service, look at the use or sales level required to be profitable. Express your capability to do the amount of work by describing how the market is available for you to capture and why clients will want to use your service to that extent. For those who want to apply financial terms, new services present financial information in a "pro forma," meaning the numbers are projections rather than historical.

2. To support an existing service, express your capabilities through historical figures gathered from financial statements. Historical figures help project future financial performance. An existing service presents financials as income statements and balance sheets with two years of operating history in the cash flow statement and the pro forma (from the initial stages of the service).

It is appropriate to use tables to present important data at a glance and to serve as reference points for your discussions. Standard tables are designed to highlight the key data (see, e.g., Table 9-1).

This information would be expanded (see Table 9-2) to be included in the appendix. However, as an introductory statement or as a portion of the executive summary, the brevity of the Table 9-1 is understood.

Table 9-1. Financial Summary Table				
Year ending 12/31 with $ rounded to nearest hundred	**Year Actual**	**Year Budget**	**Year Forecast**	**Year Forecast**
Income (or Revenue)	$	$	$	$
Gross Expenses				
Operating Surplus (Deficit)				
Percentage of Income (Revenue)	%	%	%	%
Cash Surplus (Deficit)				

Start at the beginning and work to the end of any financial statement asking, *Does it make sense to ask for support based on these figures?* Don't start at the end and work to the beginning asking, *How should this look so I can get their approval?* Try to be very critical and evaluate your service based on real information—not on what you want for support or funding. Never begin by establishing financial projections and then write a plan to suit them: your plan in this case becomes a financially driven document without a firm grounding in market research. The support or funding you receive is dependent on your proving that a market or a client group is interested enough in your service to actually use or pay for it.

As you have seen, simple tables are good ways to present key financial information or projections. Generally, budget estimates are needed to apply for outside funding or loans. Even if the business plan is going only to the library administration, estimates are still essential. Identifying a service's realistic chance of becoming cost-effective is important. For an in-house service, an estimate of what it will cost in annual expenses is needed. If the library expects the service to generate funds to support other organizational functions, an estimate is needed of when and the amount of the revenue streams can be expected to flow into the library (MacKintosh, 1999).

The financial section continues to align the service with the strategic objectives of the parent organization. It also clarifies the need for support for the growth of the service. A record of what it costs to operate your service (cost-accounting data) supports a broader range of decisions than just that of one service. "They are necessary if the institution is to run smoothly and efficiently. By knowing the cost of specific tasks or services, and comparing those costs with similar services offered by other institutions, the library can better judge what services should be offered, and whether or not those services should be provided internally or externally" (Poll, 2006: 7).

Review the example later in the chapter from the Digital Library Federation Aquifer Business Plan. This identifies project support, budget, capital requirements, and cash flow of a new project.

Table 9-2. Expanded Financial Summary Table				
Year ending 12/31	**Year Actual**	**Year Budget**	**Year Forecast**	**Year Forecast**
$ amount rounded to nearest hundred	$	$	$	$
Fees earned Grants				
Contributions				
Subsidies				
INCOME (or revenue) TOTAL				
EXPENSES				
Salaries and wages				
Payroll taxes and benefits				
Independent contractors				
Professional services				
Office supplies and miscellaneous				
Telephone and communications				
Rent				
Insurance				
Marketing and promotion				
Conferences				
Travel				
Databases				
Reference				
Web site hosting				
Server, network				
TOTAL EXPENSES				
OPERATING SURPLUS (deficit)				
% of Income (revenue)				

INCOME (PROFIT AND LOSS) STATEMENTS

This statement is completed by month for the first year and quarterly for the second and third years. It provides an overview of revenue, costs, and profits, which shows whether you are making a profit. This statement details how much money you will make after you have identified all expenses. It does not give a total picture of what your company is worth overall or of its cash position.

The income statement shows whether you have been making a profit or taking a loss for the past twelve months. It is a necessary feedback mechanism to help you keep this business plan on track. Take readings of this statement at frequent intervals. Compile it at the end of each month or the end of each quarter. The purpose is to let you have current useful information to assist in identifying trouble spots.

If appropriate for your library, specify unit costs for key items such as labor, payroll, power, communications, environmental services, etc. and forecast how these might change in the future due to inflation, currency rates, etc. Where relevant, forecast use, consumption, or utilization rates for these key items and use this to project the total costs For example, headcount multiplied by labor cost (rate) equals total labor cost (D'Angelo, 2004).

In this statement, include expenses related to delivery, mail, office supplies, equipment, materials, handouts, marketing, and accounting fees, as well as depreciation expenses of higher-cost items such as office furniture, computers, and filing cabinets. For examples of quarterly and annual income statements, see Tables 9-3 and 9-4.

Table 9-3. Income Statement—Quarterly					
Period/Quarter:	**Quarter 1**	**Quarter 2**	**Quarter 3**	**Quarter 4**	**Totals**
Sales					
Sales					$0.00
Other					$0.00
Total Sales	$0.00	$0.00	$0.00	$0.00	$0.00
Less Cost of Goods Sold					
Materials					$0.00
Labor					$0.00
Overhead					$0.00
Other					
Total Cost of Goods Sold	$0.00	$0.00	$0.00	$0.00	$0.00
Gross Profit	$0.00	$0.00	$0.00	$0.00	$0.00

(Cont'd.)

Table 9-3. Income Statement—Quarterly *(Continued)*					
Period/Quarter:	**Quarter 1**	**Quarter 2**	**Quarter 3**	**Quarter 4**	**Totals**
Operating Expenses					
Salaries and wages					$0.00
Employee benefits					$0.00
Payroll taxes					$0.00
Rent					$0.00
Utilities					$0.00
Licenses					
Repairs and maintenance					$0.00
Copyright					
Insurance					$0.00
Travel					$0.00
Telephone					$0.00
Photocopy					
Postage					$0.00
Office supplies					$0.00
Advertising/marketing					$0.00
Professional fees					$0.00
Training and development					$0.00
Bank charges					$0.00
Depreciation					$0.00
Miscellaneous					$0.00
Other					$0.00
Total Operating Expenses	$0.00	$0.00	$0.00	$0.00	$0.00
Operating Income	$0.00	$0.00	$0.00	$0.00	$0.00
Interest income (expense)					$0.00
Other income (expense)					$0.00
Total Nonoperating Income (Expense)	$0.00	$0.00	$0.00	$0.00	$0.00
Income (Loss) Before Taxes	0	0	0	0	0
Income Taxes					
Net Income (Loss)	0	0	0	0	0
Cumulative Net Income (Loss)	0	0	0	0	0

Table 9-4. Income Statement—12 Months

Period/Month:	Month 1	Month 2	Month 3	Month 4	Month 5	Month 6	Month 7	Month 8	Month 9	Month 10	Month 11	Month 12	Totals
Sales													
Sales													$0.00
Other													$0.00
Total Sales	$0.00	$0.00	$0.00	$0.00	$0.00	$0.00	$0.00	$0.00	$0.00	$0.00	$0.00	$0.00	$0.00
Less Cost of Goods Sold													
Materials													$0.00
Labor													$0.00
Overhead													$0.00
Other													$0.00
Total Cost of Goods Sold	$0.00	$0.00	$0.00	$0.00	$0.00	$0.00	$0.00	$0.00	$0.00	$0.00	$0.00	$0.00	$0.00
Gross Profit	$0.00	$0.00	$0.00	$0.00	$0.00	$0.00	$0.00	$0.00	$0.00	$0.00	$0.00	$0.00	$0.00
Operating Expenses													
Salaries and wages													$0.00
Employee benefits													$0.00
Payroll taxes													$0.00
Rent													$0.00
Utilities													
Licenses													$0.00
Repairs and maintenance													$0.00
Copyright													
Insurance													$0.00
Travel													$0.00
Telephone													$0.00
Photocopy													
Postage													$0.00
Office supplies													$0.00
Advertising/marketing													$0.00
Professional fees													$0.00
Training and development													$0.00
Bank charges													$0.00
Depreciation													$0.00

(Cont'd.)

Table 9-4. Income Statement—12 Months *(Continued)*													
Period/Month:	Month 1	Month 2	Month 3	Month 4	Month 5	Month 6	Month 7	Month 8	Month 9	Month 10	Month 11	Month 12	Totals
Miscellaneous													$0.00
Other													$0.00
Total Operating Expenses	$0.00	$0.00	$0.00	$0.00	$0.00	$0.00	$0.00	$0.00	$0.00	$0.00	$0.00	$0.00	$0.00
Operating Income	$0.00	$0.00	$0.00	$0.00	$0.00	$0.00	$0.00	$0.00	$0.00	$0.00	$0.00	$0.00	$0.00
Interest income (expense)													$0.00
Other income (expense)													$0.00
Total Nonoperating Income (Expense)	$0.00	$0.00	$0.00	$0.00	$0.00	$0.00	$0.00	$0.00	$0.00	$0.00	$0.00	$0.00	$0.00
Income (Loss) Before Taxes	0	0	0	0	0	0	0	0	0	0	0	0	0
Income Taxes													0
Net Income (Loss)	0	0	0	0	0	0	0	0	0	0	0	0	0
Cumulative Net Income (Loss)	0	0	0	0	0	0	0	0	0	0	0	0	0
Source: Entrepreneur.com (2007). Copyright © 2007 Entrepreneur.com; all rights reserved. Reprinted with permission from Entrepreneur.com.													

BALANCE SHEETS

A balance sheet shows how much the service is worth overall and lists the following:

- What the service owns
- Liabilities
- What the service is worth at the time the business plan is written

This is completed for a new service and annually for two years. At the very least, write monthly projections for the first year covered by the plan and quarterly (or annual) projections for the next 12 months. Include only high-level financial projections in summary tables. Use very simple tables or charts and place the details in appendices. The simplified balance sheet shown in Table 9-5 reflects a straightforward approach to identifying your financial situation.

Table 9-5. Sample Balance Sheet			
Name	**Balance Sheet**		**Date**
Assets			
Current Assets			
Cash	$0		
Prepaid Expenses	$0		
Total Current Assets		$0	
Fixed Assets			
Computers	$0		
Data	$0		
Furniture and Fixtures	$0		
Buildings	$0		
Land	$0		
Total Fixed Assets		$0	
Total Assets		$0	
Liabilities			
Current Liabilities			
Accounts Payable	$0		
Current Portion of Long-Term Debt	$0		
Total Current Liabilities		$0	
Long-Term Debt			
Total Liabilities		$0	
Equity (Net Worth)			
Capital	$0		
Retained Earnings (Loss)	$0		
Current Year Net Income	$0		
Total Equity		$0	
Total Liabilities and Equity		$0	
Source: Lamar (2007a).			

STATEMENTS (BASED ON PARENT ORGANIZATION'S REQUIREMENTS)

BREAK-EVEN ANALYSIS

Identify your income and balance all your resources against your expenses. Be prepared: this may be the point where you realize that the service is not viable or that it may need overhauling to become self-supporting.

Identify as specifically as possible the volume of usage or sales of your service necessary to cover costs and justify the service's existence. Completed annually for two years, the breakeven analysis describes and measures your growth in stages, showing the points at which sales will exceed costs and you begin to make a profit. This is very useful for internal planning and creating evaluation milestones.

CASH FLOW PROJECTION

The cash flow projection is an important financial statement identifying what the service is going to cost, how the income is received and distributed, and the net amounts accessible. There needs to be sufficient cash flow to support the business plan and to cover the cost of the service's existence. The cash flow projection shows if you have the cash to pay the bills. Completed by month for the first year and quarterly for the second and third years, this projection requires you to make decisions. For example, if you are estimating your usage or sales amounts, you will have to decide on a pricing and billing structure. Both of those entities will have more detailed costs of their own that you will now identify.

For each feature of the service, decide your actions and determine the specific, realistic, and tangible costs associated. As you go through the process of identifying how your money will flow, jot down your notes. These notes may assist by adding more detailed information to your earlier written description section: it is crucial your description supports the numbers expressed in the cash flow statement.

START-UP COSTS WORKSHEETS

Worksheets 9-1 ⊕ and 9-2 ⊕ will help you to compute your initial cash requirements for your business. They list the things you need to consider when determining your start-up costs and include both the one-time initial costs needed to open your doors and the ongoing costs you'll face each month for the first 90 days.

Worksheet 9-1. Start-Up Capital Requirements: One-Time Start-Up Expenses		
STARTUP EXPENSES	Amount	Description
Advertising		Promotion for opening the business
Starting inventory		Amount of inventory required to open
Building construction		Amount per contractor bid and other
Cash		Amount needed for the cash register
Credit		
Bookkeeping for Dept. Charges		
Decorating		Estimate based on bid if appropriate
Deposits		Check with utility companies
Fixtures and equipment		Use actual bids
Insurance		Bid from insurance agent
Lease payments		Fee to be paid before opening
Licenses and permits		Check with city, state offices, or copyright co.
Miscellaneous		All other
Professional fees		Include CPA, attorney, etc.
Remodeling		Use contractor bids
Rent		Fee to be paid before opening
Services		Cleaning, accounting, etc.
Signage		Use contractor bids
Supplies		Office, cleaning, etc. supplies
Unanticipated expenses		Include an amount for the unexpected
Other		
Other		
Other		
Total Startup Costs		AMOUNT OF COSTS BEFORE OPENING

Worksheet 9-2. Start-Up Capital Requirements: Repeating Monthly Expenses		
Expenses	**Amount**	**Description**
Advertising		
Bank service fees		
Credit card charges		
Delivery fees		
Dues and subscriptions		
Health insurance		Exclude amount on preceding page [Worksheet 9-1]
Insurance		Exclude amount on preceding page [Worksheet 9-1]
Interest		
Inventory		See **, below
Lease payments		Exclude amount on preceding page [Worksheet 9-1]
Loan payments		Principal and interest payments
Office expenses		
Payroll other than owner		
Payroll taxes		
Professional fees		
Rent		Exclude amount on preceding page [Worksheet 9-1]
Repairs and maintenance		
Sales tax		
Supplies		
Telephone		
Utilities		
Your salary		If applicable for first three months
Other		
TOTAL REPEATING COSTS		
TOTAL STARTUP COSTS		Amount from preceding page [Worksheet 9-1]
TOTAL CASH NEEDED		

* Include the first three months' cash needs unless otherwise noted.
**Include amount required for inventory expansion. Assume funding will generate enough cash for replacements.
Source: Entrepreneur.com (2007). Copyright © 2007 Entrepreneur.com; all rights reserved. Reprinted with permission from Entrepreneur.com.

START-UP BUDGET FOR NEW SERVICE WORKSHEET

Build a realistic budget by identifying the amount of money needed to start a new service (see Worksheet 9-3 ⓒⓓ). Note:

- This form has items already included, but you will want to alter it to suit your unique situation. For example, amounts and totals may be changed to actual and budgeted.
- Label entries to clearly identify those that are *one-time expenses or any that are not monthly.*
- Identify the anticipated calendar date when income will likely appear: in one month, within three to six months, or the number of months until a profit is expected to be generated.

Worksheet 9-3. Start-Up Budget Template						
Start-Up Budget				Amounts		Totals
Initial Expenses						
	Salaries					
	Consultants (One time or continuous?)					
	R&D (One time?)					
	Occupancy					
		Improvements (One time?)				
	Licenses					
	Equipment					
	Installation of Equipment					
	Accounting Services					
						(Cont'd.)

Worksheet 9-3. Start-Up Budget Template *(Continued)*						
	Advertising & Promotion for Opening					
		Logo Design *(One time?)*				
		Stationary				
		Handouts				
	Marketing					
	Decorating					
	Remodeling					
	Signage					
	Supplies					
	Printing					
	Moving					
Long-Term or Fixed Assets						
	Equipment					
	Furniture					
Total Assets						
Total Start-Up Costs						
Proposed Operating Capital to Break Even						

Source: Lamar (2007b).

OPERATING BUDGET WORKSHEET

Create an operating budget by identifying the amount of money needed to maintain the service. Worksheet 9-4 ⊙ has some items already included, but you will want to alter to suit your unique situation.

Worksheet 9-4. Operating Budget Template												
	J	F	M	A	M	J	J	A	S	O	N	D
Staff												
Insurance												
Rent												
Advertising												
Bookkeeping												
Supplies												
Salaries												
Utilities												
Depreciation (for profit only)												
Organization and Professional Dues												
Subscription												
Fees												
Taxes												
Maintenance												
Miscellaneous												

EXAMPLES OF FINANCIAL PLANS

Digital Library Federation (DLF) Aquifer Business Plan ⓒⒹ
Source: Kott, 2006, 9–10; © Digital Library Federation.

Project Support:
Overall project management is the responsibility of the Aquifer director. Most project activity will be distributed with various component projects managed by member libraries. Two additional full-time technical project staff will most likely need to be added centrally.

Administrative support for the DLF Aquifer initiative is provided through the DLF office. DLF resources consist of a program associate and an administrative associate. DLF Aquifer support is balanced and prioritized with other DLF administrative and program needs by the DLF executive director.

In the first phase, DLF Aquifer participant and DLF member libraries will contribute collections. Libraries are encouraged to view collection contributions to DLF Aquifer as permanent in nature. In future phases, specific targeted collections may be digitized to fill collection gaps and collections may be solicited from outside the DLF. Digitization projects may be part of an in-kind member library contribution or may be supported by grant funding. Models for procuring outside collections will be generated as the initiative develops.

DLF Aquifer technology solutions may be built or bought and integrated into DLF Aquifer. Open source solutions are preferred. Hardware will be housed at DLF Aquifer participant institutions or at other institutions, by contract on a fee for service basis. By mutual agreement between DLF and the service provider, fees may be waived. For example, discussions are underway with the University of Illinois, Urbana-Champaign, to host the collections registry as an outgrowth of their IMLS [Institute of Museum and Library Services] grant funded project. Mapping out specific locations of technology is not critical to successful implementation as long as adequate infrastructure to deliver services is present in the environment. Services will be available to users regardless of location.

Budget:
The separate draft budget spreadsheets show preliminary costs for four project phases. Each phase is estimated to be one year in duration. Phase I will begin in 2005 Q2. Costs are shown centrally, although work will actually be distributed. Project-oriented budgets will be developed as working groups get underway. Revenue is not shown. First-year revenue is assumed to be from DLF funds with possible supplemental grant funding.

Capital Requirements:
Capital equipment expenditures and initial staffing costs will be made from DLF capital funds. Most equipment needs will likely be met by in-kind contributions from participating libraries. As indicated in the support section above, service and equipment costs will be noted and in-kind contributions will be recorded as a transaction between the contributor and DLF.

Cash Flow:
Although some of the requirements of the initiative can be met through participant contributions, external funding will be needed to meet the goals of each project phase over a four-year period. It is realistic to expect that participants will contribute staff time to such

activities as developing functional specifications, setting standards, and identifying project tasks and managing workflow. The level of work that will be required in task areas such as collection analysis, data mapping, tools integration, and administrative support will require outside funding for the initiative to progress at a satisfactory rate. As outlined in the budget section, the project will require an infusion of cash.

Ontario Library Association
Cost Forecast and Funding Requirements
Source: reprinted courtesy of Ontario Library Association, the Ontario Digital Library Businesses Plan, Toronto.

7.1.2 Cost Forecast

Total costs over the 3-year plan are estimated to be $52.4 million, with over 90% attributable to ODL project activities, the true deliverables of the ODL.

Costs in Year 1 are approximately $11.4 million and grow to $23.2 million by Year 3. The main driver for the increase is the ramp up of the Content Project, with annual increases of $5.0 million. Costs over the 3-year plan are summarized in the following table.

Table 9-6. Ontario Library Association 3-Year Cost Forecast					
CDN $000s	**Year 1**	**Year 2**	**Year 3**	**3-Year Plan**	
Project Expenditures					
Content Project	5,100	10,102	15,104	30,307	57.8%
Memory Project	150	406	415	972	1.9%
Ask a Librarian Project	1,480	2,237	2,797	6,514	12.4%
Lifelong Learning Project	875	877	878	2,630	5.0%
One Place To Look Project	1,875	2,089	2,131	6,095	11.6%
Consumer Health Project	310	522	184	1,016	1.9%
Total Project Expenditures	**9,790**	**16,233**	**21,510**	**47,533**	**90.6%**
General and Administration Expenditures					
Salaries, Wages and Benefits	375	383	439	1,197	2.3%
Advocacy & Marketing Initiatives	220	225	230	675	1.3%
Portal Development, Management and Authentication	240	240	240	720	1.4%
Hardware and Telecommunications	100	100	100	300	0.6%
Professional Fees (incl. legal services)	100	100	100	300	0.6%
Committee Expenses	125	50	60	235	0.4%
					(Cont'd.)

Table 9-6. Ontario Library Association 3-Year Cost Forecast *(Continued)*					
CDN $000s	**Year 1**	**Year 2**	**Year 3**	**3-Year Plan**	
Education, Workshops & Training (incl. travel)	203	220	225	648	1.2%
Rent and Utilities	75	77	78	230	0.4%
Evaluation of ODL	—	—	75	75	0.1%
Other (contingency plus materials/supplies)	169	169	190	528	1.0%
Total General and Administration Expenditures	1,606	1,564	1,736	4,907	9.4%
Total Expenditures	11,397	17,797	23,246	52,440	100%
Sources of Funding					
Cash Contributions from Libraries	—	590	1,542	2,132	4%
In-Kind Donations from Libraries	3,682	4,680	5,261	13,623	26%
Province Funding	7,715	12,526	16,444	36,685	70%
Total Funding	11,397	17,797	23,246	52,440	100%

Projected expenditures beyond Year 3 will be determined during Years 2 and 3, once the ODL has been established and more focused and timely planning decisions can be made.

7.2 Funding Requirements

As indicated above, the ODL will need to generate $52.4 million in funding over the 3-year planning period to match the cost estimates.

7.2.1 Sources of Funding

Funding for the ODL will come from the following three sources:

- Cash contributions from the library community;
- In-kind contributions from the library community (such as professional library staff resources); and
- New provincial government funding.

Additional sources of funding may be identified as the ODL proceeds through the implementation phases, such as sponsorship and/or partnership opportunities. However, these sources of funding have not been considered for initial planning purposes.

Over the plan period the library community will contribute 30% of the funding requirements, in cash or in-kind contributions, with the remainder provided by new funding from the Province.

Sources of Funding Over 3-Year Plan

Cash Contributions from Libraries 4%
In-Kind Donations from Libraries 26%
Province Funding 70%

Annual contributions by the library community increase as a percentage of total contributions over the term, while Provincial contributions decrease, as outlined in the following:

	Year 1	Year 2	Year 3	Average Total
Library Funding	32%	30%	30%	30%
Provincial Funding	68%	70%	70%	70%
Total	100%	100%	100%	100%

7.2.2 Funding Forecast

The library contribution component (including cash and in-kind) will increase annually, on a dollar value basis, throughout the three-year plan. It is anticipated in future years libraries will increase their cash commitment to the ODL as libraries experience significant cost savings through economies of scale.

The remaining 70 percent of the ODL's funding needs over the first three years, provided on an annual basis, would come from the Province in the form of new additional funding. The Year 1 Provincial funding requirement of $7.7 million would be primarily used as "seed money," supporting the libraries' in-kind contributions to initially establish the ODL. The Year 2 and 3 Provincial funding requirement would be primarily to support the expansion of each of the projects, building on the initial products and services established in Year 1.

The Province's investment in the ODL represents an average annual investment of approximately $1 for every Ontario citizen. Tied in with a proven and tested funding model which has achieved savings of up to 50%, the ODL will make way for a better Ontario tomorrow.

For a different perspective, an overview description of the proposed application of funds is represented by the following example.

NHS London, formerly South East London Workforce Development Confederation ⓒⒹ
2006/07 Application of Funds
Source: South East London Workforce Development Confederation, 2006: 27–28; reprinted courtesy of NHS London, formerly South East London Workforce Development Confederation (SELWDC).

The Confederation's budgets are set in line with the resources received and the strategic themes within the business plan, which take account of national and sector workforce priorities. The strategic themes remain as agreed for 2005/06 and the proposed budgets for 2006/07 reflect this.

Table 9-7 shows the application of resources by strategic theme/budget heading in 2005/06 and 2006/07 based on notified/expected income levels.

93 percent of funds available are distributed directly to stakeholder organizations for the education and training of students/staff or allocated to improve recruitment and retention.

Table 9-7. NHS London Application of Resources		
Strategic theme/budget heading	2005/06 (Jan 06) in £'000	2006/07 (proposed) in £'000
Realizing the benefits of pay modernization	835	572
Improving retention	415	283
Building the workforce capacity	236	340
Working differently, promoting new ways of working	263	742
Promoting careers and supporting recruitment initiatives	700	801
To deliver education and training to support the career framework	4,238	1,673
To develop learning infrastructure	514	343
WDC establishment costs	2,761	2,699
NMET	54,757	57,745
SIFT	67,274	68,999
MADEL	64,126	65,717
Reserves	7,838	100
Total	203,957	200,015

George Eliot NHS Trust 2007
Source: Brook, 2007: 7); reprinted courtesy of Nigel Brook, Library Services Manager, William Harvey Library, George Eliot Hospital NHS Trust.

Funding

Currently, staffing costs and library services to doctors are funded through MADEL [Medical and Dental Education Levy]. North Warwickshire PCT [Primary Care Trust] provides funding for library services for their users and George Eliot Hospital NHS Trust provides funding for Nursing, Midwifery, and Allied-Health staff in the hospital. SIFT [service increment for teaching] funding is available for resources for medical students.

Recurrent funding has always been based on the previous year's allocation, with a 2.5 percent increase in MADEL funding each year but *no increase in the Trust's contribution to revenue budgets*. As a result, the budget cannot fully meet users' demands for new library resources. Annual increase in the cost of print and online journal publications coupled with rising book prices has meant that more of the available funding is required to maintain a position of status quo, with little left for forward planning.

The Library service has introduced the Blanket ILL charge to offset costs in this area, and will be looking at the development of e-learning product and Web services as a possible means of generated income in support of our Business Aims.

In 2005, SIFT supported a bid by the Library to upgrade the part-time Senior Library Assistant post to a full-time position. Funding for this was provided on a recurrent basis by the Trust.

The Library service will continue to work to attract additional funding for its resources and services, as well as further investment in resource-sharing across the region to maximize cost-efficiency.

Halifax Regional Municipality
Operating Budget Changes
Source: Halifax Public Libraries, 2006: 4–5; reprinted courtesy of Halifax Public Libraries.

Table 9-8. Halifax Public Libraries Analysis of Operating Budget Changes

Operating Budget Change Details	($000s)
2005/06 Budget	**$16,409,400**
1. Salary and benefits increase as a result of approved collective agreement with NSUPE local 14.	$454,500
2. Utilities increases in (propane, heating, fuel, electricity)	$40,500
3. Contracted out janitorial cleaning services at Halifax North (upon retirement)	($5,500)
4. Minor increases and decreases in various accounts based on actuals	$8,800
5. Increase in building maintenance costs for various branches	$8,600
6. Increase in leasing costs for Musquodoboit Harbour Library due to HRM	$20,700
7. Increase in leasing costs for various other facilities (Bedford, Tantallon, and Glendale offices)	$18,000
8. Increase in municipal taxes	$4,100
9. Manager in systems and technical services eliminated and replaced with lower level staffing	($15,138)
10. Savings from various staffing changes; employees hired at different steps than originally budgeted	($36,559)
11. Additional staffing of 0.92 FTE added to Keshen Goodman Library to deal with occupational health and safety issues	$23,811
12. Additional staffing of 2.5 FTEs in youth services to deal with Library Youth Services Strategy and in support of the Council Focus Area on Youth	$123,251
13. Elimination of mail notification service for late materials (postage, mailers, and staffing)	($31,865)
14. Elimination of Word on the Street promotion	($2,000)
15. Reduction in bindery service	($10,000)
16. Reduce office supplies	($10,000)
17. Cancel implementation of federated searching for the enhanced catalog	($14,800)
18. Musquodoboit Harbour Library lease transferred to Fiscal Services	($46,383)
2006/07 Gross Operating Budget	**$16,939,517**
	(Cont'd.)

Table 9-8. Halifax Public Libraries Analysis of Operating Budget Changes *(Continued)*	
Operating Budget Change Details	**($000s)**
2005/06 Revenue Operating Budget	**($3,716,400)**
1. Provincial grants increase to base budget	($255,500)
2. Provincial grant increase ONE time only increase	($313,200)
3. Increase in library fines and fees based on projected actuals by branch	($90,000)
4. Increase in meeting rooms rental rate charges	($6,000)
5. Decrease in photocopier fees based on projected actuals by branch	$3,200
6. Increase in miscellaneous revenues based on actuals	($7,200)
2006/07 Revenue Operating Budget	**($4,385,100)**
2006/07 Net Operating Budget	**$12,554,317**

Service Level Changes for 2006/07:

Increases:

- Additional staffing of 2.5 FTEs [full-time employees] dedicated to implementation of Library Youth Strategy Initiatives
- Additional staffing of .92 FTEs at Keshen Goodman Library to address health and safety issues (congestion caused by stacking bins of materials awaiting to return to the shelf) and improve turnaround time for returning books to the shelf for the public to borrow
- Implementation of e-mail notification for overdue materials and holds for those with e-mail addresses

Decreases:

- Reduction in staff hours in some positions
- Cancelled implementation of the federated searching service, which would have enhanced public access to online journal databases
- Unable to take advantage of summer youth employment program grants where matching dollars are required
- Reduction of bindery service
- Elimination of mail notification service for overdue materials
- Elimination of Word on the Street promotion

REFERENCES

Association of Specialized and Cooperative Library Agencies. "Surviving and Thriving: Your Business Plan." (April 24, 2007). Chicago: American Library Association. Available: www.ala.org/ala/ascla/asclapubs/surviving/yourbusinessplan/yourbusiness.cfm.

Brook, Nigel. 2007. "Library Services: Business Strategy and Business Plan 2007–2010." Warwickshire, UK: William Harvey Library, George Eliot Hospital NHS Trust.

D'Angelo, E. 2004. "Barbarians at the Gate." (Self published: Posted March 8). Available: www.webjunction.org/do/DisplayContent;jsessionid=0E37122EFC658F 25B37F3D28BA99C4C9?id=8563.

Entrepreneur.com. 2007. "Startup Capital Requirements—Repeating Monthly Expenses." Irvine, CA: Entrepreneur Media Inc. 2007. Available: www.entrepreneur.com/ contact-us/index.html.

Halifax Public Libraries. 2006. "Halifax Public Libraries Business Plan 2006–2007." Halifax, NS: Halifax Public Libraries.

Kott, Katherine. 2006. "DLF Aquifer Business Plan 2006." (May 25). Washington, DC: Digital Library Federation. Available: www.diglib.org/aquifer/AquiferBusiness Plan.pdf.

Lamar, Brad. 2007a. "Balance Sheet." Midland, TX: Western National Bank.

Lamar, Brad. 2007b. "Start-Up Budget for New Service Worksheet." Midland, TX: Western National Bank.

MacKintosh, Pamela J. 1999. "Writing an Effective Business Plan for Fee-Based Services." *Journal of Interlibrary Loan, Document Delivery and Information Supply*, 10, no. 1: 47–61.

Ontario Digital Library. 2003. "The Ontario Digital Library Business Plan: Connecting Ontarians." Guelph, ON: Ontario Digital Library. Available: www.accessola2.com/odl/pdf/ODL_BusinessPlan_Full.pdf.

Poll, Roswitha. 2006. "To Get One's Money's Worth: Library Management with Cost Data." *Bottom Line: Managing Library Finances*, 19, no. 1: 7–15.

South East London Workforce Development Confederation (SELWDC). 2006. "Business Plan 2006/07." London: SELWDC. Available: www.selwdc.nhs.uk/document_view .php?PID=0000000036&DID=00000000000000000219.

10 WRITING AN EXECUTIVE SUMMARY AND COMMUNICATING THE PLAN

Taken together, the materials described in the preceding chapters will provide you with a complete business plan. But in order to derive the greatest possible benefit from your plan, you will need to communicate its contents and conclusions in an effective, easily comprehended manner. This concluding chapter looks at specific ways to summarize and communicate your plan to your library's greatest advantage.

EXECUTIVE SUMMARY

BASIC DEFINITIONS

Even though the executive summary of the plan is physically the first section, it is completed last, after thoroughly reviewing the entire business plan. Readers may read only this section, so limit it to the main points only. As an overview of the service focusing on the fundamentals of the plan, this section outlines the general service offered, its significance and relevance, key success factors, and intended outcomes. In presenting the highlights, key facts, and opinions of the plan, this is the section that sells the service; it convinces the reader you have a sound execution strategy and realistic tactics. This section is the business plan in miniature, perhaps two to six pages of bottom-line information.

KEY POINTS TO INCLUDE

This section provides the best opportunity to make the strongest, most persuasive case. The summary has to be brief and to the point, presenting the facts concisely and persuasively, since readers may not give as much attention to the other sections. Focus here on matters of strategic importance; the details will be shown in the plan's appendices. Core elements to include in your summary are:

- High-level realistic financial projections
- Why the service will succeed, why it is compelling, and what problem(s) it solves

- Why the reader would want to invest time, support, resources, or finances

The key questions you will answer are:

- Do you have the right (best) people in place?
- Can you build or deliver it? Will it fly?
- How much will it cost to build your service?

You will focus on showing how solid your staff is, how exceptional your service is, and how huge or important the markets are that you're going after and how you'll capture them. Define your current and potential competitors in honest, realistic terms. Reduce the fear of risk and increase the idea of growth (Comaford-Lynch, 2007: 21).

WRITING AN EXECUTIVE SUMMARY

- Start the executive summary on a new page
- Give this section plenty of thought and give yourself plenty of time to write
- Do not include any material here that is not covered elsewhere in the plan
- Double-check spelling and grammar with and without software spell-check; typographical errors are the kiss of death in any plan
- Think about the words you're using; aim for succinct, affirmative statements and make every noun, adjective, and verb important and justified
- Write in the present tense and keep the length short
- Place all technical terms and detailed material in the appendices; the reader can go there for additional information
- Introduce all acronyms; better yet, don't use acronyms or jargon
- Avoid the use of personal pronouns
- Keep the style consistent; your writing style should allow the plan to be easily and concisely explainable in an oral presentation
- When you have completed a draft, ask an outside expert to review the plan and be prepared to listen to opinions, suggestions, and feedback

- Alter your language to fit the readership situation, if necessary
- Revise, refine, review, edit, edit, and edit
- Ask others for feedback

Because each business plan is quite different, creating a template for an executive summary is difficult. Generally speaking, yours may follow the pattern in Worksheet 10-1 ⓒⓓ.

Worksheet 10-1. Executive Summary Template
What is the overview of the opportunity available; what is this business plan primarily about?
Summarize your management team.
What is your purpose, intent, plan? What are the products or services proposed?
What do you offer? How do you know it will be successful? What's your advantage?
By what means will this plan be supported? How much will it cost?

(Cont'd.)

Worksheet 10-1. Executive Summary Template *(Continued)*
What is the current state of the environment? Why is "do nothing" not a better option?
What are the key risks and how will you overcome them? What are the core findings you need to share?
Use this space to rewrite your executive summary:

EXAMPLES OF EXECUTIVE SUMMARIES

EPA's Regional Libraries and Centers ⓒⒹ
Source: U.S. Environmental Protection Agency, 2004: 1.

Executive Summary

The Environmental Protection Agency's network of regional libraries and environmental center libraries provides substantial value to the Agency, its professional staff, stakeholders, and the public. Calculated conservatively, the benefit-to-cost ratio for EPA library services ranges between 2:1 and 5.7:1. Libraries and librarians are nonetheless a significant investment, costing the Agency roughly $6.2 million annually to operate and maintain. It is an opportune time to initiate an Agency-wide dialogue on the extent and nature of library services at the Environmental Protection Agency.

Digital Library Federation (DLF) Aquifer Business Plan ⓒᴅ
Source: Kott, 2006: 3; © Digital Library Federation, 2006.

Executive Summary

Business Concept:

DLF Aquifer is an initiative of the Digital Library Federation. Envisioned as a means of leveraging digital library content, DLF Aquifer will create scalable solutions to enable teaching, learning, and scholarship. Beginning with a significant, well-bounded collection of digital content in the area of American culture and life, DLF Aquifer will create a test bed of tools for selecting, collecting, and providing access to quality digital content. Grounded in the thinking that libraries add value through the organization of information, DLF Aquifer offers opportunities for collaboration among libraries and with partners building repositories, content management systems, course management systems, and other solutions that support the scholarly process. Future broader scale collaborations can be modeled on the DLF Aquifer experience.

Financial Features:

DLF Aquifer is supported by the Digital Library Federation, a membership organization, through contributions from DLF capital funds and by grant funding. DLF Aquifer will not generate revenue with service charges in the first phase but may develop fee-for-service models during the course of the initiative.

Financial Requirements:

Development of collections, tools, and services will require systems resources and staff. Potential sources of revenue are DLF capital funds, DLF operational funds, grant funds, and contributions by DLF Aquifer participant libraries and others. DLF members are already investing heavily in the project with DLF capital funds.

Current State:

DLF Aquifer is in the project planning and prototype stage.

Principals:

The DLF Aquifer director leads the initiative and reports to the president of the Digital Library Federation board of trustees.

Major Digital Library Federation Achievements Underpinning Aquifer:

Promulgation of Open Archives Initiative (OAI) metadata standards and best practices, collection registry support, user evaluation, and tools registry development have laid the groundwork for the DLF Aquifer initiative

Maroochy Shire Libraries, Maroochy Shire Council ⓒᴅ
Source: Maroochy Shire Council, 2006: 2; reprinted courtesy of Maroochy Libraries, Maroochy Shire Council.

Executive Summary

To assist in developing a strategic approach to the delivery of library services in Maroochy Shire, the Council has undertaken a review of its Library Service. This report is based on three key premises.

1. That Council is in a budget constrained environment and that operational funding for improvements to the library service will need to be found largely from within the existing library budget.

2. That Council already has a well-established asset in libraries and collections in the community, which is clearly highly valued by users and nonusers alike. There is a clear need to maintain and develop this asset.

3. There are significant opportunities to build on the social capital and information infrastructure already established to provide better learning and community outcomes through innovative service delivery and strategic partnerships within and beyond the Shire.

This report provides options for the development and maximization of Council's library asset and explores opportunities to consider some alternative mechanisms for service delivery. The conduct of the development of the strategy involved an iterative process that can be summarized into the following main phases:

- Environmental Scan: Review of existing policy and planning frameworks, demographic trends, Best Practice models, and library trend data, including research on the economic and social value of libraries.
- Market Research and Consultation Program: Conducting user and nonuser surveys, staff and stakeholder interviews, direct market research, and staff and community workshops.
- Process Analysis: Assessment of opportunities for refinement of processes to gain labor savings.
- Needs Analysis: Identification of service gaps within the current delivery model and identification of the strategic directions to inform future service planning and delivery decisions.
- Development of the Service Delivery Model and Funding Strategy

Calgary Public Library
Source: Calgary Public Library, 2006; © Calgary Public Library, All Rights Reserved, 2006–2008.

The Calgary Public Library is pleased to present its Business Plan for 2006 to 2008, "Building Community, Building Capacity."

Building on previous successes, the Business Plan is based on a thorough analysis of the changing environment which the Calgary Public Library will operate in during this period, and the challenges which may arise.

This plan is designed to convert these challenges into opportunities. Three key areas of strategic focus have been identified:

- Increasing awareness, visibility, and value of library services
- Extending the Library's reach into the community served
- Building organizational capacity to ensure continuing future success

The Business Plan also contains updated statements of vision, mission, and values, as well as specific action plans in support of each strategic focus area.

Highlights of the action plans include:

- Introduction of community consultation strategy
- New programs and services for Calgarians at risk

- Implementation of new Master Plans for library collections and facilities
- New customer service and convenience features through technology
- Strategies to ensure the effective management of information technology infrastructure and human and financial resources
- Building staff capacity and increasing depth in key operating areas

The actions outlined in this Business Plan will increase awareness, visibility, and value of library services, programs, and collections. It will help extend the Library's reach into the communities we serve and build the organizational capacity required to sustain the delivery of excellent public library service to Calgarians into the future.

Port Stephens Library
Source: Port Stephens Library, 2004: 23; reprinted with thanks and acknowledgment to Port Stephens Library, NSW, Australia.

Business Plan Summary
- We will provide a customer-focused public library service to the community of Port Stephens through proactive management of resources and partnerships.
- We will be responsive to community learning and development needs through equitable access to information, recreation, and technology resources.
- We will provide facilities that recognize community needs for meeting spaces and social interaction.
- We will stimulate community creativity and connectedness through opportunities for cultural appreciation and programs that educate and entertain.

Unit/Division Association for Library Collections & Technical Services (ALCTS) ⓒⅅ
Source: Association for Library Collections & Technical Services, 2001: 1; reprinted courtesy of Association for Library Collections & Technical Services (ALCTS).

1.1 Objectives of Plan

The plan is intended as a guide: to help take the message of ALCTS to members of the library community who create, collect, organize, and preserve all types of information; to continue to evaluate ALCTS' present products and services to meet a changing library and information landscape; and to provide a framework from which current and future ALCTS members can draw in developing member related activities.

1.2 Mission

- ALCTS' mission statement is appropriate to state here. Although not specifically aimed for a membership business plan document, it does outline ALCTS in a very succinct way.
- "ALCTS provides leadership to the library and information communities in developing principles, standards, and best practices for creating, collecting, organizing, delivering, and preserving information

resources in all forms. It provides this leadership through its members by fostering educational, research, and professional service opportunities. ALCTS is committed to quality information, universal access, collaboration, and lifelong learning."

1.3 Keys to Success

The keys to success for ALCTS are:

- attracting and maintaining the traditional ALCTS member, librarians working in ALCTS areas;
- identifying a pool of potential members including but not limited to library support staff, those working in nontraditional information positions, students, and vendors, then attracting them to ALCTS;
- providing high-quality products and services, not only those that ALCTS has traditionally provided, but also new ones to meet a changing membership;
- strengthening and then emphasizing the role of ALCTS in continuing education for both members and the library community at large;
- "branding" ALCTS as THE authority in the fields of technical services, including cataloging and classification, acquisitions, collection management, and development, serials, and preservation and reformatting;
- maintaining a high visibility in the development of standards, policies, and procedures in technical services and related fields for the library community, nationally and internationally;
- ALA [American Library Association] support and advocacy in areas represented by ALCTS;
- Cooperating with other ALA units and other national and international library groups on common interests and endeavors.

Franklin Templeton Global Research Library
Source: Brigevich, 2004; reprinted courtesy of Franklin Templeton Global Research Library.

Library Services: Summary

- Global initiatives to leverage organizational resources, especially those in the United States, to achieve superior investment performance and effectively compete on a global scale.
- Manage information overload to filter and distribute needed information in an actionable format; accomplished through library professionals with information organization and searching expertise.
- Demonstrable increase in investment professionals' efficiency and productivity through better information solutions and value-added information services.
- Professionally managed resources and services meet the increasing information demand across business units and geographic locations worldwide.
- A focus on in-house original research from various sources (independent research, academic sources, and government materials) fulfills a

strong need for ensuring a level of quality information no longer available from Wall Street.

- Duplication of effort and cost reduced across the organization.
- An increase in awareness of the availability and use of external research systems and information sources results in higher return on investment.
- Faster integration of acquired companies into Franklin Templeton family resulting from availability of knowledge management.

The Ontario Digital Library
Source: Ontario Digital Library, 2003: 1–8; reprinted courtesy of Ontario Library Association, the Ontario Digital Library Business Plan, Toronto.

1 EXECUTIVE SUMMARY

The Transformation of the Information Economy

Ontario citizens need current, accurate, and high-quality information to support them throughout their lives—as they learn to read, move through the education system, develop professional and job-related skills, and look for consumer, leisure, and health care information. While the Internet has opened a vast world of information and data, much of the most valuable information, which comes at a high cost, remains available to only a few.

Public, school, university, and college libraries have always played a key role in providing the information that Ontario citizens need. In the past, much of this information has been in print form. However, technology now allows Ontario libraries to provide information and services to users whether they are in the library building, in a neighboring city or town, or in an isolated or remote location hundreds of kilometers away.

The change in the way that information is being delivered and the way Ontarians use that information to learn, improve, and compete globally necessitates a *transformation* in the way that Ontarians seek, find, and evaluate the information they need. Libraries, schools, and academic institutions must partner together to play a central role in this *transformation* to an information literate society, making content, training, and services available, making access across Ontario more equitable, and supporting the education, research, and government sectors.

Ontario Information Transformation Challenges

In Ontario, libraries spend up to $150 million each year to purchase resources for their users (including such diverse materials as picture books, current fiction, news magazines, audiovisual kits, and scholarly journals). While the estimated 6,500 individual libraries spend these funds wisely within their own mandates, they have no mechanism currently in place to coordinate how the money is spent in order to take advantage of economies of scale or to develop services that could be offered to all Ontarians. Large libraries have the ability to purchase expensive and valuable electronic information products while small libraries, particularly those in the public and school communities, have minimal budgets and resources to purchase and provide access to similar products.

Furthermore, all libraries in Ontario have been hampered in their provision of services and collections to Ontarians since the mid-1990s with continued funding rollbacks and restraints and increased costs. Ontario school libraries are in particular danger with many downsized or eliminated completely. Unfortunately this comes at a time when students, workers, professionals, business people, health care workers, and citizens have increased expectations about the information they need to be informed, competitive, literate, and well-educated. Ontarians increasingly expect, and need, access to all of the information that is available for them to make day-to-day decisions and life/career choices.

Cooperation is very strong among libraries within the college sector and within the university sector. Within each sector, libraries have worked together on a large number of projects that have resulted in a greater equality of resources and services being available to students across the Province. The same level of cooperation has not been possible among public and school libraries, although the results of some current cooperative projects indicate that working together could have significant benefits for Ontarians. Even though libraries often serve overlapping constituencies, cooperation between the sectors has been hampered by different mandates and focus and different funding mechanisms.

Without the needed coordination in the purchase of products and services, the Government of Ontario (the "Province") and libraries have paid a premium, being unable to realize the economies of scale and to develop the needed strength in the marketplace that could be realized by working together to purchase Province-wide licenses and virtual services. Libraries need to find a way to create a strong voice and a mechanism to meet the challenges in today's information economy and to work more effectively together. The Ontario Digital Library (the "ODL") is that vehicle.

The Ontario Digital Library: Ontario's Solution

The ODL will coordinate the purchase and delivery of electronic information and virtual services on behalf of all Ontarians and Ontario libraries. It is a partnership among Ontario's libraries and academic and educational institutions working with the training, business, and health care communities with the assistance of all levels of government. The services provided will assist Ontarians at all ages to learn about, find, and locate the information they need. The ODL will transform how libraries in the Province interact with one another and with those who use their collections and services.

With the development of the ODL as a means to encourage cooperation, to share resources, and to provide Province-wide information services, there will be enhanced provincial buying power that will provide appropriate and needed resources and services for Ontarians to learn, be competitive, and drive economic performance and development.

Without the ODL, the digital divide will become a chasm, creating have and have-not students, educators, and information-seekers and resulting in lost global competitiveness, long-term deterioration of Ontario's education system, and an inefficient use of public funds. The Province and libraries across Ontario have a unique opportunity to narrow the gap of these inequities and to be on the leading edge in the development of digital tools that will give all Ontarians the resources they need to thrive in an information economy. Through strong financial support for the ODL, Ontario will become a leader in research, education, and community economic development and will transform how Ontarians learn, grow, conduct their business, and interact with one another.

The ODL will support Ontarians as they move through their lives, from cradle to grave. Children in Ontario will first use the ODL through their local public or school library Web site, finding resources that provide graphics and audio about Ontario's history, its people, and its wildlife. A librarian will be as close as an e-mail to help them find the information they need at any time of the day or night.

As children move into the upper grades, this information and assistance will help them gather background on their projects, giving them accurate, quality, and interesting information about their local community and its pioneer families. While at college or university students will access the ODL through their university or college library Web site in support of their assignments and research work.

After graduating they will use the ODL through their public library Web site to upgrade their job skills, seek information on business competitors, and find out more about exporting the products they produce and services they provide.

As they move through life stages, through child-rearing, home purchasing, volunteer work, and caring for their parents, they will use the ODL and its services through the public library to inform their decision-making and find out about valuable government services and activities and local and provincial resources that will support their needs.

The core objective of the ODL is to enhance information access for all citizens by strengthening local Ontario libraries. Through the collaborative framework of the ODL, users of their local library (be it the public library or the libraries at their school, college, or university) will experience a greater array of services and resources. The ODL is not a new library. The ODL is a way for existing libraries to become more effective both individually and collectively.

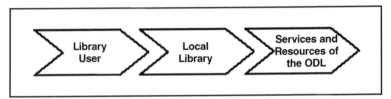

Why the ODL Is the Right Solution

(i) Proven Approach in Other Jurisdictions

Other provinces and numerous U.S. states have successfully met the information needs of their citizens by providing a coordinated approach to the purchase and delivery of digital information and services. Key to the success of these initiatives has been leadership from state and provincial governments working in partnership with the library, education, academic, health care, and business communities. Best examples include digital library programs in Georgia, Michigan, Colorado, and Ohio. The ODL solution is tried, tested, and proven. Similar to other province and state-wide digital library initiatives, the ODL will provide support to Ontario citizens through:

- Enhanced access to electronic information, interactive tools, graphics, and e-Learning materials (the "Content Project")
- Providing a gateway to local memory and heritage products (the "Memory Project")
- Providing reference and assistance services staffed by professionals, 24 hours a day, 7 days a week, throughout Ontario (the "Ask a Librarian Project")
- Developing state-of-the art searching and locating tools (the "One Place to Look Project")
- Collaboration among the library, education, and training sectors, and the business and health care communities (the "Lifelong Learning Project" and the "Consumer Health Project")

Products and services will be delivered seamlessly through local library, school, college, or university Web site, moving with Ontarians throughout their lives.

(ii) The ODL Vision is Strongly Supported by the Ontario Library Community

The ODL is a collaborative effort addressing the concerns and visions of the Ontario library community. The following library communities have played an integral role in the development of the ODL:

- Public libraries
- University libraries
- College libraries
- School (K–12) libraries

One group that has not participated as yet in the plan is the special libraries: "Special Libraries come in many flavors. They can be specialized collections in the not-for-profit sector like associations, charities, hospitals, research institutes, government, etc. Due to their small size they often do not have the buying power to acquire access to the resources they need to succeed. The ODL, when fully formed, creates the framework for these important research entities to participate as partners so as to offer good service and provide better research to their own clientele. In the long run, for-profit libraries (such as law, consulting, finance, corporations, etc.) could also benefit from a workforce that is more information and research literate as well as from the economic advantages of an Ontario as a learning and knowledge economy. There are thousands of special libraries in Ontario serving the specialized needs of researchers" (Stephen Abram, MLS, Special Libraries Association).

This large cross section of the library community and its leaders believe that significant cost avoidance can be realized through an effective consortia partnership and Province-wide collaboration in the purchasing of electronic content and services and are willing to commit people and resources to the project. However, this can be accomplished only with an infusion of new funding to leverage cooperation and realize this new business model. Libraries are already straining to meet the needs of their users with existing budgets. The transformative vision enabled by the ODL is possible only if Ontario's libraries are assisted with both transitional and sustaining funds to build and maintain the powerful Province-wide library cooperation that is the foundation of the ODL.

(iii) The ODL Fully Achieves the Province's Stated Objectives

The ODL can be a catalyst to achieving the Province's objectives and priorities related to e-Learning, lifelong learning, professional development, upgrading job skills, and training, as well as to reducing the "digital divide" among the population by helping to create an educated, informed, and "digitally aware" population. As an example, the ODL:

- Supports the Ontario e-Learning strategy by providing a single point of contact interface to the resources of Ontario's libraries
- Provides improved access and flexibility for learners at all ages and stages in their education, thereby supporting the Province's lifelong learning strategy
- Increases the ability of the Province to distribute information to citizens and to support their education, career, and community objectives
- Addresses emerging job skill shortages and facilitates school-to-work and job-to-job transitions through upgrading skills with the necessary information and knowledge supports and tools
- Supports business development growth and opportunities in Ontario
- Provides digital and electronic services to smaller, remoter, rural, and First Nations libraries that do not possess a high level of in-house technological expertise

Planned Milestones and Achievements

The ODL has developed an ambitious but achievable three-year business plan to develop its products and services. The human resources, technological, and governance foundations for the ODL will be built in these years, allowing it to coordinate access to and create important products and services that will gain momentum and importance over time. The ODL will provide its products and services in both English and in French and will make every effort to meet the needs of those speaking other languages and in need of specialized services. Initial projects will focus on the:

- Access to digital and electronic content
- Creation of an Ontario memory/history portal
- Development of a Province-wide virtual "Ask a Librarian" reference desk similar to Telehealth
- Training for Ontarians in the development of critical analysis and life-long learning skills
- Development of a unique provincial access gateway (One Place to Look) accessible only through local libraries

Overriding all of the service and product projects will be advocacy and marketing campaigns, which will be directed by the ODL Board of Directors (the "Board") with the support of all library sectors. A summary of the intended achievements at the end of each year of the business plan include:

Year One

- The members of the Board, Steering Committee, and Project Committees will be named, the Chief Executive Officer ("CEO") hired, the initial projects will be chosen, decisions made about how long the services and products will be offered, and early marketing efforts will begin.
- A Province-wide virtual reference service will begin to operate, electronic text and files will be made accessible to everyone in Ontario, the launch of a virtual Librarian via real-time electronic communication, and a gateway will be launched to help Ontarians to locate historical digital collections from libraries, museums, and archives throughout the Province.

Year Two

- The initial products and services will be expanded, building on the identified needs and work done in the first year. Additional partnerships will be sought.
- Students will see more resources to support their curriculum, additional content will be made available to all Ontarians and an easy-to-use gateway will be launched to help them access credible, reliable information.

Year Three

- An evaluation will take place of the work completed to date. A marketing campaign will focus on citizens and students.
- Electronic and digital content will continue to expand the ODL, along with the development and launch of a Province-wide infrastructure and portal that will support and train Ontarians in developing critical analytical skills for using and accessing information.

Financial Highlights and Funding Requirements

The principles for establishing the ODL have been based on a phased approach focused on developing the necessary foundation for the ODL and building on this foundation on a pragmatic basis over time. This phased approach is predicated on the prudent management of costs and funding, ensuring that all expenditures are incurred effectively, as and when required, and that the funding requirements properly match the expenditure needs and timing. Outlined below [see Table 10-1] is a summary of planned expenditures over the first three years of the ODL's operations.

Table 10-1. ODL Planned Expenditures			
Total Expenditures ($000s)	**Year 1**	**Year 2**	**Year 3**
Project Expenditures			
Content Project	5,100	10,102	15,104
Memory Project	150	406	415
Ask a Librarian Project	1,480	2,237	2,797
Life-Long Learning Project	875	877	878
One Place to Look Project	1,875	2,089	2,131
Consumer Health Project	310	522	184
Total Project Expenditures	**9,790**	**16,233**	**21,510**
Total General and Administration Expenses	**1,606**	**1,564**	**1,736**
Total Expenditures	**11,397**	**17,797**	**23,246**

In Year 1, projected expenditures total $11.4 million, and are primarily focused around the establishment of core products and services along with the human resources, technological, and governance foundations for the ODL. As products and services are expanded in Years 2 and 3, expenditures will increase accordingly. Over 90 percent of the ODL's expenditures are focused on project activities, the true deliverables of the ODL. Projected expenditures beyond Year 3 will be determined during Years 2 and 3, once the ODL has been established and more focused and timely planning decisions can be made. The ODL's operations will be funded by both the library community and the Province, as outlined below [see Table 10-2].

Table 10-2. ODL Funding Sources				
Total Funding ($000s)	**Year 1**	**Year 2**	**Year 3**	**% Total**
Library Communities	3,682	5,271	6,802	30%
Province	7,715	12,526	16,444	70%
Total	11,397	17,797	23,246	100%

Over the first three years, 30 percent of the total funding will be provided by the library community through cash and in-kind contributions. The remaining 70 percent of the ODL's funding needs over the first three years, provided on an annual basis, would come from the Province in new funding. This includes the initial "seed" funding in Year 1 to help establish the ODL. The Province's investment in the ODL under this funding model represents an average annual investment of approximately $1 for every Ontario citizen. The funding model proposed for the ODL is based on other tested and proven models that have resulted in savings of up to 50 percent. A savings that will result in a better Ontario tomorrow.

North and East Yorkshire and Northern Lincolnshire (NEYNL)
Source: North and East Yorkshire and Northern Lincolnshire Workforce Development Confederation, 2004: 19; reprinted courtesy of North and East Yorkshire and Northern Lincolnshire (NEYNL).

Summary of the Project Brief

Context:

The Strategic Health Authority (SHA) is the Headquarters of the NHS for North East Yorkshire and Northern Lincolnshire and is responsible for the performance of the 14 autonomous NHS Trusts that provide health care services across primary and acute care.

One of the responsibilities of SHAs is to enable these service delivery organizations to develop adequate capacity and capability to meet the health needs of the population. This involves developing new models of care, understanding the changing roles and needs of the workforce within these, and ensuring that programs of recruitment, retention, education, and development are in place to deliver this capacity and capability. It is important that the SHA creates a high-performance environment within which all 14 organizations are fully empowered and enabled to develop to their full potential.

The Knowledge Information and Library Services Strategy Group (KILS Strategy Group) has submitted a Strategic Plan titled "From Knowledge to Health," which calls for the appointment of a Project Manager to map services and staffing against identified strategy drivers in order to provide a sound basis on which to build improvements.

Project Purpose:

To ensure that the KILS Strategy Group has the information necessary to make a sound case for allocation of funding and resources to ensure its members are able to fulfill the Mission Statement (see the Strategic Plan "From Knowledge to Health").

Project Components:

- Conduct an audit of funding for Knowledge Information and Library Services across the organizations comprising the NEYNL SHA.
- Assess the impact on these organizations of a reduction in, or withdrawal of, funding.
- Measure Knowledge Information and Library Services provided to organizations within the NEYNL SAH against nationally accredited standards (HeLICON).
- Produce a gap analysis of differences that exist between existing Knowledge Information and Library Services and those specified within the national standards.
- Map Knowledge Information and Library Services against the strategy drivers identified in the Strategic Plan "From Knowledge to Health."
- Make initial recommendations on ways to improve Knowledge Information and Library Services.

Project Outcomes:

- An interim report, to be produced by January 2005
- A final document, to be produced by the end of March 2005, to report on all of the listed Project Components

---

Oakville Public Library 💿
Source: Oakville Public Library Executive Director's Team, 2005: 1–10); reprinted courtesy of Oakville Public Library.

1.0 Introduction

In December 2002 the Library Board approved the "Oakville Public Library Business Plan 2002–2005." Since that time staff have been implementing Business Plan priority initiatives and maintaining current service commitments. One key initiative undertaken was the development of a brand strategy, and this led us to revise the wording of our Vision and Mission statements. In addition, since 2002, new initiatives have been identified which address our branding objectives and respond to changing community needs.

The Library's accomplishments against the Business Plan outline have been recorded in the annual Integrated Business Plan documentation that is part of the annual budget preparation process. They also form part of the Library's "Annual Report to the Community" and the Town's annual report.

A key initiative that is underway in 2004 and 2005 is the Master Plan for Parks, Recreation, Culture, and Library. Once this is completed (midyear 2005) the recommendations adopted by Library Board and Council will form the basis for the Library working on a new 3–5 year strategic plan document and the subsequent annual business plans flowing from that direction.

The following pages provide the detail of the Library's "Business Plan 2005" and is the result of OPL directors and managers meeting to review past efforts and discuss and brainstorm what is required for 2005. The process resulted in a number of identified projects that have been placed into two main categories—Customer Service Priorities for the efficiency and improvements for serving our customers and Corporate Priorities, those that are critical for the administration of the library as a municipal service.

Priorities were arrived at by determining eight decision-making criteria and by a rating system by which to rate all the projects. Projects were also given an approximate start and completion date, a team leader, and the resources required to successfully complete the project.

The key projects are as follows [see Table 10-3].

Table 10-3. Oakville Public Library Business Plan: Key Projects

Corporate Priorities	Customer Service Priorities
Strategic Planning • OPL Business Plan—Communication • Service Strategy—Master Plan (Parks, Recreation, Culture and Library) • Strategic Planning—2006–2011 • Glen Abbey Expansion • Glen Abbey Enhancement Project • Team and Committees	Collections • Collection Satisfaction Survey • Language Learning Centers • Collection Agency Review • Age-Specific Collections—Children's Research • Local History (Images)

(Cont'd.)

Table 10-3. Oakville Public Library Business Plan: Key Projects *(Continued)*	
Corporate Priorities	**Customer Service Priorities**
Performance Measures/Surveys • Statistics Management Reports • Key Performance Indicators	Brand Integration/Implementation • Interior Design Strategy—Central Adult Service Desk • Interior Design Strategy—Glen Abbey Expansion • Lifestyles, Topics, and People Events • Merchandising and Display • Branding for Teens
Advocacy • Board/Council Relationships • Staff Relationships with Town	Outreach Services • YO! For Grades 7 and 8 Outreach • New Book Nooks • BookPlay
Human Resources • Employee Satisfaction Survey • Training Survey—Town • Succession Planning/Competencies • Reward/Recognition Events • Health and Safety Audit • Compensation Study	Early Childhood Literacy • Research/Redesign Children's Area—Iroquois Ridge • Family Connections • Early Literacy Awareness Campaign
Contract/SLA Reviews/Budget • Halton Community Services Database—Funding and Governance Model (HIP) • "Sustainability of Initiatives Policy"	Teen Services • Teen Book Club
Town as Partner • Wireless Research and Implementation • Horizon • Corporate Information System	Customer Service Impact • Telephone/E-Reference Customer Service • Self Checkout Research for Glen Abbey • Glen Abbey Closure and Mitigation Strategies • IRIS—Online Registration • OSCR (Ontario School Curriculum Resources)

2.0 Vision, Mission, and Core Values [see also Figure 10-1]

VISION

The Centre for Learning—Your Gateway to Knowledge

MISSION

To provide the ideal environment for our customer's learning experience and to support, educate, motivate, and recognize staff and volunteers in providing the ideal environment for learning.

CORE VALUES

Accountability   Taking responsibility for meeting the library service needs of the community in an efficient and effective manner. The Library's accountability to all of its stakeholders, including Town Council as its major funder, is measurable and managed.

Communications   Engaging in open dialogue, listening attentively, and responding in such a way as to cultivate understanding and strengthen relationships.

Equitable Access	Facilitating access to all expressions of knowledge and intellectual activity.
Innovation	Constantly challenging current practices, initiating breakthrough improvements, and creating new standards of performance.
Partnerships	Seeking mutually beneficial partnerships and links with the community. Working together with other community and private organizations in achieving synergies and common goals promotes a progressive community. Partnership opportunities are seriously explored, analyzed, and implemented when win-win situations are derived.
Trust and Respect	Acting in good faith and understanding and appreciating differences.

Figure 10-1. 3.0 OPL Direction 2005 at a Glance

VISION
The ultimate goal, a future state, a picture of what we want to be.

"The Centre for Learning — Your Gateway to Knowledge"

MISSION
The purpose of the organization, for all stakeholder groups.

To provide the ideal environment for the customer's learning experience.

To support, educate, motivate, and recognize staff and volunteers in providing the ideal environment for learning.

OBJECTIVES
Measures how well we achieve our mission.

- Increase awareness
- Increase value in the community
- Increase usage
- Align organizational culture with external position in the community

STRATEGIES
The means used to achieve the mission and move towards the vision.

Corporate Priorities
- Strategic Planning
- Performance Measures/Surveys
- Advocacy
- Human Resources
- Contract/SLA Reviews/Budget
- Town as Partner

Customer Service Priorities
- Collections
- Brand Integration/ Implementation
- Outreach Services
- Early Childhood Literacy
- Teen Services
- Customer Service Impact

GOALS/TARGETS
Specific measures of success.

Effectiveness Measures

VALUE	Maintain ranking in Citizen's Survey
	Maintain Cardholders per capita 70%
USAGE	Number of service transactions per capita > 47.56
AWARENESS	Overall awareness of breadth of programs & services improved
ALIGN	Dollars spent on training as a % of personnel budget
CULTURE	Satisfaction measure through informal customer satisfaction surveys

Efficiency Measure

ROI	Number of Service Transactions > 1.0 / Annual Expenditures

Source: \Executive\Business Plan\Business Plan 2005 - 2007\BP 05 v9 OPLB Summary.doc

4.0 Current Service Commitments

The core services offered by the Oakville Public Library are as follows:

4.1 Collections

The library acquires and makes available a broad range of resources, including books, magazines, audiovisual materials such as DVDs, CD-ROMs, and compact discs and subscriptions to full-text books, magazines, and newspapers in electronic formats. To ensure the continuing relevancy of these resources to the community, the library is developing a strategy for the ongoing evaluation of user satisfaction. All library branches will expand the concepts of merchandising and "retail roaming," modeled after the success of the Iroquois Ridge Branch. These concepts encourage use of the in-house collections and help facilitate users' access to relevant information. This year, there is an emphasis on the system deselection process, its implication on the Glen Abbey closure and subsequent expansion, and a review of the collection agency process.

4.2 Children's Programs

The library offers a wide range of programs for children up to age 12, with the goals of introducing children to children's literature and instilling a lifelong library habit. Many of these programs are inclusive of parents. They are offered within and outside the library. The priority over the next few years will be to focus on children from birth to six years of age and to include programs that are delivered beyond the walls of the library to nontraditional users.

4.3 Librarians' Assistance to the Public

Library staff information skill sets are increasingly essential to help the public find what they need within the complex wealth of information available in print and electronic formats. Staff assistance is available through the in-house service desks, telephone service, e-reference, and the development of recommended Web sites. It will be important to communicate to the public that staff can not only assist with collections but also facilitate the navigation of electronic resources and the World Wide Web, that they are "knowledge management experts."

4.4 Adult Learning Programs and Services

As well as assisting the public directly in finding information (i.e., reference service), library staff will provide instruction that supports self-sufficiency in the use of the Internet and the library's growing number of electronic databases. This instruction will be in a variety of formats: one-on-one instruction, online tutorials, and group sessions such as the Web-wise workshops. This instruction will assist in maximizing the public's awareness and use of the library's electronic resources. Lifestyle and hobby-related programs will also be delivered to enhance our customers' learning experience.

4.5 Online Commercial Resources

The library must provide information in formats that the community needs and values. It subscribes to electronic databases to ensure that the public has access to required information. Current examples include electronic databases such as full-text magazines and newspapers, government documents, health and drug information, encyclopedias, and books on business and information technology. As more and more information becomes available electronically, the library will expand its online commercial resources, reallocating monies from the print budget.

4.6 Local History and Community Information

The library is a clearinghouse for information, both current and historical, about the local community. The format varies—print, microfilm, and electronic information. In its business plan, the library will expand electronic access to unique local historical and contemporary resources such as documents, photographs, and newspapers as well as Town of Oakville information and will act as an electronic publisher to assist others in the community to provide access to their information over the Web; will enhance the access to the Halton Community Services and events databases, partnering with other community agencies to promote awareness of their services and provide specialized views of the database; and will support the shared development of Halton-wide access to local information.

4.7 Community Space

The library is a "gathering place" for the community. It provides meeting room space for community events and library-sponsored programs. It provides study and reading lounge spaces for those using library resources in-house. The adequacy of library facilities will be addressed within the terms of the Master Plan research.

4.8 Outreach and Convenience-Based Services

The library provides services outside library walls to encourage use of library resources and services. Currently these services include book nooks, classroom promotional events, and speaking engagements. The library's Youth Online initiative is an outreach service designed to promote the library's electronic products and services for high school students and educators.

4.9 Special Needs Services

The library provides services to assist with access to information for library users who have difficulty accessing the facility-based collections. Currently, the library offers a volunteer-based delivery service and deposit collections at six seniors' residences/day care centers. Available formats include large print books, descriptive videos, unabridged books-on-tape, and a variety of special reading aids. As well, it provides access to the collections of the CNIB [Canadian National Institute for the Blind] in a partner relationship.

4.10 Electronic, Networked and Web-Based Resources

The library is continually updating and enhancing its Web site (http://www.opl.on.ca), its Web-based catalog, subscribing to new commercial sources of full-text information, and developing new database services to assist students, researchers, and readers of all ages. The convenience of being able to place holds, renew items, do research, and browse through the library's Web site is more and more appreciated in the community. Recent improvements include adding BookArt, reviews, first chapters and tables of contents to the new Web-based catalogue, launching a newly designed Web site with a new teen-designed Teen section. Further development will include enhanced "One Place to Look" technology and convenient borrower self-service checkout and wireless hotspots.

5.0 Decision-Making Criteria and Assumptions

Balancing the areas of effort and ensuring maximum effectiveness and accountability is critical for the Oakville Public Library in 2005. In order to achieve these objectives, it was imperative that decisions relating to where our organization spends its time and energy be based on a number of set criteria that have been generated and agreed on. Through a multi-voting tool, the Executive Team has determined eight decision-making criteria to be used for prioritizing existing and new projects. They are as follows:

1. The Oakville Public Library Mission and Vision is supported—provides an ideal environment for a customer's learning experience

2. Local needs are met first—where local accountability to the Oakville tax payer is evident and well communicated to relevant stakeholders

3. Service improvements and project goals are measurable

4. The project or service improvement advantageously positions the Oakville Public Library in the eyes of its stakeholder groups (Town, public, donors, etc.)

5. Stable resources are available (including strong passionate leadership for a project), and sustainability is likely

6. Public satisfaction can be maximized or improved

7. The project or service improvement moves the public forward in its perception of libraries and library staff

8. A community need is met (e.g., growth-related, demonstrated public demand, or staff anticipated)

The above-mentioned criteria have been applied to all Oakville Public Library projects for 2005. Using an evaluation matrix tool, each project was evaluated against all eight criteria and were assigned point values. Equal weighting is given to each criteria. The results have been divided into Mandatory, Medium, and Flexible categories based on the point ratings of each project.

Projects listed in the Mandatory category have definitive timelines and resources dedicated for their successful completion. After which, those projects in the Medium category have been designated start and completion dates depending on the resources available within the 2005 timeframe. Any projects listed in the Flexible category will take place only if staff time resources (beyond 2005 budget allowance) become available in 2005. If not, these Flexible projects will be reevaluated using a list of decision-making criteria in 2006.

These projects are as follows [see Table 10-4].

Table 10-4. Oakville Public Library Project Prioritization	
Corporate Priorities	**Customer Service Priorities**
Mandatory	
• OPL Business Plan—Communication • Service Strategy—Master Plan (Parks, Recreation, Culture, and Library) • Strategic Planning—2006–2011 • Glen Abbey Expansion • Glen Abbey Enhancement Project • Statistics Management Reports • Board/Council Relationships • Succession Planning/Competencies • Reward/Recognition Events • Health and Safety Audit • Compensation Study • Halton Community Services Database—Funding and Governance Model (HIP) • "Sustainability of Initiatives Policy" • Wireless Research and Implementation • Horizon • Corporation Information System	• Interior Design Strategy—Central Adult Service Desk • Interior Design Strategy—Glen Abbey Expansion • Lifestyles, Topics, and People Events • BookPlay • Teen Book Club • Telephone/e-Reference Customer Service • Self Checkout Research for Glen Abbey • Glen Abbey Closure and Mitigation Strategies • IRIS—Online Registration
Medium	
• Key Performance Indicators	• Collection Satisfaction Survey • Language Learning Centers • Collection Agency Review • Merchandising and Display • YO! For Grade 7 and 8 Outreach • New Book Nooks • Research/Redesign Children's Area—Iroquois Ridge • OSCR (Ontario School Curriculum Resources)
Flexible	
• Team and Committees • Staff Relationships with Town • Employee Satisfaction Survey • Training Survey—Town	• Age-Specific Collections—Children's Research • Local History (Images) • Branding for Teens • Family Connections • Early Literacy Awareness Campaign

COMMUNICATING THE PLAN

The business plan will open the door only to a project being heard. A formal presentation brings it to life and generates the trust necessary to build successful relationships. It develops the very important interpersonal factors that no amount of accurate paperwork can provide. Your delivery will develop belief in the value of your planning and the integrity of your intentions. When you tell them the client will be satisfied because the marketing data supports it—they will believe you.

RECOMMENDATIONS FOR IMPROVED COMMUNICATIONS

1. Every library committee member and member of management should get a copy of the plan after it is ready.
2. Consider distribution of or highlights from the plan to everyone in the library. Even the newest staff member will gain quick context, appreciation, and meaning from a review of the business plan.
3. Put copies of the plan in the library collection.
4. Publish the plan on the Web site.
5. Post your mission and vision statements on the walls of your offices.
6. Publish portions of your plan in your regular newsletter and in advertising and marketing materials (brochures, ads, and so on).
7. Ask the in-house publication to publish the plan or a summary of it—including the local newspaper for public institutions.
8. Train everyone from board members to employees on portions of the plan during orientations.
9. Include portions of the plan in policies and procedures, including the employee manual.
10. Consider copies of the plan for major stakeholders, for example, foundation members, supporters, funders or investors, trade associations, potential collaborators, vendors or suppliers, and so on.
11. In designing an e-mail message to share your plan consider this: if receivers have to scroll down to a second page, it's too long.
12. If you are not confident in your writing skills, the services of a good PR (public relations) person or copy editor will help.

13. Always network and keep in front of potential clients and supporters. Always communicate where the service is and how it is progressing.

14. Have a prepared message ready to leave on voice mail or an answering machine. Remember to leave your phone number or contact points twice: once at the beginning of the message and once at the end.

PRESENTING AND DISTRIBUTING THE PLAN

> There are two types of speakers: those that are nervous and those that are liars.
>
> —Mark Twain

Distribute the executive summary to the reviewing board or upper management before making the presentation for approval. This gives them an opportunity to review it and come prepared to comment. However, your reviewing board or upper management should be well aware of your efforts when writing the plan and should be invited to review the progress as you move along in writing. "It's not unusual for the board and/or top management of large organizations to provide major input primarily to the contents in the body of the document, that is, the mission and vision and values statements, and the goals and strategies" (McNamara, 2006).

Distributing the Plan

Before distributing anything to inform stakeholders, prepare a succinct elevator pitch: about 30 seconds worth of "commercial" for your plan. Thirty seconds forces you to focus on the most important elements of your message and how it relates to your listener. Begin by identifying three things:

1. What you do and the problems you'll solve
2. How you will be successful
3. Why they should care

Determine what makes your service unique. Differentiate each and every project and back it up with facts. Write down your pitch, which should be similar to an executive summary of the business plan, but shorter, much more concise, and with snappy sentences. Practice its delivery, developing a conversational style, steady eye contact, and positive body language.

Either way you choose to prepare your pitch, always make sure it's short and that anyone could understand it. Ask to hear other people's reactions to your pitch. Be ready to answer your listener's questions. Have a list prepared of ten questions that interested parties might ask after listening to you. Know the answers to these questions as well as you know the pitch itself.

When the time is right to distribute copies of the plan, keep a distribution record. This allows you to update your plans as needed and keeps you on top of who has a copy. You may not want the plan distributed more widely than those on your initial list. If appropriate, include a disclaimer limiting the ability of individuals to distribute or otherwise copy the plan without the consent of the writers.

When asking someone to review your plan, get buy-in from stakeholders and decision makers by assuring them that you have reduced as much risk as possible and not left any holes in your plan. When sharing the plan, remember that every interaction will involve two-way communication. This is the perfect opportunity to gather feedback and input.

Presentations

You and your team have spent much time and energy creating a concise, well-thought-out plan. Now you'll need to present it in the same manner, with the additional pressure of trying to convince your audience to support or fund your creation. Just as in writing the business plan, there is a simple but sometimes difficult rule of thumb: when speaking, be brief.

Less is more in presentations. A successful presentation requires preparation. Design your message to be passionate, clear, and concise. Fifteen minutes is the length of the average attention span. If you haven't reached the point within that time then most in your audience will have mentally checked out. Deliver only the basics of what they need to know. If they seek more information, they will have a copy of the full business plan or they can make inquiries.

When presenting, think of your talk as more information sharing or talking with them rather than lecturing. The difference in effectiveness is dramatic: the least effective form of presentation is a lecture that goes in one direction; the most effective form is through creating a dialogue. Motivation is stirred through emotional connection. That connection is created through a relationship—and a relationship is created through dialogue.

You'll want to determine three things before presenting to any group:

- What do they need?
- Do you have a strong belief in your message?
- Do you have an action to request of the audience?

People generally like an idea if it helps them reach their goals or satisfies their needs. Present your idea or plan from the perspective of the audience. You already know the immediate needs of the library and its current focus of activity. The groups with whom you talk will realize you have done the research and are the acknowledged expert source. By addressing them individually and making eye contact, they will understand you are sincere and your information is substantial, based on facts. Persuasion is the result of sincerity, and you will be speaking from the heart. At the end of the talk, ask the group to take some action or create a challenge for them. If you don't, then why are they there? (Garrett, 2006: 10; Russell, n.d.; Zahorsky, n.d.).

The philosophy of speaking with them, not to them, carries over to the question and answer period: When taking questions, look audience members in the eye and be sincerely interested in their thoughts. Don't look around the room for a better questioner or someone more interesting. When an individual is talking or speaking to you, make him or her the only person in the room.

Dos and Don'ts of Public Speaking

- Go prepared to win—preparation is everything.
- Erase all jargon and acronyms; be concise in your language and speech.
- Pay attention to details: the presentation and the plan should say the same thing.
- Breathe.
- Reduce terminology to plain words ("saving money" instead of "driving cost reduction," or "working better" instead of "optimizing a library process").
- Speak in a regular tone, no monotones.
- Humility is good; being a doormat is not. Find a comfortable medium.
- Mimic your audience: dress well, as defined by the group you're speaking to.
- Videotape yourself for critique when practicing—it's painful but it gets results.
- Practice, practice, practice; compensate for fear by being prepared.
- Speak, don't read.
- Do not use any jokes.
- Treat your audience with respect.
- Use facts to back up your assertions.
- Stay away from PowerPoint.
- Forget yourself.
- Remember why you are there—focus on the group, your subject, and your purpose.
- Be simple and short.
- Learn from each presentation—even if it's unsuccessful.

- Be confident.
- Be action-oriented, using dynamic verbs.
- Speak in short, direct sentences.

Note: compiled from Cohen, 2005; Gleeson, 2007; Goodwin 2006; McCarthy, 2005; "Presentations," 2003; Western New York Venture Association, 2003.

RECOMMENDATIONS FOR APPENDICES

The appendices can include any information that could be useful to the plan's readers but may not be appropriate to everyone receiving the plan. Appendices are usually bound separately from the other sections of the plan and provided on an as-needed basis to readers.

Appendices might include:

- Résumés of key managers
- Pictures of the service
- Professional references
- Description of planning process used
- Action plans—the detailed report
- Market studies
- Analysis reports
- Budgets
- Operating plan
- Financial reports—the detailed report
- Published information: magazine or news articles
- Patents
- Licenses
- Contracts
    —Leases
    —Sales contracts
    —Purchase contracts
    —Employment or compensation agreements
    —Noncompete agreements
    —Insurances: errors and omissions or general liability (Ernst & Young, 1997)

REFERENCES

Association for Library Collections & Technical Services. 2001. "Membership Business Plan Outline FY 2002–2005." (February 26). Chicago: American Library Association Available: www.ala.org/ala/alcts/divisiongroups/membershipdiv/businessplan0205.doc.

Brigevich, L. 2004. "Business Plan, Franklin Templeton Global Research Library." Fort Lauderdale, FL: Franklin Templeton Global Research Library. Franklin Templeton Investments.

Calgary Public Library. 2006. "Building Community, Building Capacity Business Plan 2006–2008." Calgary, Alberta, Canada: Calgary Public Library Available: http://calgarypubliclibrary.com/library/pdf/businessplan06.pdf.

Cohen, Carolyn. 2005. "Ladies and Gentlemen." *CAmagazine* (November): 47–48. Available: www.camagazine.com/2/8/5/5/3/index1.shtml.

Comaford-Lynch, Christine. 2007. "Make Your Financing Pitch Sizzle." *Business Week Online* (February 22). Available: www.businessweek.com/smallbiz/content/feb2007/sb20070219_940216.htm.

Ernst & Young LLP. 1997. "Outline for a Business Plan: A Proven Approach for Entrepreneurs Only." Available: www.techventures.org/resources/docs/Outline_for_a_Business_Plan.pdf.

Garrett, David. 2006. "The Lost Art of Presentations." *Certification Magazine* (June): 10.

Gleeson, Alan. 2007. "How to Deliver a Winning Business Plan Pitch." Bytestart.co.uk (May 15). Available: www.bytestart.co.uk/content/businessplans/30_1/business-pitch-tips.shtml.

Goodwin, Bill. 2006. "Prepare Well to Win Over the Board." *Computer Weekly* (May 23): 30.

Kott, Katherine. 2006. "DLF Aquifer Business Plan 2006." May 25. Washington, DC: Digital Library Federation. Available: www.diglib.org/aquifer/AquiferBusinessPlan.pdf.

Maroochy Shire Council. 2006. "Library Strategy 2006: Executive Summary with Outcomes and Recommendations." Queensland, Australia: Maroochy Shire Council. Available: www.maroochy.qld.gov.au/maroochylibraries/documents/Maroochy%20Strategy%20Executive%20Summary%20Internet.pdf.

McCarthy, Barbara. 2005. "Make Your Point with Real Power, Not Projections." *The Sunday Times* (May 1): 2.

McNamara, Carter. 2006. "Basics of Writing and Communicating a Strategic Plan." Adapted from *The Field Guide to Nonprofit Strategic Planning and Facilitation* by Carter McNamara. Minneapolis, MN: Authentic Consulting. Available: www.managementhelp.org/plan_dec/str_plan/writing.htm.

North and East Yorkshire and Northern Lincolnshire Workforce Development Confederation. 2004. "A Report on a Study Funded by the NEYNL Workforce Development Confederation for the NEYNL Knowledge Information and Libraries Services Strategy Group: NEYNL WDC Business Plan 2004–2005." York, UK: North and East Yorkshire and Northern Lincolnshire Workforce Development Confederation.

Oakville Public Library Executive Directors Team. 2005. "Oakville Public Library Business Plan 2005 Summary." Oakville, ON: Oakville Public Library. Available: www.opl.on.ca/BP_05_v9_OPLB_Summary.pdf.

Ontario Digital Library. 2003. "The Ontario Digital Library Business Plan: Connecting Ontarians." Guelph, ON: Ontario Digital Library. Available: www.accessola2.com/odl/pdf/ODL_BusinessPlan_Full.pdf.

Port Stephens Library. 2004. "Port Stephens Library Business Plan 2004–2005." Port Stephens, Australia: Port Stephens Library.

"Presentations: How to Make Effective Presentations." 2003. *Personnel Today* (July 22). Available: www.personneltoday.com/Articles/Article.aspx?liArticleID-19829&PrinterFriendly.

Russell, Wendy. "12 Tips for Delivering a Knockout Business Presentation." About.com: Presentation Software (n.d). Available: http://presentationsoft.about.com/od/powerpointbusiness/p/bus_delivery.htm.

U.S. Environmental Protection Agency. 2004. "Business Case for Information Services: EPA's Regional Libraries and Centers." Washington, DC: U.S. EPA. Available: www.epa.gov/natlibra/epa260r04001.pdf.

Western New York Venture Association. 2003. "Business Plan Presentation Outline." Buffalo, NY: Western New York Venture Association. Available: www.wnyventure.com/presentationoutline.html.

Zahorsky, Darrell. "8 Secrets to a Knockout Business Presentation." About.com: Small Business Information (n.d.). Available: http://sbinformation.about.com/od/sales/a/presentationtip/htm.

INDEX

ABOUT THE AUTHOR

Joy HP. Harriman has worked for more than 20 years in the health care industry in marketing, library and information management, training and research. She has more than 18 years' experience in the library management and staff development field. She was formerly the Director of the Medical Library at the Mobile Infirmary, in Mobile, Alabama, and a consultant with Right Management Consultants, Inc. She was also the CEO of InfoResearch, an information brokerage specializing in business, legal, and medical information. Most recently, she was the Associate Director, Library of the Health Sciences, Texas Tech University Health Sciences Center of the Permian Basin, Odessa, Texas. She is currently a Development Officer for Texas Tech University Health Sciences Center of the Permian Basin, Odessa, Texas and is an adjunct faculty member at the Physician Assistant Program, TTUHSC, Midland, Texas.

Harriman graduated from the University of West Florida, Florida State University, and the University of South Alabama. She holds a BA in Journalism and Communication Arts, an MLS, and an MBA. She holds a distinguished level of certification from AHIP, the Academy of Health Information Professionals and Medical Library Association.

The Medical Library Association, founded in 1898, is an educational organization of more than 700 institutions and 3,300 individual members in the health sciences information field committed to education health information professionals, supporting health information research, promoting access to the world's health sciences information, and working to ensure that the best health information is available to all.